Fashion Journalism

Fashion Journalism presents a comprehensive overview of how fashion journalism operates and how to report on fashion. Encompassing skills for print and online media, the book includes many case studies and interviews with fashion journalists working for newspapers, magazines, broadcasters and websites, as well as with stylists, PR executives, photographers and bloggers. The first-hand explanations of these roles and practical tips and advice are accompanied by analysis of examples from their work.

The business of fashion and fashion PR is explained for the trainee journalist, offering practical guidance on how to report effectively on fashion – from sources and research to writing and layout – with chapters including suggested exercises and further reading.

Covering a broad range of subject areas, from law and ethics and using social media to fashion theory and reporting the catwalk, this text offers everything a student or trainee needs to know to excel in fashion journalism.

www.facebook.com/fashionjournalism

Julie Bradford is programme leader for BA Fashion Journalism at the University of Sunderland, UK.

Fashion Journalism

Julie Bradford

Routledge
Taylor & Francis Group

LONDON AND NEW YORK

First published 2015
by Routledge
2 Park Square, Milton Park, Abingdon, Oxon OX14 4RN

Simultaneously published in the USA and Canada
by Routledge
711 Third Avenue, New York, NY 10017

Routledge is an imprint of the Taylor & Francis Group, an informa business

British Library Cataloguing in Publication Data
A catalogue record for this book is available from the British Library

Library of Congress Cataloging in Publication Data
Bradford, Julie.
Fashion journalism / Julie Bradford.
1. Fashion writing. I. Title.
TT503.5.B73 2014
070.4'9--dc23
2013046151

ISBN: 978-0-415-68660-0 (hbk)
ISBN: 978-0-415-68661-7 (pbk)
ISBN: 978-0-203-13086-5 (ebk)

Typeset in Garamond
by Taylor & Francis Books

Printed and bound in Great Britain by
TJ International Ltd, Padstow, Cornwall

To my mother, Jean, and father, Peter, for their lifelong support.
And to my sister Jill, my fashion partner-in-crime.

Contents

List of figures		ix
Note on contributor		x
Acknowledgements		xi
Preface		xii

1	Working in fashion journalism	1
2	Ways in to fashion journalism	13
3	Fashion media and audiences	35
4	The fashion industry	61
5	Ideas, sources and interviewing	81
6	Writing fashion news and features	104
7	Reporting the catwalk	127
8	Reporting the trends	145
9	Styling	164
10	Photography and video for online	187
11	Fashion blogging and social media	199
12	Fashion journalism and PR CAROLE WATSON	219

viii   *Contents*

13 Law and ethics   234
      CAROLE WATSON

      Glossary   246
      Bibliography   253
      Index   264

Figures

3.1 Early edition of *Vogue* (CN/Fairchild)   36
4.1 Liz Lamb feature on fashion students (Liz Lamb/NCJ Media)   62
5.1 Liz Lamb fashion feature (Liz Lamb/NCJ Media)   82
6.1 Zoe Beaty feature on 'A day at the races' (Grazia/Bauer Media)   105
7.1 Chanel runway show (CN/Fairchild)   128
7.2 Cara Delevingne on runway (CN/Fairchild)   130
8.1 Jennifer Lawrence at the Oscars (CN/Fairchild)   146
9.1 1950s fashion shoot (CN/Fairchild)   165
9.2 *Fabulous* fashion shoot (Tracey Lea Sayer/News UK)   167
10.1 Phill Taylor picture of Kellydeene Skerritt (Phill Taylor,
     www.philltaylor.com)   188
10.2 Phill Taylor picture of Elena Perminova (Phill Taylor,
     www.philltaylor.com)   190
11.1 Madeleine Bowden Instagram pic (Madeleine Bowden)   214

Contributor

Carole Watson was deputy editor of *Grazia* magazine, head of features at the *Daily Mirror* and features editor of the *News of the World*. She is now a senior lecturer in fashion journalism at the University of Sunderland.

Acknowledgements

Thanks first of all to the fashion journalists, editors, stylists, photographers and PRs who were interviewed for this book, and who were so generous with their time and advice. They are: Hannah Almassi, Emma Bigger, Madeleine Bowden, Jessica Bumpus, Jess Cartner-Morley, Aaron Christian, Hattie Crisell, Phil Cullen, Caryn Franklin, Amber Graafland, Emma Hart, Peter Henderson, Louise Gannon, Liz Lamb, Tracey Lea Sayer, Luke Leitch, Siobhan Mallen, Fiona McIntosh, Adam Mooney, Arieta Mujay, Alex Murphy, Charlie Porter, Melanie Rickey, Phill Taylor, Polly Vernon, Harriet Walker, Elizabeth Walker, Victoria White, Sasha Wilkins and Lucy Wood. Thanks, too, to Rachel Richardson, Marianne Jones, Victoria Kennedy and Julie McCaffrey for their invaluable tips for students.

I am also grateful to designer Mick Dixon and Loraine Davies of the Professional Publishers Association for sharing their expertise with me.

Thanks, too, to the fantastic fashion journalism students at the University of Sunderland, who always come back from work placements buzzing with stories, some of which are included in the book – special mention goes to Melody Small and Stephanie Currie, as well as to avid bloggers Shannon Hodge and Amy Fitzsimmons of the North East Bloggers network.

I'd like to say a huge thank you to my colleague Carole Watson, who has been unfailingly supportive over the past year. As well as writing two chapters of the book and contributing to interviews, she also read and commented on drafts of the other chapters, though any mistakes and omissions are my own. Senior magazine journalism lecturer Lee Hall was also generous with his time and advice.

Special thanks to Chris Rushton, without whom it simply would not have been possible to write this book, and to Maureen, for her wise advice. Finally, I am endlessly grateful to my family – Chris, Jack, Peter and Max – for putting up with me these past six months. I promise to be human again from now on.

Preface

It has always seemed to me that fashion journalists got a bad press, both from colleagues in other parts of the industry and from the academics who write about them.

They've been accused of being PR poodles (see Andrew Marr's book *My Trade*), of being shallow and trivial, of promoting consumption, and of letting women down by focusing on appearance rather than political or social issues.

There are no textbooks about fashion journalism – unlike, say, war reporting or sports journalism – and studies of women in journalism have all but ignored the fashion media, staffed and run largely by women.

Yet fashion and lifestyle journalism are the top choices of specialism for students (Hanna and Sanders, 2007), and there are hundreds of graduates chasing every job that comes up in the industry.

What's more, fashion coverage has exploded in newspapers and magazines, and has found a natural home on the Internet. Sites like *Style.com* and live-streamed catwalk shows have opened up the fashion industry to a public hungry for more.

Fashion has become a branch of the broader entertainment industry. Not only are celebrities intertwined with fashion like never before, but industry figures like designers and stylists have become celebrities themselves.

Fashion editors say they're astonished at this appetite for behind-the-scenes coverage and how fashion-savvy today's audiences are.

Jess Cartner-Morley, the *Guardian*'s fashion editor, says: 'Fashion has become part of the national conversation. It's part of the blurring of boundaries between the public and private spheres' (2011b).

So fashion journalism is hugely popular, both in terms of people wanting to get into it, and audiences wanting to read or watch it. That's not shallow or trivial.

And neither is the subject itself. Fashion is a massive industry, worth $1 trillion worldwide a year (Tungate, 2012). In the UK, fashion contributes £21 billion to the economy, employs almost a million people and is as big as the food industry or telecommunications industries (British Fashion Council, 2010). That's not silly or shallow, either.

The fact it's also peopled by larger-than-life characters makes it a great news story. 'Fashion has everything – industry, beauty, history, characters, money, drama, intrigue', says Jess.

And that's still not all. Culturally and socially, fashion is an important part of our lives. It's how we choose to communicate things about ourselves to others, and it has an effect on how we feel.

Fashion editor and commentator Caryn Franklin said the best moment of her career was delivering lorry-loads of clothes to teenagers in refugee camps in the former Yugoslavia. It was part of an appeal by BBC TV's *The Clothes Show*, which she presented at the time.

She says:

> It showed me the power of fashion – the magic of clothes as a show of confidence. The clothes made them feel they were just the same as other teenagers around the world. Fashion was shorthand for having things in common.
>
> (2013)

Far from being defensive, then, fashion journalists feel very privileged to do what they do.

Charlie Porter, who has worked for the *Guardian*, *GQ* and *Fantastic Man*, says:

> The thing about fashion is that it is one of the broadest topics you can write about. There's so much depth to it that people don't realise is there.
>
> There is the surface attraction of things that are beautifully made, but then there's the whole sociological side of why we wear clothes, what meaning clothes have and why we make certain choices, both conscious and subconscious.
>
> There's a whole ecological discourse, which comes and goes, and there's the psychological aspect to understanding what it is that makes us buy clothing. And there's the corporate side and the business side, which are also incredibly personal because there are such alpha males and females in charge.
>
> There are all these things you can do within fashion that make it a very open world to work in, if you decide to do that.

Of course, there are contentious issues within fashion journalism. There's the influence of advertisers, the relationship with PRs and the arguments about how narrow its representations of beauty can be.

This book addresses those issues, but also gives fashion journalists the chance to explain how they see them and the ways in which they work round the constraints they sometimes face.

All the journalists, editors, stylists and photographers I interviewed for this book are thoughtful, dedicated and talented individuals who have worked very hard to make it in a highly competitive industry.

They appreciate how difficult it is to get onto that first step on the ladder – indeed, even to know where to start – and are helpful and generous in their advice to would-be fashion journalists.

Like the rest of us, they're in the dark about the future of their industry at a time of great upheaval in media in general. Fewer people are buying print products (newspapers and magazines), publishers are still trying to work out how to make as much money from the Internet, and retailers are muddying the waters further by becoming magazine publishers themselves.

But whatever happens, they promise that fashion will still be the place to be.

Peter Henderson, a blogger and journalist who writes for an online retailer, admits:

> I find it really hard to place myself in five or ten years, because I just don't know what's going to happen to the whole landscape. I might be working on a mobile phone magazine, or app, or augmented reality!
>
> But I'm sure it will be something that lets me appreciate what we love about fashion so much – madness, creativity and energy – whatever the medium might be.
>
> (2013).

Author's note: all quotes in the book were taken from original interviews, unless otherwise stated in the text.

1 Working in fashion journalism

Introduction

The *good* news is that there have never been so many ways to be a fashion journalist. It has become what *Daily Telegraph* fashion editor Lisa Armstrong describes as a 'mass sport' (2009).

There are the glossy monthlies that everyone associates with fashion – *Vogue* or *Elle* – as well as the relative newcomers in the weekly market such as *Grazia* and *Look*.

There are the national newspapers, where the likes of Lisa Armstrong write news, features and reviews.

But with the expansion of platforms for journalism, and the huge appetite for fashion as a subject, there are now many new ways for a fashion journalist to ply their trade.

A national newspaper doesn't just need writers for its print edition. Luke Leitch, deputy fashion editor at the *Daily Telegraph*, explains: 'We've got a fair amount of fashion pages to fill, but we've also got a brilliant online operation and several different magazines' (2013c). Writers will generally work across all platforms, but new posts have opened up for online editors, while burgeoning newspaper supplements require freelance contributions.

Then there are big stand-alone websites like *Never Underdressed* (now closed), set up by the publishers of free magazines *Shortlist* and *Stylist*.

Other fashion websites like Style Bubble (www.stylebubble.co.uk) or LibertyLondonGirl (www.libertylondongirl.com) are one-woman brands, set up by bloggers who have developed enough of a following and a strong enough appeal to advertisers, partners or sponsors to be able to earn a living off the back of their writing, photographs or videos.

Retailers have latched onto the Internet to become fashion publishers in their own right. Where Net-a-Porter led, with its blend of e-commerce and magazine content, many others have followed, providing a host of new opportunities for both established and aspiring fashion journalists.

This has crossed over into print, too. It's hard to believe customer magazines were once seen as naff, now that *John Lewis Edition* and *Asos* magazine are two of the three biggest-circulating fashion magazines in the UK.

On top of this, there are well-respected fashion journalists working free-lance, pitching ideas and selling stories to a variety of magazines and websites, as well as writers and stylists working in regional publications.

Now for the *bad* news ... for every job in fashion journalism, there are hundreds of people chasing it. Victoria White, editor of *Company* magazine, says: 'We have only 17 people at *Company*, and we get at least 200 people applying for every job, including those who've done work experience with us' (2011).

There are no set routes into a job, either, and no guaranteed professional paths. In a study of specialists back in 1971, academic researcher Jeremy Tunstall found that fashion journalists tended to be younger than other journalists, without professional training and without having gone through the tried-and-tested route of regional newspapers that many other types of journalist follow.

It's still a free-for-all now, though there are signs that this is changing with younger fashion journalists tending to having degrees and with more specialist degrees like magazine or fashion journalism springing up.

This chapter will look at where fashion journalists work, what they do there and how they see their role. Chapter 2 will go on to explain how they got there, and what the main routes into the industry entail.

Before we start

Bear in mind that fashion journalism is a vague phrase that covers two disciplines – writing (editorial) and styling (fashion).

Most fashion journalists tend to be one or other, a writer or a stylist, and it's as well to find out where your strengths or interests lie before applying for an internship or a job.

Harriet Walker, news editor on the *Never Underdressed* fashion and beauty website, tells a cautionary tale:

> When I started, I hadn't realised there was a writing route and a styling route. I thought if I turned up at a magazine they'd figure out what I wanted to do and they'd put me in the right place.
>
> But obviously they weren't going to do that – it was 'go into the fashion cupboard and fold these clothes'. So that was an eye-opener.
>
> (2013a)

Luckily, alongside her internships and her assistant's job on a glossy, Harriet also wrote – unpaid – for newspaper and magazine websites, and was thus able to get a permanent job as an assistant on the *Independent* newspaper, where she could focus on editorial.

On so-called quality newspapers like the *Independent*, fashion journalists are often writers first and foremost, working alongside either freelance stylists or a stylist on staff.

On general interest women's magazines, like *Company* or *Marie Claire*, the fashion department (assistants, junior and senior editors, directors) tend to be stylists, although they'll write captions, blurbs and short pieces to accompany their pages.

More fashion-focused magazines like *Vogue*, *Elle*, *Grazia* and *Look* have the luxury of employing both fashion writers – generally called fashion news or fashion features assistants/editors – and stylists, generally called fashion assistants/editors.

Of course, it's way more complicated than this. On a magazine, general features writers might also chip in with fashion features, while freelancers have to be able to turn their hand to a variety of subjects. The fashion desk might be called upon to write more than the standard blurbs (a paragraph or so introducing a shopping page) – the *Company* fashion team, for example, does everything for its *High-Street Edit* spin-off title.

A tabloid newspaper, as opposed to a 'quality' newspaper, might require its fashion team to do all its writing and styling. Meanwhile, a newspaper supplement might be so fashion-focused it will employ magazine-style fashion editors who are stylists rather than writers – the *Sun on Sunday's Fabulous* magazine has fashion director Tracey Lea Sayer, a stylist, who has a fashion editor, shopping editor, two assistants and a web fashion assistant in her team.

And to further confuse things, young fashion journalists in particular are finding they have to have more than one string to their bow in these days of multiplatform publishing. *Grazia* fashion editor Hannah Almassi, who began in fashion news and features, says:

> There are a lot of fashion journalists who don't like to style, and vice versa – but I think nowadays there is less and less opportunity to be that narrow in your job spec.
>
> Although there's no styling in my title, it's something I am encouraged and often needed to do. I've been at *Grazia* for five and a half years and my job has changed enormously, there are so many facets to it now.
>
> (2012b)

Wisely, Hannah carried out test shoots in her spare time early in her career, so now she's in a position where she can style a fashion week wardrobe for a celebrity like Olivia Palermo, or a key model or industry figure, as well as interviewing them for the accompanying feature.

With bloggers changing the rules still further – many write and style, as well as do their own photography and video – fashion journalism may move further along the road of multi-skilling.

But as things stand, when you apply for a placement or internship on a magazine, there will be two types on offer – fashion (styling) and editorial or features (writing) – so make sure you choose the one that best suits you, or try a mix of both.

Where fashion journalists work

Fashion media are explored in more depth in Chapter 3. Despite publications increasingly being discussed more in terms of brand (voice, tone, purpose) than platform (print, broadcast, online), fashion journalists still see their roles differently depending on which area of the media they work for. The main types are discussed here.

Newspapers

Newspapers can be broadly divided into three types – local newspapers, national tabloids, like the *Sun* and the *Daily Mirror*, and the 'quality' newspapers like *The Times*, the *Guardian* and the *Independent*, which used to be called broadsheets before many of them shrank.

Fashion has become increasingly important to newspapers as they try to appeal more to female readers. Amber Graafland, fashion director at the *Daily Mirror*, says newspaper coverage is better than ever before, too. 'Newspapers are much more sophisticated with their layout and the way they present their fashion, almost to magazine standard' (2013).

Amber is one of a team of three who, together with an intern, produce two fashion shoots a week as well as a host of fashion stories and trend reports. Because they're aiming at a general newspaper reader, rather than a full-blown fashionista, they have to take a very different tack from, say, a *Vogue* writer.

'We have to be useful', Amber says. 'We try to give tips and advice, and add value. It can be quite prescriptive. You're not just going to do a spread on an item from the runway – you're going to say what body shape it's good for, what to look out for, advice.'

Luke Leitch, deputy fashion editor at the *Daily Telegraph*, likewise is careful to explain the world of fashion to his readers, rather than revel in it. 'Even though you're in a very specialised world, you're trying to translate it to a much broader audience so you're negotiating a tension in a way, but also you're trying to be a bridge between the two.'

Of course, newspapers of all types also appreciate the colour that fashion can add to their pages, especially the celebrity or runway pictures. 'You'd be lying if you didn't say that sometimes it's a bit of light relief, a bit of glamour,' says Amber.

Local newspapers may also have fashion coverage as part of their features mix, although by 2013 that was becoming rarer as cutbacks meant redundancies and centralised features 'hubs'.

Liz Lamb, who gained a fashion journalism degree at the London College of Fashion, joined the *Newcastle Chronicle and Journal* as a features writer who specialised in fashion, organising shoots and finding local angles on national fashion news. 'I knew I wanted to do features but that I would never be able to do fashion full-time in the North East because that job doesn't exist. This was a good mix without having to go to London again,' she says (2011).

Newspaper supplements

Most national newspapers carry magazines at the weekend to attract a broader readership and as a platform for different advertising. Examples are *The Times Magazine* on a Saturday, the *Sun on Sunday's Fabulous*, the *Guardian Weekend* magazine and the *Mail on Sunday's You* magazine.

They may have some dedicated staff – a much smaller number than a stand-alone consumer magazine – as well as writers who also work for the newspaper and freelancers who get paid for their contributions.

Polly Vernon, a freelancer who was deputy editor of *Observer Woman* before it folded, and now writes mainly for the Saturday *Times* and *Grazia*, says supplements have much greater freedom than stand-alone magazines.

> Selling a newspaper is hard but not as hard as a stand-alone magazine because you've got a very loyal contingent of readers who will pick you up regardless of the front cover. You can do whatever you want with the magazine within that, as weird or as fabulous as you want.
>
> (2012)

And though they may not be quite as aspirational as the likes of *Vogue*, they are known to have clout with the consumer. *Fashion Babylon* (Edwards-Jones, 2007), a novel purportedly put together from real-life accounts of fashion insiders, says that a design studio's phone will ring off the hook after an item has appeared in the midmarket *You* magazine, which comes with the *Mail on Sunday*, as opposed to *Vogue* or *Tatler*.

Consumer magazines

Consumer magazines, especially biannuals and monthlies (the 'glossies'), are what many people think of when they imagine a fashion journalist at work.

There are the magazines where fashion is the main focus, like *Vogue*, *Elle* and *LOVE*, which give us 'the wit and sensuality of fashion' as opposed to the more utilitarian newspaper approach, according to former fashion editor Brenda Polan (2006: 166).

On top of that, there are the glossy weeklies like *Grazia* and *Look* that launched in 2005 and 2007 respectively and shook up the magazine market with their ability to keep pace with the latest drops in shops, twists and turns of celebrities' lives and hot-off-the-press trends.

All these magazines will have two separate teams working on fashion – the stylists and the writers – though both will liaise on stories, says *Look* senior fashion news editor Lucy Wood.

'We work very closely with stylists. As a writer, if New Look, say, offer Kelly Brook for a shoot, I will go to our fashion team and ask if there is a stylist free to do it, because that's their forte,' says Lucy (2012).

'Likewise, they might have seen a really cool new trend but not quite know what it is or how to describe it. So they might call over a writer for a look, and we'd come up with a name, headlines, references.'

The different departments and editors are given responsibility for their own pages, like main fashion (the shoots), shopping pages, trend reports, features and news, though on the busier weeklies they will pitch in and help with other sections when required.

'I'm fashion news, so if there's a new collection launching, a shop doing a new range of prom dresses, Kate Moss doing a campaign with Mango, a celebrity spotted carrying a new Chanel handbag, that's me,' says Lucy. 'But we have the opportunity to pitch and write across the different subjects.'

Customer magazines

For new students of journalism, it can come as a shock to look at the 100 biggest-circulating magazines in the country and see that many of them are customer magazines for the likes of Tesco and Asda.

The charts for women's lifestyle magazines are no different. By the first half of 2013, *John Lewis Edition* was the biggest magazine for women, with *Asos* magazine in second place. Free magazine *Stylist* was third, while the highest-circulating paid-for magazine was *Glamour* in fourth, with a circulation of just over 400,000, according to Audit Bureau of Circulations figures (*Press Gazette*, 2013).

Customer magazines are either produced in-house by the brand itself, like *Asos* magazine, or contracted out to a specialist company like John Brown Media, which produces *John Lewis Edition*. They're available in store, or sent directly to customers or subscribers on the brand's database.

Journalists once sniffed at customer magazines, which were seen as compromised by having to feature the brands' own goods, and extremely uncool. Now, some of the biggest names write regular columns for customer magazines, which are protected from the advertising downturn by the brands' marketing budgets.

Customer magazines don't just exist for the behemoths of the corporate world; many companies from shopping centres and high street stores to hotels and airlines have their own magazines.

Hattie Crisell, a freelance journalist who writes fashion and lifestyle pieces, says:

> It's often better paid than consumer publishing. A lot of successful journalists are balancing the two, so you might be reading an amazing article in *Vogue* by a fantastic fashion journalist, but what you might not know is that she's also doing some freelancing for *Asos* magazine or M&S magazine but she's not going to be shouting about it from the rooftops as much as she would about *Vogue*.

(2012)

Guardian fashion editor Jess Cartner-Morley and *Daily Telegraph* deputy fashion editor Luke Leitch have both written regular columns for *John Lewis Edition*, for example.

The main difference between customer and consumer publishing, Hattie says, is that

> in customer publishing the client is king. It can be quite difficult, because your client is a business person, they're not a journalist, and they have ideas about what they want to see. You have to relinquish some of the editorial control you'd have in consumer publishing.

Trade magazines

Another branch of the magazine market is business-to-business, or trade, magazines. They're written not for the general reader but for members of a specific trade or profession, and as such contain specialised information as opposed to general interest or consumer-led features.

They can be costly, as the information is not available elsewhere and gives readers a commercial advantage, and most are sold through subscription rather than on the news stand.

Women's Wear Daily is the leading US trade magazine for fashion while in the UK, *Drapers* describes itself as 'the voice of the fashion industry' for more than 100 years (2012).

Drapers' print circulation of 8,671 (ibid.) is tiny compared to a consumer magazine, but almost two-thirds of these readers are hugely influential owners, heads or senior managers of fashion brands, retailers, e-tailers and manufacturers. Besides, it claims that five people read every copy purchased, and it also has 92,000 web users a month.

It covers industry news, interviews and analysis that will be of interest to those working in fashion. Like consumer magazines, it also does shoots, covers catwalk shows and compiles trend reports, but more from the point of view of the retailer (helping buyers) than the consumer. Its journalists also travel the world reporting from trade and textile fairs and graduate fashion shows.

The reporting is rigorous and respected, and Polan describes trade magazines as 'an excellent training ground for young journalists, immensely improving the nose for news of any would-be fashionista' (2006: 167).

Websites

Although most fashion journalists will work for the Web in some way, some are hired specifically to work online, either for a magazine's website or for a stand-alone site.

Jessica Bumpus, fashion features editor for *Vogue* online (www.vogue.co.uk), describes how the site has grown since 2007. 'When I started there were two full-time and one part-time members of staff. Now there are seven of us and an intern – it's a massive site and we've relaunched about four times' (2013b).

Jessica compiles the shopping section of the website, reports on catwalk shows, writes news and features, and does interviews, sometimes on video.

Vogue.co.uk grew, she says, because it worked as an entity in itself, breaking news and doing exclusive content, as opposed to other magazine websites that acted as an online front for the print edition. 'The magazine can't break news. They can do an amazing interview, but we can get it up first.'

The online team still work in unison with the magazine staff, but have to repurpose content into a web-friendly format. 'For example, we'd turn a 2,000 word feature into a gallery spin-off – there are different ways to translate it for a different audience,' she says.

Another difference between the website and the magazine is the fact that *Vogue* online is often accessed by searches, rather than an active decision to land there. 'When we put something online, it's in its own world, whereas with the magazine you've made a conscious decision to buy it,' Jessica says.

'So we are writing for the more general online audiences, as well as followers. We have to tell the story directly and clearly. People use the content for information gathering and don't spend as much time reading.'

Blogs aside, most fashion-only websites tend to be part of an existing brand. Web advertising generally brings in less money than print advertising – discussed further in Chapter 3 – so it is difficult for a stand-alone site to generate enough money to pay staff wages.

Never Underdressed, a fashion site set up by publishers Shortlist Media, aimed to break that mould when it launched in 2013 with 14 full-time fashion journalists. It closed in July 2014.

Its news editor Harriet Walker said it was trying to combine the speed of online with the beauty and luxury of glossy magazines in a way that nobody had managed before:

> We are doing something that is very different from print – our updates are much more regular, they're much more quick, there's more of them. We're also doing something that's very different from magazines' websites because we have shoots and these amazing graphics, and the whole thing is meant to feel like it's art directed in a way those websites don't.
> (2013a)

At the time of writing, free newspaper company Metro International was also trying to launch a fashion website. It had advertised a job spec for style editor that not only required the traditional skills of a fashion journalist – the ability to spot trends, strong content ideas, coverage of shows and events – but also online and digital skills, including multimedia packages, viral-ready copy and a strong social media presence.

'If you're not adept at Twitter and Facebook, if you rarely check out Instagram, Pinterest, Vine or Tumblr, you're probably not ready to apply,' it warned (*Fashion Monitor*, 2013). The names of the social media channels will change, but more and more job specs will probably look like this.

E-commerce sites

By 2013, many of the new jobs in fashion journalism being advertised were at e-commerce sites, rather than editorial.

Despite initial scepticism that fashion, and especially luxury fashion, would not work on the Web, sales of online fashion soared by 152 per cent between 2005 and 2010, and were expected to reach almost £7 billion a year by 2015 (Mintel, 2011).

So retailers have scrabbled to have a strong online presence, which increasingly includes editorial – magazine-style trend reports and shoots – as well as commerce, the business of selling clothes.

It's good news for fashion journalists, who are getting hired for roles once considered as copywriting or marketing. 'Journalists have a different skill set. They know how to engage the reader, and engage communities of readers,' says Julia Hutchison of the Content Marketing Association (in Greene, 2011).

Some e-tailers have gone in guns blazing with lavish, well-staffed digital magazines, like Net-a-Porter's *The Edit* and its male equivalent, Mr Porter's *The Journal*. Others have introduced a stronger editorial feel to their main website, such My-wardrobe.com which hired *Grazia* founding editor-in-chief Fiona McIntosh as consultant to add a magazine-style gloss to its online presence.

As well as sending out printed style guides to the site's top 100,000 customers, Fiona worked on giving the site a stronger 'look' and feel. 'We wanted to get a modern, sharp identity into the pictures, and we kept the copy really short and punchy, not cold and fashion-y,' she says (2012).

Alex Murphy, a young journalist who was editor of *Elle*'s Edited by the Interns edition in October 2012, got her first job as product writer for My-wardrobe.com.

She wrote descriptions of all products – about 100 items a week – and sets them live on the site. She wrote emails to customers showcasing new drops, and contributed copy to an inspirations section of the site.

> I see all the product, and I spot certain micro-trends – for example, I've seen lots of ombre dip-dyes in watery colours, a lot of fish prints, so to tie in with our holiday shop we did a feature called 'The Life Aquatic'.
>
> Because My-wardrobe.com is quite a small company, if someone sees something that would make a big impact on the website or would make a good email, or make a good category, even, for merchandisers to put together, then they can make a suggestion, and we can see if that works.
> (2013)

Alex's editorial eye worked together with commerce in ways that online has made possible.

This is happening at a local, as well as a national, level. Online, even regional boutiques can have the presence of a global e-tailer and the fashion content to match.

Jules B, a Newcastle-based chain of independent boutiques, has worked on its web content with the help of Sunderland University journalism graduate Adam Mooney to the extent that its online turnover was around £4.5 million per year by 2013.

Adam wrote his own job description based on a role he found on the Net-a-Porter website when he joined Jules B in 2009. 'My job was to describe products in a way that was editorial in nature and with Google keywords built in,' he says (2013). As fashion coordinator, he also styled and coordinated photo shoots of all the garments.

He's proud of how the website (www.julesb.co.uk) has developed.

> When I started, it had been up for less than a year, and it was a really basic site. But as an independent retailer, you've got to keep up with what's happening with the big guys. Now the website is our bread and butter. In store, your catchment is a 10-mile radius but online it's endless if you do it well.

A host of big-name journalists now work in e-tail – *Esquire* ex-editor Jeremy Langmead at Mr Porter, *Harper's* ex-editor Lucy Yeomans at Net-a-Porter and former *Grazia* associate fashion director Siobhan Mallen at Asos, to name but three.

Those still in traditional media agree it's a good option, especially for young journalists. Amber Graafland, fashion director at the *Mirror*, says: 'It's a really good side to get into, because these people have money!'

Freelance

A lot of fashion editors who have jobs on magazines or newspapers also do freelance work, either on the writing or styling side. Employers are normally quite happy for this to go on because they know they don't pay very well themselves.

But some journalists make their entire living as freelancers – pitching and writing stories for a variety of outlets, or contracted to contribute regular features for a specific publication. If you see 'editor at large' or 'contributing editor' against someone's name on a magazine masthead, they are freelance rather than a full-time member of staff.

Polly Vernon is a freelance writer who regularly contributes to the Saturday *Times* and *Grazia*. She has to make sure she can write about more than fashion – 'the more you can do the better, for any paper or magazine' – and believes she's got more freedom than other magazine journalists because 'I'm a little bit immune to having to please advertisers. I can push things a little bit further' (2012).

But she has to have tremendous self-discipline to forge a successful career:

> I'm really quick. I've never skipped a deadline in my 15-year career. I don't drink and work. I get up and write better in the mornings. I walk a hell of a lot because it really clears your head.

Hattie Crisell has done a huge variety of freelance work, from covering London Fashion Week for *New York Magazine*'s The Cut website to editing a magazine for French fashion company La Redoute.
'It has pros and cons,' she says.

> It's financially insecure and you're not guaranteed work. You might go through periods where you're not entirely sure when you're going to be paid, and it can be labour-intensive because you have to spend a lot of time nurturing the contacts you've got.
>
> On the other hand, it often pays more than a permanent staff role, and there's so much variety, freedom and opportunity to do different kinds of work, meet different kinds of people.
>
> The secret to doing well in freelancing is to be a safe pair of hands. It's as simple as don't mess things up and get on well with people.
>
> (2012)

Hattie believes freelancing will become increasingly common in journalism. 'There are fewer staff jobs, and it works better for companies because they don't have that much obligation to you.'

Highs and lows of fashion journalism

Like all work, fashion journalism has its pros and cons, and they're worth bearing in mind when considering a job in the industry.

One drawback might be long and unpredictable hours. Stories have to be completed, whether or not the working day is officially over, and there'll be evening events to attend. Shows are frantic, and shoots abroad generally hectic.

On newspapers and websites, this is exacerbated by daily deadlines. Amber Graafland, fashion director of the *Daily Mirror*, says: 'On a paper you don't get bank holidays off, so you don't get all those holidays you could share with your family and friends, and that can get you down after a while.'

Lucy Wood, senior fashion news editor of *Look*, says it's just as hard work on a weekly magazine. 'You get 30 minutes to write a story and you're non-stop between 9.30am and 6pm; then you have events in the evening. Beyond that, looking for stories never stops.'

The pay is not great in the lower ranks of the profession compared to other graduate jobs, either. A first job at a magazine may only be paid £16–18,000 a year, and that's in central London. Lucy says it leads to a weird dichotomy, where you're writing about things you can't afford to buy yourself. 'We are taken to really lovely places for launches, but we have beans on toast for dinner when we get home,' she adds.

However, that's offset against free travel, discount shopping cards for high street and designer stores, and the odd freebie as a thank you from a PR.

Besides, fashion journalists are far more forthcoming about the things they love about the job. Many say they're grateful to be writing about something they love and are fascinated by. 'I'm in the minority of my friends in having a job I'm genuinely interested in,' says *Never Underdressed*'s Harriet Walker. Luke Leitch, of the *Daily Telegraph*, says: 'I find the fashion world constantly fascinating, and the only thing I try and do is recognise what the most entertaining things are and pass them on in copy form.'

Add to that a job where no two days are the same, you're meeting new people all the time, travelling to new places, being creative, working with clothes and knowing what's coming into shops, and you can see why so many people want to get into fashion journalism.

'It's exciting and it's changing all the time, and I've never once in my five and a half years at *Grazia* sat down and thought, "I'm bored today, I've got nothing to do,"' says fashion editor Hannah Almassi. Quite a recommendation.

Recommended reading

Edwards-Jones, I. (2007) *Fashion Babylon*. London: Corgi.

Jackson, T. and Shaw, D. (2006) *The Fashion Handbook (Media Practice)*. London: Routledge.

McKay, J. (2013) *The Magazines Handbook*, 3rd edition. London: Routledge.

McNair, B. (2009) *News and Journalism in the UK*, 5th edition. London: Routledge.

Press Gazette: www.pressgazette.co.uk.

Professional Publishers Association: www.ppa.co.uk.

2 Ways in to fashion journalism

Introduction

The first job is the hardest to get – on that all fashion journalists are agreed, apart perhaps from the *Daily Telegraph*'s Luke Leitch, who was surprised to end up in fashion (more of that later). Once you've got the crucial first foot on the ladder, it's much easier to go from job to job.

In news journalism, it's relatively simple. You get industry qualifications, you join a local newspaper or news agency as a trainee, you sit further exams 18 months later and become a senior journalist, and you might then try your chances in London on a national.

In fashion, there is no officially sanctioned route in. But the backgrounds of a range of well-established fashion journalists and those just starting on their careers throw up some recurring themes, outlined in this chapter.

The main route is still the internship, and this chapter will explain the different types of internship, how to apply for them and what you do when you're there.

There are problems with internships, though – not least the pay, or lack of it, and the fact that you could intern for years without ever getting a job – and so other ways into fashion journalism will be explored.

Company editor Victoria White, in particular, says it's incredibly naive to focus just on the glossies, where jobs are scarce and competition fierce. She says interns confuse wanting to work on a fashion magazine with wanting to be a journalist, adding: 'Any way in is a good way in.'

Finally, it will look at the old clichés of the terrifying designer-clad fashion maven immortalised in books and films like *The Devil Wears Prada* – a fiction that still seems to haunt fashion journalism hopefuls of every generation – and will hopefully put their mind at rest.

Although some of the advice in this chapter might seem a little daunting, especially if you haven't started university yet or are in your first year, don't be discouraged. You can learn the skills on your course, and get support from tutors and careers advisers on applying for placements as you go.

Do you need a degree?

Like many professions, journalism is increasingly made up of graduates. Victoria White, editor of *Company* magazine, says: 'Of all the editors I'm close to [*Elle*,

Cosmopolitan, *Glamour*], I'm the only one with a degree. That's because I'm the youngest of the bunch – the next generation will all have degrees' (2013).

As magazine and newspaper budgets shrink, universities are taking on the responsibility of training would-be journalists. Moreover, it's easier to take on students as unpaid interns than people already in the job market; National Minimum Wage guidelines don't apply to students in full-time education, even when they're taking a year out on a sandwich course.

Given that a degree is highly useful, and likely to become more so, does it matter what type of course you do?

Because of the internship system, graduates from all types of degree courses do make it into fashion journalism. Professionals quizzed for this book did degrees ranging from politics, philosophy and economics to religious studies to American studies.

But that might be changing. The *Guardian*'s fashion editor Jess Cartner-Morley, who studied history, said: 'I don't have specialist training in fashion. None of my peers did. But the younger ones coming through tend to have either a journalism or a fashion qualification' (2011b).

Some younger journalists studied fashion design, like *Grazia*'s Hannah Almassi who said it left her with a hatred for sewing machines but an appreciation of what it takes to produce a fashion garment.

Others believe it's more useful to do a journalism degree. Charlie Porter, ex of the *Guardian*, *GQ* and *Fantastic Man*, says: 'Fashion needs to be treated just like any other features or news subject – pretending it's special, being all aloof and exclusive, can actually denigrate it' (*Press Gazette*, 2003).

Interns and assistants also find that having a journalism background gives them the confidence to suggest they try writing, even if they're largely confined to the fashion cupboard.

Madeleine Bowden, a University of Sunderland journalism graduate who had a year's internship at *Elle* magazine, says:

> Having a journalism degree is amazing. If you're interning and mention you've done journalism and can write, a magazine may let you do a little piece for online and see how that turns out; then it can develop from there. It makes you stand out.
>
> (2013)

Some journalism degrees are accredited by industry bodies like the National Council for the Training of Journalists (NCTJ), the Professional Publishers Association (PPA) or the Broadcast Journalism Training Council (BJTC), which means students have to have covered certain subjects and skills, and, in the case of the NCTJ, passed industry standard exams.

There are a handful of specific fashion journalism degrees in the UK: at the London College of Fashion, University of the Creative Arts in Epsom, Southampton Solent University and the University of Sunderland. There are also degrees called fashion promotion, or writing fashion, or fashion communication, which will include elements of fashion journalism.

All these degrees will involve varying levels of styling, too, but there are specific degrees in fashion styling at London College of Fashion and Southampton Solent University, and joint honours degrees that include styling at the University of Central Lancashire and Middlesex University.

Graduates of any discipline can also do a journalism or fashion journalism master's degree – effectively a conversion degree that lasts a year.

If you're looking for a suitable degree course, it's worth thinking about what added value it will give you. The London College of Fashion has a strong reputation and its graduates can be found in many fields of fashion journalism.

Meanwhile, degrees with industry accreditation are recognised by employers as guaranteeing a certain professional standard. Doing NCTJ exams at the same time as your degree (as you can at Sunderland, the only fashion journalism course to be NCTJ-accredited) keeps your options open when you graduate, as you'll be qualified to work at a newspaper, magazine or news agency if your first job doesn't turn out to be in fashion (not uncommon).

Subjects like shorthand and law are worth their weight in gold for a working journalist in any discipline. Louise Gannon, a freelancer who writes for *Elle*, *Grazia* and the *Mail on Sunday*, says: 'I was in an interview with Madonna and my tape recorder batteries were running out, and if I didn't have shorthand I'd have been screwed!' (2012b).

Loraine Davies, training director at the Professional Publishers Association, says prospective students should also look for digital as well as traditional skills on any university course. 'Magazines have an enormous skills gap, and courses whose focus is entirely traditional are not working,' she says.

> You have to learn how to tell a story, how to edit copy, what the law is, but you also need to understand how to get winning copy out on the various platforms available, and how to be just as good in 140 characters as you would be in 5,000 words.
>
> (2013)

Just how multi-skilled fashion journalists need to be is evident in fashion editor Hannah Almassi's description of covering a Kenzo catwalk show in Paris for *Grazia*.

'Not only did I write the report, but I'd learned how to use the content management system, Photoshop my own pictures, do the headlines, and make sure everything was tagged for search engine optimisation,' she says (2012b).

The problem is, not all publications are agreed just what multimedia skills a graduate entrant needs to have because of their different approaches to the web.

It's a tricky question for the PPA, which has to decide on the skills degree courses should teach before it will accredit them. Loraine Davies says:

> I was with a group of editors recently, and one said a graduate has to be able to podcast and put together a really good video.

Another editor from a different company said they didn't care, because they outsource those skills. We at the PPA just have to hold the middle ground.

Internships

The closest thing to an accepted way into fashion journalism is work placements or internships, where you work for anything from two weeks to a year at a magazine, newspaper or website assisting fashion writers and editors there and learning on the job.

Not only do you learn vital skills and get a taste of the industry, but you start to make the contacts so essential in the relatively small world of fashion journalism.

A two-week placement on *Elle* changed stylist Madeleine Bowden's life. While there, she applied for and got a year-long internship assisting *Elle's* market and merchandising editor. On the strength of that, she moved from Newcastle to London.

> Going to *Elle* was the best thing that happened to me because I was talking to everyone, daily, from Chanel, Gucci and Lanvin to Next. I was meeting all the PRs at press days and going to call-ins. It opened up my world.
>
> (2013)

On the strength of that, she has enough work to operate freelance, still doing shoots for *Elle* and other magazines, but also a stint assisting *X Factor* stylist Laury Smith and dressing one of the show's judges, Nicole Scherzinger, along with singer Jessie J.

Not only that, but the internship gives employers the chance to cherry-pick talented journalists. The hope is always that you'll be given a longer-term contract as an assistant on that particular publication or be recommended when jobs come up elsewhere.

Emma Bigger, fashion editor on *Company*, had a fairly typical start:

> At university, doing English literature, I did lots of placements during holidays – once you have one or two under your belt it's a lot easier to get other ones.
>
> I did a post-graduate journalism degree and after graduating, I did a three-month placement at *Glamour*, being paid travel and lunch, and then they kept me on on a rolling contract, so I was a freelance fashion assistant, basically. The position came up at *Company* and because I knew that was permanent, I took that.
>
> (2012)

Grazia fashion editor Hannah Almassi was so organised she lined up a year's worth of placements starting the week after she graduated. Like Emma, she was asked to stay on at *Grazia* on a rolling contract to assist fashion news and features editor Melanie Rickey, and ended up doing it for 18 months before getting a permanent job there.

So valuable are these freelance assisting roles that Lucy Wood, senior fashion news editor at *Look*, stayed at *Grazia* assisting Melanie Rickey for the whole of her final year at university, seeing her tutors once a week and writing her dissertation in the evenings.

It's worth pointing out that you'd be extremely lucky to swan into your favourite fashion magazine and be picked up immediately. Most people who make it have done dozens of placements, some a lot less glamorous than others. They have proved they want to be journalists, not just fashion journalists.

Company's Emma Bigger worked at two local newspapers in Northern Ireland as well as contract publishers before she got the *Glamour* role. Alex Murphy, now in e-tail, may have been the high-profile head of *Elle*'s Edited by the Interns issue in October 2012 but she also interned for a contract publisher producing in-flight magazines for easyJet and Ryanair.

Company editor Victoria White says:

> The more work experience you get the better, and it's so naive to stick to the glossies. Weeklies are a great training ground; they have a huge staff compared to monthlies. My first job was *Inside Soap*, and it was still the best job I've ever had.

> (2011)

Applying for a placement/internship

A placement generally lasts two to four weeks, is meant to be a learning experience, and is unpaid, while an internship is longer than a month, involves specific tasks and … well, the pay issue is a problematic one and will be discussed below (pp. 22–24).

Most magazines and newspapers have continuous fashion and editorial placements or internships, but many are booked way in advance, so it pays to be organised.

Placement opportunities also come up on Gorkana (www.gorkanajobs.co.uk), Twitter and the Bauer Media and O2 website GoThinkBig (www.gothinkbig.co.uk), so keep an eye on those.

And remember, don't restrict yourself to the glossies; retailers like Asos, local magazines, weeklies, trade magazines, newspapers, news agencies and contract publishers all provide invaluable experience.

Your application – normally by email – will consist of a covering letter in the main body of the email, with your CV attached.

Make sure you address the email to the right person … the editor is NOT the right person, however friendly they may seem on Twitter. Most magazine websites give you the name and email address of the relevant person under their 'contact us' section, but if you're in any doubt ring up the magazine and ask who it is.

Jessica Bumpus, fashion features editor at *Vogue* online, says:

> I get lots of CVs sent to me and not only am I not the right person to send them to but they won't even have been addressed to me within the main body of the email and will just say 'To whom it may concern'. This looks like you haven't taken any time whatsoever to find out who is the right person, and suggests you'd do the same given any other task.
>
> (University of the Arts London website)

That's one of the main gripes about intern applications – another is not being familiar with the publication you're applying to. *Grazia*'s Hannah Almassi says: 'If you're applying for a job somewhere it should be because you're interested in working there, so know the pages, know what they're called, the kind of products featured, the way they're written' (2012b).

It's also useful to get hold of the publication's media kit (usually available online; see Chapter 3 for more details) where it describes its typical reader and how it appeals to them.

Next, consider what editors are looking for in an intern and how you might meet that. Another common mistake in application letters is to write it from the point of view of what the publication could do for you, rather than what you could offer.

What do editors want? Of course they want great writers, with immaculate spelling and grammar, but a lot of them cite fresh ideas and enthusiasm as vital. 'We can train writers to knock a story into shape but we can't teach fresh, innovative, finger-on-the-pulse ideas,' says Marianne Jones, deputy editor of *Grazia* (2012).

Victoria Kennedy, deputy editor of *Now* magazine, adds: 'Be enthusiastic – we've got the best jobs in the world! There is nothing more off-putting that someone who isn't passionate about what they do' (2012).

Your email or letter should:

- state what you're applying for, and when you're available to work;
- say why you'd love to work there – show enthusiasm and a strong knowledge of the brand;
- summarise your strengths and experience, and point to the CV attached as having further details;
- thank the employer and say you're looking forward to hearing from them soon.

All in two or three beautifully written, grammatically perfect paragraphs!

Anything that might make your application stand out is worth including – a little joke, anything that makes you sound really keen to work there. 'Anything creative or sparkly, anything that makes you sound grateful, will make it stronger,' says *Company* editor Victoria White (2011).

Above all, your letter must be professional. It should not include a single spelling mistake or lapse into text speak, and if in doubt start with 'Dear such-and-such' rather than 'hi!' ... and don't sign off with kisses.

If you're sending out several applications at once, using the same basic letter, check that you have changed the name and publication title for each one; otherwise your application will go straight in the bin.

There is a lot of guidance online on how to write a CV, and schools, colleges and university careers services will also help. Some CVs can be very creative; a design specialist might create theirs to look like a magazine page, for example, to show off their skills, or someone might create a video CV.

But a simple, clear Word document of one or two pages is good enough, as long as it's clear enough to be taken in at a glance.

There are no hard-and-fast rules, but it's useful to put your name in large type at the top instead of Curriculum Vitae (everyone knows it's that), with your address, date of birth, telephone number and email address underneath.

A personal statement of one or two sentences is worth including to summarise who you are very quickly, tailored to whichever job you're applying for. Include concrete details ('I'm a final-year fashion journalism student ... ') rather than just personal qualities.

The most important categories on your CV will be your education/qualifications and your employment record, including work placements and internships. It's useful to include a line under each post explaining what it involved and what you achieved. Start with the most recent qualification or post, and work backwards in time.

Any other categories are optional, but skills, interests or other achievements can enhance a CV. Some jobs require a clean driving licence, for example. A good knowledge of French might be an asset, and you could also list skills like use of Adobe InDesign and Photoshop here (which editors may not know are part of your course).

Christina Simone, workflow director at *Elle*, looks through all the CVs the magazine receives and forwards them on to the relevant department if she thinks they're strong enough.

What is she looking for? 'I try to find fashion interns that have experience in other magazine fashion departments, art/pictures interns who know how to use InDesign and have a portfolio, and features interns who write a good cover letter and have a well-written CV,' she says (2013).

What do you do on a placement/internship?

Editorial

On an editorial internship, you'll be assisting the writers, be they features, news, health or celebrity. Hattie Crisell, freelance writer, began her career with a four-month editorial internship at *Red* magazine:

I'd ring up PRs [public relations executives who deal with the press on a brand's behalf] that the writers needed something from, did research, photocopied, made cups of tea, did little bits of writing, and any little job that needed doing.

(2012)

When Hannah Almassi assisted *Grazia* fashion news and features editor Melanie Rickey, she'd do background research for her, found catwalk pictures, sourced products for a page she was editing, and shadowed her on interviews.

On a placement of less than a month, you might also find yourself distributing the office post, putting calls through to the right people, transcribing recorded interviews and doing the coffee run. It's not unknown to have to pick up the editor's dry cleaning! But you will also get to research stories and pictures and write short pieces, especially for the Web.

Fashion

This is where the infamous fashion cupboard comes in – the small room where all clothes and accessories called in for shoots pass through. If you're on a placement or short internship, it's where you'll start, like generations of fashion editors before you.

Your main task there will be to take delivery of garments sent by PRs, log them, sort them and, if necessary, pack them for fashion shoots, and then return them back to PRs. 'Everyone on staff has too much to do, so they need people in to clear the cupboards,' says Madeleine Bowden, the stylist who interned at *Elle*.

When clothes come in, Madeleine advises interns to check them for damage, take a picture and email the PR straight away to let them know; otherwise you might be blamed when the garment goes back. You'll hang the clothes on a rail ready for the fashion editor to make a selection – depending on your editor, you'll hang them according to brands, to items or to colour.

If they're to be photographed as products on a page, you might have to write the details of each piece on a form so you can do the credits, pack them up and send them to a photographer. If they're for a shoot, you'll have to put everything in tissue paper, hanging bags and cases for the fashion team.

When the clothes come back, you have to get them dry-cleaned if they're dirty, pack them and send them back to the PR. You'll have to handle any fallout if samples are damaged or have gone missing, liaising with the PR to sort it out.

It might sound tedious, but it's a good test of initiative and dedication, says Madeleine:

> It's sink or swim, and they take that as a sign of how good you're going to be as a fashion assistant.
> At the end of the day, it's only fashion – but for that shoot, it has to be your life. It has to be the most important thing in your world at that time.

Madeleine also used her time in the cupboard to memorise and test herself on which brands went back to which PR companies. 'So now, if someone names me a brand, I can say the PR company and the contact straight away. It's useful, and it stopped me going insane in the cupboard!'

If you do a longer internship or are given a rolling contract, you'll be basically doing the job of a fashion assistant. This might mean compiling the fashion team's diary, going to press days they can't make, and calling in clothes for fashion shoots.

'They'll go through *Style.com* and pick looks, about 40–50 for main fashion. You'll put them in preference order and try to secure them from the PR company,' says Madeleine.

> We have massive boards and all the looks are pinned to them, so you can cross them off as they're confirmed or come in. On *Elle*, you'd probably get 20–25 looks in, though the story is only ever going to be six looks.

You'd attend shoots with your fashion editor, acting as a kind of production manager, prepping props and locations, unpacking and ironing clothes, and helping to dress the models.

A fashion assistant might also suggest and compile shopping pages, where products are gathered in themes, with a short blurb and captions. They'd assemble a selection of high-resolution images of the products (either from the press office, downloaded from the brand's site or taken from a site like PRshots.com), and then put it to the editor for approval before either calling in the products to be photographed or using the brands' PR images.

Your first permanent job in a fashion department would be at assistant level (some have junior and senior assistants), before rising to fashion editor.

How to be a good intern

Tales of bad interns abound – people who turn up late or not at all, one intern who rang in to say she'd be working from home that day, and others who are only interested in making a splash without putting in the hard work.

So every fashion journalist is full of tips for interns. This is what they boil down to:

- Be enthusiastic. 'Be super friendly, super enthusiastic; never roll your eyes when you're asked to do something really basic even though you've got a degree!' says freelancer Hattie Crisell. Tackling everything that comes at you with relish and offering to do other tedious tasks nobody else wants to do are the only way to get on.
- Know when to ask. You should show initiative, but ask for advice when you're really not sure. 'We don't expect you to know everything to begin with, so if in doubt do ask,' says Jessica Bumpus of *Vogue* online (University of the Arts London website).

- Be thorough. Don't rush work and check it carefully, says Jessica. 'If you end up making more work for the people you're supposed to be helping, it's not going to be so great' (ibid.).
- Be realistic. You have to earn the right to go on shoots or write for the magazine. 'Don't expect to be writing cover profiles, but if you're good and do the boring stuff well, you'll probably get asked to do amazing things,' says *Company* editor Victoria White (2010).
- Do as lengthy an internship as possible. Tracey Lea Sayer, fashion director at *Fabulous*, says it's hard to be remembered when you're only there for two weeks. 'But if someone's with you for a long time and makes themselves indispensible to you, they're really at the forefront of your mind if any vacancies come up. Or you can recommend them to people you've worked with' (2013).
- Keep in touch. 'Don't be afraid to get back in touch with people you have worked with; otherwise it's easy to be forgotten about. My intern kept emailing, became friends, came in to freelance and now she works at *Company*,' says the magazine's fashion editor Emma Bigger.

Other interns are another good source of advice and support. Melody Small, a 20-year-old student from Canterbury who did a two-week editorial placement at *Grazia*, said: 'Make friends with other workies – it's meant people have sent me their cover letters to help with my own, given advice on getting other placements and told me where vacancies are open' (2013).

Another tip from Melody is to be remembered:

> I always buy the desk I've been working on some biscuits or something to say thank you for having me. One magazine tweeted their appreciation. It means they might remember you for something, even if it's as the biscuit girl!

The trouble with internships

For many, internships have acted as a kind of apprenticeship system, where they prove themselves by working alongside a fashion editor, get picked up as a fashion assistant, secure a permanent job and eventually rise to be a fashion editor themselves.

So what's the problem? It's whether you get paid or not for the work you're doing, and who exactly can afford to intern in London before getting a permanent job.

The rules about payment are still vague. According to the Professional Publishers Association, you should not expect to be paid on a work placement of two to four weeks as it's a learning experience rather than work. Many publications will offer expenses of £10–15 a day for travel and food.

There is no direct legislation about pay for interns, but National Minimum Wage guidelines do say that anyone who contributes to the business, has set duties and works set hours SHOULD be paid at least the minimum wage, unless they're full-time students on a sandwich course.

Unpaid interns who have taken employers to court in the past have won their case; see, for example, the case of Keri Hudson, who was awarded five weeks' pay after interning at online review site My Village (Malik, 2011).

The Professional Publishers Association advises magazines to pay interns:

> not just because there is legislation guiding employers to make payment, but because we believe those who don't pay perpetuate the lack of social diversity in our industry by excluding those students who simply can't afford to work for no pay.
>
> (PPA, 2012a)

Some magazines, like *Elle*, pay interns. Some, like *Fabulous*, will only take full-time students who are interning as part of their course, so it doesn't have to pay them anything beyond expenses. Others will pay something, but not a full-time wage, when they take someone on as assistant on a rolling contract.

Amber Graafland, fashion director of the *Daily Mirror*, worked for almost two years unpaid before she got a fashion assistant's job, about 12 years ago. 'Things have changed; you can't do that any more', she says. 'But I do think some of these girls have to go and work for nothing for a while, or with just a tiny bit of money.'

Interns are so desperate for a break, though, they'll do it. Lucy Wood, who worked on *Grazia* for a small wage during her final year at university, says:

> I was doing it for the title and the pages and my own byline and a portfolio filling up.
>
> Having a business card with *Grazia* on and being on the masthead [the list of staff, published near the start of a magazine] is enough when you're starting out in fashion. You have to be prepared to do that for little or no money.

But to do this, you have to have somewhere to live in or near central London, where most internships take place, and you often have to have a family in a position to help you out. Lucy admits: 'I was very lucky: my parents helped me out a lot. But it got to the point where my dad gave me six months after graduation to get a paid job.'

The internship system is inevitably skewed in favour of people from middle-class backgrounds who live in or near London. Some break through – Harriet Walker, of *Never Underdressed*, comes from Sheffield and worked in a pub and as an au pair to be able to intern in London.

Fabulous fashion director Tracey Lea Sayer, from Liverpool, lived in a squat until her mum came and got her! Even after that, she says, 'I slept on a lot of people's couches and called in a lot of favours from friends of the family.'

But many others fall through the net. Liz Lamb, from Darlington, graduated from the London College of Fashion and worked for three years at the likes of the *Sunday Times* magazine and the *Independent* before eventually giving up.

'Even when there were jobs going, it was either work for free for a year or on very, very low pay,' she says. 'You get a lot of society girls for whom it's a second job really. And other people from my course were from London and living with their parents.'

Liz returned to the North East, did a training course with the regional newspaper group and worked as a general news reporter before getting a features and fashion job in Newcastle.

It's something even fashion journalists who've made it in London feel uncomfortable about.

Harriet Walker says: 'The internship system is impossible. The most dreadful thing about it is that it doesn't necessarily lead to anything.'

She also feels uneasy that it means that people applying for entry-level fashion assistant roles are often overqualified, having done that very job or higher for years on temporary contracts.

She herself had worked for 18 months at *Glamour* as a temporary assistant on a small wage when she got a permanent assistant role at the *Independent*:

> I got it on the strength that they could see I could write, but also they knew they were getting a junior fashion editor whom they could pay as an assistant.
>
> Had I literally been an assistant who hadn't done any writing, didn't have any training and didn't have any experience, I wouldn't have got it. They advertise for a certain job when what they want is something different.
>
> It's misleading for a lot of people. As a graduate, you're applying for jobs at entry level and not even getting them because you're up against people who've been doing it for five years, which is crazy.

There are campaigns to change this, like Intern Aware, which has a video interview with London College of Fashion head Frances Corner saying interns who have graduated should all be paid at least the minimum wage plus expenses. 'Attitudes are changing, but we have to keep pushing,' she said (www.internaware.org/media). The National Union of Journalists also has a 'cashback for interns' campaign.

In the meantime, people desperate to get into the industry will carry on doing stints of work for little or no money, in the hope it will pay off. Lucy Wood of *Look* has these consoling words:

> You do see girls who are interning all the time and the jobs aren't coming up. But I firmly believe that if you put the work in, to the right standard, and are going to all the events in the evening and socialising and networking, then there's nothing to stop you getting one of these jobs.

Other ways in

For those who don't have the wherewithal or the stomach to intern, there are other ways into fashion journalism, especially on the writing side.

Newspapers and news agencies

Some journalists will get their first job at a newspaper, perhaps in a general or features role, and gradually feel their way to fashion.

Fashion journalist Charlie Porter couldn't afford to take up a place on a fashion journalism master's course at Central Saint Martins, and instead got a job as a researcher on the *Daily Express* newspaper. He moved on to arts journalism, working as commissioning editor at *The Times* and as arts editor at *Esquire*, before landing the job of deputy fashion editor at the *Guardian*.

'At the *Guardian* they prefer to have a view of fashion that isn't necessarily linear, but has a broader, features-based viewpoint. Having had wider journalism experience helped me approach fashion as a multifaceted thing,' he says (2013b).

He went on to *GQ* as associate editor, then to *Fantastic Man* as deputy editor. Now he is menswear critic at the *Financial Times* and works on his website charlieporter.net.

Jess Cartner-Morley, fashion editor of the *Guardian*, landed at the newspaper as a general features researcher, then commissioning editor at its *G2* supplement before moving into fashion. Lack of fashion training didn't put her off – 'It's more about knowing how to write a story,' she says. 'It's always story-based journalism. I learned the rest on the job' (2011).

Lorraine Candy, editor of *Elle*, began her career on the *Cornish Times* and *Wimbledon Times*, while a predecessor of hers, Fiona McIntosh, was trained and put through university by the *Melbourne Herald* in her native Australia. One of her peers is now on the *Wall Street Journal*, but Fiona came to London, where she has edited *Company* and *Elle*, and was the founding editor-in-chief of *Grazia*.

One of the most unexpected leaps across to fashion journalism was made by Luke Leitch, deputy fashion editor of the *Daily Telegraph*. Luke did a postgraduate journalism degree and worked as a news reporter and arts correspondent for the *Evening Standard* before moving to features on *The Times*.

The Times' deputy fashion editor went off on maternity leave and, out of the blue, the newspaper asked Luke to cover for her. 'It was perfect newspaper logic – I was available and I was cheap,' he says.

> Within a week or two I was in New York for the shows.
>
> It was very confusing at first; it's a largely female world and I made some naive mistakes, but people were tolerant. And, I think, slightly amused as well because I really was quite shambolic.
>
> (2013c)

On the fashion side, he had to feel his way, but his journalism stood him in good stead.

> The area you're covering is unique, but the fundamental thing is finding and writing entertaining copy. It's also about being outgoing and interested in other people, and trying to think of your readership.
>
> Fashion journalism is a very seductive world and it's important not to be too reverent about it, but also not to be too snide or apologetic about it either because it's wonderful.

As we've seen, fashion journalism graduate Liz Lamb gave up on internships and did a regional newspaper training programme, working as a general reporter before coming back to fashion.

Company editor Victoria White says it's possible to carve out a role for yourself once you're in a newspaper. 'It's still a very male industry, so chances are if you go and tell your male boss you want to write about fashion, he'll say, "Oh really? Go on then," because nobody else wants to do it.'

It's important not to overlook news agencies, either, which are fantastic training grounds for a young journalist. Most cities will have an agency, which will pitch and sell news and features from its patch to national newspapers and magazines. Not only does agency work develop reporting skills and a nose for a good story, but journalists there make good contacts on the national newspapers and magazines they sell stories to.

Zoe Beaty, a journalism graduate from the University of Sunderland, got her first job at North News in Newcastle. After two years, she secured her dream job of features writer at *Grazia*.

Other types of magazine

It's possible to start out on a magazine unrelated to fashion, perfect your skills and then move to a publication that more suits your interests.

Company editor Victoria White began as features writer on *Inside Soap* magazine. From there she went to Australia to edit *Inside TV*, moved to a gossip magazine and then went to Los Angeles as a celebrity correspondent. She returned to the UK as deputy editor of *B* magazine, then went to *Company*.

'It's not just me – someone like Louise Court, editor of *Cosmopolitan*, worked on weeklies for most of her career. Jo Elvin [editor of *Glamour*] worked on *TV Hits* and Jane Bruton [editor of *Grazia*] started on *Chat*,' she says.

> It's a career; it's not just something you like doing. So getting into fashion magazines, you have to decide what your expertise is. If you're a writer, you could write about anything.
>
> There is a naivety around what being a fashion journalist is, and that it's just something you start doing and end doing. But you've got to be good at something.

Other magazine roles

Magazines don't just have writers and stylists: they also have people on the design side. Picture editors will research and secure the best images and perhaps manage shoots. Subeditors conjure up eye-grabbing headlines and brush up journalists' copy, making sure it's the right length, factually and legally correct and as lively as it can be.

Designers and art directors are responsible for the look and layout of the magazine – hugely important in such a visually appealing medium – and increasingly for designing a publication's website and apps.

If you've learned InDesign and Photoshop at university, and have a flair for visuals, it's a dynamic area to go into, says *Company*'s Victoria White:

> Art and graphic design is going to be a massive growth area – visuals are the currency of a magazine on all its platforms, and the art department creates the look and feel across all our touchpoints. We're pretty reliant on them.

Some famous fashion journalists started in the art department. Caryn Franklin, who fronts the Clothes Show Live and runs the campaign group All Walks Beyond the Catwalk, got into *i-D* magazine as a graphic designer before becoming fashion editor there.

Elizabeth Walker, former executive fashion editor of *Marie Claire*, began as assistant art director at *Harpers and Queen*. Her graphic design training helped her in her later role as fashion editor, she says. 'Proportion and understanding the balance of things is one of the hardest things to teach a stylist – knowing how paintings work, with the triangles and the space, helps you very much when you're directing photographs' (2012).

Blogs

It's still quite rare, but there are stories about people getting their first job on the strength of their blog.

Company gave a job to a young woman they met at their bloggers' awards.

Victoria Kennedy, deputy editor of *Now* magazine, says: 'We recently hired someone else for a role who didn't have that much experience but she blew us away so much with her enthusiasm and online blogs at her interview that we actually created a role for her.'

Aaron Christian, video editor at Mr Porter, the male version of Net-a-Porter, perfected his video and online skills by working on a collective blog, Individualism (www.individualism.co.uk), for years. He still juggles the two. 'I'm learning a lot of stuff at Mr Porter that is useful at Individualism and vice versa,' he says. 'I can see both sides of the fence – the blogosphere and the corporate environment' (2013).

Even if your blog doesn't directly land you a job, it could still play a vital part, says Peter Henderson, whose Hapsical blog (http://hapsical.blogspot.co.uk)

has garnered press attention and landed him an invite to a cultural event from his idol, Christian Dior designer Raf Simons.

It certainly helped him get a job as a writer for an e-commerce site that combines retail with editorial:

> A blog is such a great thing to show employers. You can sit in an interview and say, 'I love fashion, I keep up with everything that's going on, I have opinions about it,' but if you keep a blog, you have something concrete to back that up.
>
> (2013)

E-commerce

As we saw in Chapter 1, by 2013 most of the entry-level jobs in fashion journalism were coming up at retailers' websites.

On some sites, the posts will be called product writers, but on others like Asos they'll be called news and fashion writers, producing content for the home page and mobile apps.

Skills required, according to a 2013 job ad for Asos, were the traditional ones of a fashion writer – an eye for a great story, sparkling writing skills, an ability to spot new trends and to meet deadlines – and those of an online content creator, including an ability to use a content management system, an understanding of search optimisation and strong engagement in social media.

Some writers for e-tailer sites do hanker after an editorial job, where the motivation of a story is (slightly) less commercial and it's not likely to get pulled if a product isn't selling.

But some journalists on the editorial side believe e-tail is the place to be. Melanie Rickey, consultant and contributing editor for *Grazia*, says:

> One of my most enjoyable consultancies was at Asos, and I'd never have thought 10 years ago that an online retailer would have 100 editorial staff who probably trained at fashion journalism school.
>
> I talked to them about trends, what we talk about at *Grazia*, but one day the tables will be turned and they'll be the editorial powers, and they'll hire the top editors in the world who'll edit their collections. Net-a-Porter has the potential to be the biggest fashion magazine in the world.
>
> (2012)

The mentor

This isn't a way in as such, as you'd normally meet a mentor through other means like an internship. But there are definitely some inspirational people in the industry who take promising writers under their wing and give them a vital leg up.

One such person is Melanie Rickey, who's worked on the *Independent*, *Daily Telegraph*, *Sunday Times Style*, *Nova* and *Grazia*, consults for top brands and blogs at www.fashioneditoratlarge.com. She has mentored many young fashion journalists and helped them get their first job by introducing them to other editors.

Hannah Almassi worked as her assistant, which turned into a permanent role at *Grazia*. 'I learned so much from Mel. She's a fantastic writer and her mind works well ahead of all the trends.' Lucy Wood was another Melanie protégée, and got her job at *Look* on her recommendation.

Melanie herself says it's a two-way thing:

> When you're in your 30s, you can't pretend you're a 24-year-old going clubbing, so you need a 24-year-old. I'm vicariously living through my assistants! But equally I've got access to people they only dream about, and they need to learn from me, so it's a really good combination.

Not everyone is lucky enough to forge such a career-changing relationship, but you can approach potential mentors for guidance. Sasha Wilkins, who blogs as LibertyLondonGirl, says this is much more common in the United States. 'It's worth contacting someone you really admire, and asking for their advice,' she says (2013b).

Personal qualities required

So far we've discussed the training and experience required to break into fashion journalism – but what about the mindset, attitude and things you can do in your spare time?

Here's a round-up of what fashion journalists say is needed to make it into the industry, and to prosper there when you do:

- *Social skills*. Journalism of any type requires calling people on the phone, speaking to them face to face, getting them to help you and drawing information out of them. Even in the office, you need to work well with other members of your team. 'It's a very social, creative thing when you're on a fashion shoot and all working together to create something,' says Tracey Lea Sayer of *Fabulous*. 'We've had some girls in that don't have great social skills – we have to train them up in how to speak to PRs, how to deal with people around the office, because they're very social online but not in person.' Any part-time or voluntary work will help build up your social skills, and get used to picking up a phone instead of texting or emailing.
- *Volunteer*. Stylist Madeline Bowden says: 'When I was at uni, I bled everything I could out of the North East. Any fashion show going on, I'd offer to style it. Any shoots for the local newspaper or magazine, I'd style them even though I was never paid. Practice makes perfect.'

- *Make and maintain contacts.* Mr Porter's Aaron Christian once saw *Esquire* editor Jeremy Langmead walking through Topman, where Aaron worked at the time. He approached him, talked his way into a two-week placement, and kept in touch via Twitter. It was Jeremy, in his role as editor-in-chief of Mr Porter, who alerted Aaron to the video editor's job when it came up. Contacts can be sources for stories, too – at university, meet as many people as you can, go to events, talk to people, swap numbers. You never know when they'll be useful.

- *Go the extra mile.* You will need dedication both to get a job and once you're in it. Fashion editor and commentator Caryn Franklin tells the story of going to *i-D* to show editor Terry Jones her portfolio at 11 a.m. He said he was going out and asked her to answer the phones and continue some graphic work he was doing. 'I absolutely believe that if I'd said, "Really sorry, I'm meeting a friend for lunch," that would have been that,' she says. 'So I dropped everything and stayed.' She stayed until 7.30 p.m., came back the next day and carried on until she was taken on.

    The same will happen once you're in a job. Louise Gannon, celebrity writer, says:

    > It's not a job: it's a vocation. Your editor will say, 'Research those clothes for me,' and she means now even if it's 6.30 p.m. and you've planned a meal with your boyfriend. I know people who've missed weddings in their own family for work.
    >
    > You have to really want it, and do it incredibly well. You can't go into this half-heartedly.

    (2012b)

- *Suck it up!* Not very pretty, but a phrase you'll often hear from experienced journalists urging you not to be precious about your own work. A piece of writing you've lovingly crafted may be slashed in half, dropped altogether or rewritten, and an interview you've helped set up may be handed over to someone else. 'When you're starting out, it feels quite personal and painful when you write something you're really proud of and it gets changed, but you have to learn to let things go once you've written them,' says freelancer Hattie Crisell (2012).

- *Have confidence, without being cocky.* As an intern or a journalist just starting off, it's natural to look around and feel that everyone else knows what they're doing and you don't. Every single fashion journalist has felt that at some point. *Grazia* fashion editor Hannah Almassi says: 'Some people just have the chat. It doesn't mean they're better than you: they're just better at projecting themselves' (2012b). Confidence comes with experience, when you realise you can do what's asked of you without messing up.

    Until then, fake it – in an interview, if you don't look confident you can do the job, why should an editor take you on? Once in a job, don't let yourself be intimidated by either sources or your colleagues, says freelancer

Polly Vernon. 'Don't sit at the back of the room in a conference or a meeting. Congregate round the boss. And don't ever think your opinions are stupid,' she says (2012).

But don't get too cocky – a little insecurity drives you on, says freelancer Louise Gannon. 'If you felt confident about how you wrote, you wouldn't write well,' she says (2012b).

- *Leave your comfort zone.* 'It's essential as a journalist to be brave. All the successful journalists are the ones pushing themselves all the time,' says Hattie Crisell. She realised this when she was made redundant at the age of 24, to her horror, but then forged ahead with her freelance career. Even when you stay in a job, new things will be thrown at you and it's essential you cope. *Grazia*'s Hannah Almassi had to start producing video reports at the September 2012 shows. 'I was terrified going up to the front-row celebrities with a camera. But you just have to be tactful and smiley and quite brave, and after a while you get over it and wonder why you ever got scared in the first place' (2012b).

  Even in your own time, push yourself go to new places, try different things and meet new people. Getting out of your comfort zone will make you braver and more receptive to new ways of seeing things, new trends and different lifestyles. 'Everything informs what you write,' says Polly Vernon. 'The more you know about life and the world, the better you'll be.'

- *Be yourself.* Editors want someone with a personality and opinions, so don't be afraid to show them. Alex Murphy believes she got her job at My-wardrobe.com because she went to town in the product write-ups she did as a test, dropping in Greek mythology and literary references. 'They said they liked the fresh approach. There are so many people and so few jobs, you have to stand out, and the easiest way to stand out is being yourself.' This is where blogs and other social media are useful – they can showcase your opinions and personality. Rachel Richardson, who won awards as editor of *Fabulous*, always checks a candidate's Facebook, Twitter and blog. 'It's a window on a person, and I hire a personality and skills as a package, not just skills,' she says. 'Magazines live and die by their tone of voice, so it's really important' (2012).

  On the styling side, a portfolio of tests that you've done in your spare time is another way to demonstrate your ideas to an employer. 'Testing is so important because people can't see what's inside your head; they need to see a portfolio,' says Tracey Lea Sayer, of *Fabulous*. 'I encourage the girls who work with us at assistant level to test at weekends, so they've got some of their own work coming to life.'

- *Clean up your digital footprint.* If your heart stopped when you read above that editors check candidates' Facebook and Twitter, perhaps it's time to start managing your online reputation. Rachel says: 'If you've done some-thing inappropriate on Twitter or are moany, it would put me off. If I saw pictures of you on Facebook vomiting in the street, I just wouldn't hire you.' Check your Facebook privacy settings, and treat your Twitter feed as an outward-facing, professional tool – opinions and some personal detail will bring it to life, but moaning about university or work, or going into lurid detail about your hangover, won't impress employers.

- *But do use social media.* Increasingly, this is a requirement of a journalism job, especially for commercial brands like Asos which require you to have a strong presence online. Peter Henderson, who writes for an e-tailer and runs his own blog Hapsical, says:

  > Having a knowledge of social media is something all students should be shouting about. Most companies know they need to do it but some still find it all quite mysterious. If you can prove you can set up a blog and use Twitter, it could be valuable.

- *Build up your skill set.* Platforms for journalism change all the time, so who knows what skills you'll need for a job? Ten years ago, it was unthinkable that a journalist would need computer coding skills, but by 2013 many fashion writers said they needed to know the basics to work effectively on websites. This will only increase, as fashion journalism increasingly takes place online. Sasha Wilkins, ex-fashion editor and LibertyLondonGirl blogger, says the one thing she'd tell students is: 'Take as many courses as you can, at university or wherever, on photography, video, editing and search optimization.'

- *Think like a journalist.* Ideas and contacts are two of the most valuable commodities in journalism, so start building up your contacts book, and start filing tears (ripped-out pages) from magazines and newspapers that spark a story idea. Every fashion journalist you'll meet is obsessed with reading websites, magazines and newspapers, to hoover up knowledge and visual inspiration.

  'What we're looking for in a candidate is someone who is obsessed with magazines (all of them, from *Vogue* to *Waitrose Food Illustrated*) and also blogs and websites,' says Victoria Kennedy, deputy editor of *Now* magazine. 'They'll have a book full of tears and thoughts, not just about what to do but how it could look on the page. Come to an interview with ideas, even if you're not asked to bring them.'

The devil in Prada?

Finally, the one thing that seems to scare would-be fashion journalists the most before they start getting internships is the idea that fashion editors are terrifying harpies who will sneer at their clothes.

'I was terrified about interning because you have this vision of fashion magazines being these horrible, bitchy, scary places where you're kicked to the kerb the very first day if you're not wearing the right shoes,' says Hannah Almassi (2012b).

Of course, she found the contrary – the team at *Grazia*, she said, were 'warm, welcoming and incredibly talented', and she's stayed there ever since.

Ask many interns what they found most surprising about magazines or newspapers, and it's always how friendly everyone is. 'I wish I'd known how relaxed it was, how casually people dressed and how friendly everyone was so I wouldn't have worried so much beforehand,' says Steph Currie, a 20-year-old student who went to *Heat* magazine's fashion department.

It's not that dressing the part isn't important, though. If you're in fashion, you should have a demonstrable interest in it. And if you're taking on the role of telling other people what to wear, you should take care of your own grooming and style.

It's also of commercial importance, said Rachel Richardson when she was *Fabulous* editor. 'You're representing the brand. My team go out and talk to advertisers and PRs, and I wouldn't feel comfortable if one of them met L'Oréal looking an absolute state,' she says. 'Superficial as it sounds, it's incredibly important.'

That said, your choices do NOT have to be high-end, trend-driven or uniform, and you won't be judged on your personal style as long as it doesn't conflict with the magazine's brand image. Assistants and junior editors will rarely have the money to buy designer clothes.

Alex Murphy, who interned at *Elle*, said she was surprised that the first member of staff she saw had bright pink hair and a nose piercing. But then she realized that 'Any style seems to be fine, as long as there is some. As long as there's some kind of passion and interest, you get away with it.'

Elizabeth Walker, former executive fashion editor at *Marie Claire*, used to send interns home if they looked like they'd just tumbled out of bed, but again it was the lack of interest that annoyed her, not how much they'd spent on their clothes.

'Fashion assistants should look young and stylish. When you see what's in the likes of H&M, there's no excuse not to look stylish and inspiring, however broke you are. Even if you have to make it yourself!'

Other journalists say that fashion is MEANT to be diverse and creative, so nobody will judge you on what you wear. 'If you want to come to work in Doc Martens, shredded jeans and an old 80s rock T-shirt, and that's your look, then that's fine,' says Lucy Wood of *Look*.

'You dress to emanate your personal style, and you need to have all those different mixtures on a magazine.'

So we've established that fashion editors don't go around sneering at each other's clothes. But does fashion deserve its reputation for bitchiness and back-stabbing?

No, not really, according to those that work in it. Journalists writing about men's fashion say everyone is very down-to-earth and friendly, and those in womenswear say that while it is highly competitive – like all types of journalism – the fashion community is inspiring rather than undermining.

Harriet Walker, news editor at *Never Underdressed*, says: 'It's a nice bunch of people with the same interests, and though there are some people who are less friendly than others, it's certainly not the cartoon pack of wolves they're made out to be.'

Some commentators have pointed out that fashion journalism's reputation for bitchiness is a lazy sexist cliché directed at an industry largely staffed by women. The *Guardian*'s Hadley Freeman says of films like *The Devil Wears Prada*:

> Fashion magazine employees are invariably depicted as childish, narcissistic bitches. See what happens when you let the silly billies work together in a closed environment?
>
> Fashion is a multibillion-dollar industry, and it would be awfully hard to keep that afloat if its movers and shakers sat around all day fretting about the high sugar content in grapes, pausing only to stab one another in the back.
>
> (2009: 80–81).

Harriet Walker thoroughly agrees.

> What's most amazing about this community is that it's one of the few careers where you can be a woman and have a family and be a boss and be respected and get somewhere. The fashion industry is full of incredible women. Whether they're editors or writers or on the commercial side, it's mostly women. There are so many good role models.

Recommended reading

Broadcast Journalism Training Council: www.bjtc.org.uk.
Fashion Monitor: www.fashionmonitor.com.
Gorkana Jobs: www.gorkanajobs.co.uk.
GoThinkBig: www.gothinkbig.co.uk.
National Council for the Training of Journalists: www.nctj.com.
National Union of Journalists: www.nuj.org.uk.
Professional Publishers Association: www.ppa.co.uk.

3 Fashion media and audiences

Introduction

The relationship between fashion media and the fashion industry is a lot closer than in most other journalistic fields. Fashion was a driver for the spread and popularity of early magazines, and its rhythms, needs and – crucially – advertising still sustain the print media today.

In fact, journalist, commentator and campaigner Caryn Franklin goes so far as to say: 'Fashion is an industry that has very cleverly created its own media to support it' (2013).

Other journalists argue that the relationship is more subtle than this, and applies to some media more than others.

This chapter will look at the various types of fashion media and the juggling act that editors have to pull off to keep their publishers, readers and advertisers happy.

It will discuss the centrality of the brand, and the importance of the target reader: two things that editors say they wished new recruits were more aware of when they join them from university. It will also look at practical issues like lead times and media kits.

The move online will be explored, along with the rise of branded editorial – the two developments that have most changed fashion journalism in the last ten years.

And one of the key issues plaguing fashion journalism – the accusation that it is largely uncritical and kowtows too much to advertisers – will be addressed from both sides of the fence, from critics and from those who deal day-to-day with advertiser relations.

What this chapter will NOT do is give a comprehensive overview of all the newspapers, magazines and websites covering fashion. There are many textbooks devoted to doing just this, and there is a recommended reading list at the end.

The symbiotic relationship between fashion and media

On a theoretical level, many academics have pointed out that fashion has to be written about and represented in some way to exist – otherwise it would just be a bunch of clothes with no backstory.

Figure 3.1 Early edition of *Vogue* (CN/Fairchild)

A famous study by French linguist Roland Barthes called *The Fashion System* looked at how fashion writing spun a 'veil of images, of reasons, of meanings' (1967: xi) to turn mere garments into desirable fashion, and mere detail into a new trend.

A rather more accessible book is Yuniya Kawamura's *Fashion-ology: An Introduction to Fashion Studies* (2005), which explains how journalists are a crucial cog in the fashion wheel, acting as gatekeepers declaring what is in fashion and what's out, making new trends sound desirable and explaining a designer's ideas to the public.

Whether or not they've read the theory, editors and journalists, too, comment on the way the media are bound up with the fashion system. One obvious connection is frequency – how magazine publication dates fit round new collections.

For example, biannuals come out twice a year to fit with the two fashion seasons – autumn–winter and spring–summer. So when Condé Nast's *LOVE* comes out in August, it will show the collections that were sent down the catwalk in February/March.

The trouble is, people can now see these collections instantly online, and in some cases buy them from July onwards, so where does this leave biannuals? 'They served a more genuine purpose under the old season system, whereas now they have to find their purpose,' says Charlie Porter, who was deputy editor of biannual *Fantastic Man*.

'The men's biannuals don't come out until October. In reality the clothes they've been shooting for those issues will have been in stores for three months. So their usefulness in a real sense has disappeared' (2013b).

Quick-thinking publishers can actually harness these changes in the fashion system to produce a new type of magazine. That was the case with *Grazia*, says Fiona McIntosh, who was the magazine's editor-in-chief when it launched as the UK's first weekly glossy in 2005.

'It was at the point when all the retailers were beginning to do much faster fashion. Even the designers were churning out cruise and pre-fall collections on top of their standing collections,' Fiona says.

> So we knew how important it was to have a fashion weekly that could really keep up with the change of pace.
>
> Girls started taking the magazine into shops and saying, 'I know this has just dropped, and I want it.' You can't overestimate how critical that was to its eventual success.
>
> (2012)

More so than frequency, though, advertising and editorial mentions – discussed later in this chapter – bind magazines the most strongly to the fashion industry.

Charlie Porter describes it as the industry propping up the media for as long as it wants to. 'Fashion is a bubble that protects its own,' he says. 'As long as fashion wants there to be certain magazines like biannuals, whom they'll support with advertising and supply with tickets to their shows, then biannuals will exist.'

A brief history of fashion and print media

The fashion system we know now grew up alongside the development of mass media. It was partly the hunger to share latest styles of dress that drove the first women's magazines, and the desire of advertisers to promote their goods that supported an explosion of lifestyle publishing in the Victorian era.

Fashion was always a preoccupation of social elites, especially at royal courts. But news about what, say, the French aristocracy was wearing that year could only be transmitted via letters and sketches sent home from those who had seen it.

By the seventeenth century, however, illustrations of the latest dress styles could be engraved, hand-coloured and reproduced as fashion plates. As printing improved, these plates could be gathered into collections and distributed throughout Europe.

Early magazines like the *Le Mercure Galant* in France from 1672 used fashion plates as part of their mix of fashion, gossip, songs, letters and news. The first women's periodical in the UK to really take off was the *Lady's Magazine or Entertaining Companion for the Fair Sex*, launched in 1771.

It promised elegant dress patterns and 'engravings to inform our distant readers with every innovation that is made in the female dress', beauty, health, cookery, readers' letters and advice columns – a formula that looks surprisingly familiar today (Ballaster *et al.*, 1991).

It spawned many imitators, and they found a ready-made audience in the newly affluent upper middle-classes thrown up by the Industrial Revolution in the latter part of the eighteenth century who were striving for social respectability.

Media historian Martin Conboy describes the magazines as providing 'imaginary communities' for female readers, who had no real way of meeting other women in groups (2004: 135).

But these first magazines also set the pattern of addressing women in the private world of home, rather than the public world of work, and of defining their looks as the most important thing about them, academic authors say (see, for example, Ballaster *et al.*, 1991).

The nineteenth century saw a huge boom in magazines thanks to new leisure time, mass literacy, railways to distribute them and improvements to colour publishing. There were 50 new titles between 1870 and 1900 in England alone (Craik, 2009), many based in London, where huge department stores like Selfridges, Harvey Nichols and Harrods were opening and thriving.

Shopping and consumption were the driving force behind women's magazines, which were often 50 per cent made up of advertising pages (Ballaster *et al.*, 1991). No longer was magazine reading confined to the wealthy, as advertising gave publishers the confidence to diversify in search of new markets. The *Englishwoman's Domestic Magazine* from 1852 was the first to target the lower middle-classes, while sister publication *Queen* was aimed at society ladies.

At the same, in the United States, magazine giants *Harper's Bazaar* and *Vogue* were launched.

Vogue was a social gazette when it first came out in New York in 1892, and the fashion industry was still in its infancy. There were few famous designers and no catwalk shows, so fashion coverage consisted of what the rich were wearing at social events. Most clothes were made to measure, so *Vogue* gave pages of minute detail about specific garments to help dressmakers run them up, and launched its own pattern service in 1899.

When *Vogue* was taken over by lawyer Condé Nast in 1909, he set about turning it into one of the first specialist magazines deliberately targeted at a wealthy niche audience with the aim of pulling in high-end advertising.

It worked. By shunning a mainstream audience, *Vogue*'s circulation in 1910 was only 30,000 but it had 44 per cent more advertising pages – at the highest prices – than any of its competitors (Oliva and Angeletti, 2006).

Today, *Vogue* and other high-end fashion glossies pursue much the same strategy. Though their circulations appear small (in the first half of 2013, British *Vogue* sold 193,000 copies a month, *Harper's Bazaar* 113,000 and *Tatler* about 84,000, according to the Audit Bureau of Circulations – see *Press*

Gazette), the spending power of their readers and the luxury advertising this attracts gives them profitability and credibility.

Quite what a priority this is for them is brought home when you read their media kits or packs – the information they compile about their readers to attract advertisers. '*Tatler* delivers ... a glamorous environment, a rich audience, an acquisitive attitude' (*Tatler* media pack, 2010).

Even the more mainstream glossies and other consumer magazines secure around 60 per cent of their revenue from advertising (McKay, 2013), and it is this reliance that has led to accusations that their editorial is compromised, as will be discussed later.

Women's magazines continued to boom in the early twentieth century and reached what was probably an all-time high in the late 1950s and early 1960s (Ballaster *et al.*, 1991). As those figures subsequently began to fall, publishers increasingly sought to target new areas of the population, segmented by age, gender, attitude and lifestyle, in a bid for new readers and – more importantly – new audiences for advertisers.

In the 1960s, teenagers were identified as a separate market with their own disposable income, and the likes of *Honey* (1960), *Petticoat* (1966) and *19* (1968) were launched, showing young fashion-conscious women how to assert their difference from older generations.

Similarly, in the 1980s, publishers began to chase the male market that advertisers were desperate to reach. It was a famously difficult audience for a general lifestyle magazine – 'Men don't define themselves as men in what they read, they define themselves as people who are into cars, who play golf, or fish,' said an article in *Campaign* magazine (in Nixon, 1996: 130) – but *The Face*, launched in 1980, and other members of the so-called style press, like *i-D* and *Blitz*, showed how fashion and consumption could be promoted to young men.

As a result, *Arena* was launched in 1986 and *GQ* in 1988, setting themselves up as lifestyle manuals for men. Fashion – or rather style – was represented as unfussy, classic and timeless to avoid accusations of triviality, while articles about news, sport and women kept everything reassuringly masculine.

Throughout the twentieth and twenty-first centuries, the high cost of publishing meant the development of large corporations owning a stable of magazines, with only a handful of independents.

Foreign capital has also entered the UK market at various points, such as Condé Nast launching *Vogue* in Britain in 1916, and Hearst launching *Good Housekeeping* in 1922. Both now own a host of British magazines, while European publishers like Bauer (German) came into the market from the 1980s.

In historical accounts, magazines are sometimes taken to task for concentrating on women's looks and domestic skills, and ignoring other aspects of their lives, while also focusing on consumption of new products as a way of constructing feminine identity (see Winship, 1987, Ballaster *et al.*, 1991, McRobbie, 1991, Conboy, 2004).

But it's interesting to look at the history of the ultimate glossy, *Vogue*, and see also the changes it has both wrought and represents. It has featured the work of artists like Salvador Dali and writers like Arthur Miller and it pioneered the use of photography in magazines, with the first photographic cover in 1932.

It has also captured in pictures the vast changes to women's lives over the course of the twentieth century, from aristocrats in corsets to the 'youthquake' of the 1960s (a phrase coined by then US *Vogue* editor Diana Vreeland) to the laughing, jeans-clad woman in the street that was Anna Wintour's first cover in 1988.

Art historian Kohle Yohannan says *Vogue* didn't just chronicle these changes, but it actually helped propagate them in the early days by showing women new images of themselves they could identify with. 'Transmitting the female roar soon to be heard round the world was the written word, the image,' he writes (in Oliva and Angeletti, 2006: 123).

Fashion coverage in newspapers was largely a post-war development, but even then it was largely limited to a weekly slot in the qualities (McRobbie, 1998). It was generally in the form of a fashion editor's report on couture shows, trends and on what to wear for various social occasions (Polan, 2006).

It began to be taken more seriously from the 1960s, buoyed by the strong trade press, and writers began to analyse fashion in a social and economic context to appeal to the general reader (ibid.).

From the 1980s, fashion reporting grew yet more prominent along with other forms of lifestyle journalism as newspapers sought women readers and introduced colour printing. Fashion stories began to appear on news pages, stylists were hired to produce shoots for feature pages, and colour supplements became a natural home for extended coverage.

The likes of *Sunday Times Style* and the *Mail on Sunday's You* magazine have strong followings, and the *News of the World's Fabulous* supplement was the only section to survive the newspaper's closure in 2011 when it moved to sister publication *The Sun*.

Today's print market

Magazines

The British Fashion Council estimates that fashion magazines employ 3,101 people and contribute £205 million to the UK economy each year (BFC, 2010).

They can be roughly divided into three types – the biannuals, monthlies and weeklies.

The biannuals include the likes of *LOVE*, *AnOther Magazine*, *Fantastic Man* and *The Gentlewoman*, and tend to feature high production values, luxury brands and lavish photo shoots with top models and photographers, together with wider arts and culture coverage.

They have relatively small circulations but are read by many people in fashion. 'Biannuals have huge importance – they're very industry-based magazines,' says Charlie Porter, who was deputy editor of *Fantastic Man*.

They are supported by luxury advertising, have fantastic access to industry figures and get top photographers, stylists and models to work for them even though pay rates are low. 'They work for a pittance because it's a great place to be seen and the hope is you'll land a commercial job through it,' says Charlie.

Weeklies were once associated with traditional older women's magazines and downmarket titles, like *Woman's Weekly* or *Bella*, but 2005 onwards saw a wave of new fashion-and-celebrity titles for younger women.

Now they have been so successful it seems they've always been here, but it was a very delicate balancing act in the early days trying to put together an appropriate mix of 'news and shoes' that didn't upset upmarket advertisers, says *Grazia*'s founding editor-in-chief Fiona McIntosh.

'It was nerve-wracking trying to create a fashion weekly for the first time in the UK, make it tasteful, try to get the right voice and look and stories,' Fiona recalls of the launch which, at £16 million, was the UK's biggest ever.

'Advertising and sales soon told us when we got it wrong! Nowadays, though, it's very sure-footed.'

Like the vast majority of fashion magazines, weekly circulations were on the decline by 2013 – *Grazia* sales were down 11 per cent year-on-year in the first half of 2013, and *Look* was down almost 20 per cent, according to the Audit Bureau of Circulations (ABC) (*Press Gazette*, 2013).

But the drops were even worse at many monthly magazines, squeezed in the middle between arty biannuals and fast-paced weeklies. *Company* magazine had a circulation of more than 230,000 in the first half of 2009; by 2013, 60 per cent of those purchasers had disappeared, with circulation down to 90,726, in print at least.

In fact, the January–June 2013 figures were difficult reading for all magazines apart from the frees (*Stylist*, *Asos* and *John Lewis Edition*). Even the previously unassailable *Vogue* was down by 6 per cent year on year, and *Elle* by 10 per cent.

However, *Vogue* also reported advertising up by 6 per cent and its most profitable year ever (Halliday, 2013). Luxury titles were undoubtedly faring a lot better than the squeezed middle market.

Victoria White says that when she started on *Company*, it was enough to be a generic women's magazine, like *Marie Claire*, *Cosmopolitan*, *Glamour* and *New Woman*:

> It was enough to be in the middle, because there were enough readers and enough advertisers to fund all of them.
>
> Now, advertisers aren't spending as much as they used to, and consumers aren't buying as much as they used to because they're online. Now you have to stand out, have a point of difference.
>
> (2013)

She says her main competition as *Company* editor is not other titles so much as things like smartphones and social media that take young women away from reading magazines.

> We still fill the luxury time-out time, but what we no longer fill is the commute time, the dead time. When I get on a train I see people watching films on their iPad or listening to music on their phones, whereas they once would have been leafing through a magazine.

It's a conundrum that all editors are desperate to crack. What Victoria finds most galling is that magazines are seen by young women as an unnecessary expense. 'I don't know how we've got to the situation where a magazine has become seen as a luxury purchase,' she says.

> Even an expensive magazine like *Elle* at nearly £4 is around half the price of a packet of cigarettes. *Company*, at £2.50, is probably half the price of a shot or vodka and tonic and some people go out and drink 10 of those in an evening.

She believes it's partly to do with the way monthlies have marketed themselves, with price discounts and cover mounts, and the non-luxurious way they're sold: 'We're sold alongside weeklies in a supermarket or a newsagents where they could be chucked on the floor next to *CBeebies* magazine.'

Magazines have responded by extending their brands – into biannual runway editions, offshoots like *Company's High-Street Edit*, websites, iPad versions, apps and events (see below).

This has inevitably led to more pressure for journalists. One editor said that six years ago she had twice the staff, twice the budget and one magazine to produce … now they have to stretch their resources to produce two magazines, the website, apps and events.

Yet monthlies still command a lot of respect in the fashion industry. 'Probably the core value of the monthly is the great shoots, great access and the articles – the depth that they can bring to fashion coverage and features,' says Fiona McIntosh.

Newspapers

Newspapers were likewise having a torrid time by 2013, with declining advertising revenue and plummeting sales.

Their circulation figures are logged and published every month by the ABC, and you can read analysis of the latest figures on trade website *Press Gazette* (www.pressgazette.co.uk) or in the *Media Guardian* (www.theguardian.com/media).

Despite this, they are still well respected in the fashion industry, and some of fashion's best-known journalists, like Lisa Armstrong and Hilary Alexander, write for them.

'Regardless of the political leaning of the newspaper, or the readership, if you are working at a newspaper you've got that name behind you and you get a lot of access,' says Harriet Walker, former style editor and columnist for the *Independent*.

'People want to be in newspapers, whether readers are buying them or not.'

And newspapers want fashion because it adds colour to their pages, and hopefully attracts more female readers. Only the *Daily Mail* has more female readers than male; the rest of the nationals are chasing to catch up.

'The newsdesk don't want men in suits on every page: they need something more vibrant,' says Jess Cartner-Morley, fashion editor of the *Guardian*.

A crucial difference between newspapers and magazines is that papers aren't anywhere near as reliant on fashion or beauty advertising, and don't work with brands as closely as the glossies.

As a result, newspaper fashion journalists often describe themselves as freer and more ethical than magazine journalists. Melanie Rickey started out on the *Independent* and *Daily Telegraph* before going to *Grazia* as fashion features and news editor, and says: 'Naively I didn't realise that most journalists are basically slaves to their advertisers on magazines. To this day I will not accept a gift unless it's a thank-you present, and I make a big distinction between the two.'

Likewise, Jess Cartner-Morley says: 'We can be independent because we are not supported by their advertising. I can go to a show and write a review saying it's rubbish – a magazine can't do that.' (She keeps her word – see her review of Tom Ford at www.theguardian.com/fashion/fashion-blog/2011/sep/19/london-fashion-week-tom-ford.)

Another big difference between newspapers and magazines, touched upon in Chapter 1, is that newspaper journalists are writing for a general audience who may or may not be interested in fashion.

Melanie Rickey, for one, says she loved the challenge of making fashion relevant to the wider world.

> I liked reporting on things that anyone could be interested in.
>
> For example, I wrote about Hardy Blechman, who had a label called Maharishi which was only ever written about by the style press, and he told me that finally his uncle knew what he did because it had been in the *Telegraph*. These sorts of moments are what I'm in fashion journalism for.
>
> You don't want to write for five people in Hoxton or ladies who lunch in Chelsea. You want to write about it for people who may or may not know about it, and open their minds to it.

Explaining fashion and setting it in its economic, political and social context are part of how newspapers will make it relevant to the general reader. This means anything from looking at government support for the fashion industry to debating what the prime minister wears on holiday.

Or a tabloid newspaper might peg fashion to celebrity to make it interesting to readers, rather than simply writing about designer fashion and the catwalks.

Like magazines, some newspaper fashion desks are finding themselves squeezed. When Harriet Walker started on the *Independent*, there were five full-time journalists on the fashion desk. By 2013, there were two.

And they have to turn shoots and copy around much quicker than most magazines. Amber Graafland and her team of three at the *Daily Mirror* produce two fashion shoots a week, whereas she says her friends on the glossies will do six shoots a year.

Sometimes, too, the fashion desk on a newspaper find there's a culture clash with their newsdesk (the news editors who coordinate coverage from all the departments).

Amber, at the *Daily Mirror*, says she has to stand up to news editors who want to cover high fashion by ridiculing it. 'We on fashion are always fighting that tendency,' she says. 'If you're covering it, you should cover it properly.'

Interestingly, other types of journalists accuse the fashion desk of being too separate from the rest of the newspaper and too unwilling to pitch in with hard news stories.

Louise Gannon, who has worked on the *Sun*, *Daily Mail* and *Express*, and now does celebrity interviews for the likes of the *Mail on Sunday*, *Grazia* and *Elle*, says:

> Fashion journalists can be considered fluff on a newspaper.
>
> They're not particularly loud. They know their stuff but are considered as being in their own little area. When a news editor wants to do something, they physically have to walk across to talk to them.
>
> What fashion journalists should do is look out for stories (for example, 'at the shows, I noticed so-and-so wasn't wearing her wedding ring') and then make that walk themselves to the news editor and give them that information, and so become more part of the team.
>
> (2012b)

The move online

It's no exaggeration to say that the Internet has turned journalism upside down, with far-reaching impacts that were still unclear at the time of writing this book.

While editors know they have to go where the audience is – and by 2013 the audience was online, increasingly on smartphones and tablets – the problem is making money out of their websites and social media channels.

Most website content is free, so there's no money from sales. And advertising, which provides the bulk of a magazine's income, is nothing like as expensive online as it is in print.

Newspapers and magazines have been trying everything to monetise digital content: launching paid-for iPad editions and apps; working with advertisers on sponsored content; putting up a paywall round their website (like the *Sun* and *The Times*), and bringing in shopable content, where readers can click through to a retailer's website to buy a product and the publication gets a small percentage of the sale.

But by 2012, income from digital publishing contributed only 8 per cent to the total revenues of consumer publishers, according to the PPA's Publishing Futures report – not enough to pay the wages of all those journalists producing the content.

'Online is where all journalism is heading, including fashion,' says Amber Graafland of the *Daily Mirror*. 'But the problem is that nobody's sure where the money is coming from at the moment.'

When magazines and newspapers first launched websites in the late 1990s, it was very much a case of print product first, and website off the back of that, either reproducing the print content or acting as a shopfront.

Now, they've radically changed their thinking to become what Loraine Davies at the PPA calls 'omniplatform'. At the centre is the brand, which will simultaneously take the form of, say, a monthly glossy, a digital tablet version, a daily app, an online store and an exhibition or awards ceremony.

'We've had to change our definition of a magazine,' Loraine says. 'We used to talk about magazines and websites; now we talk about brands. It's not about a print product any more; it's about curated, trusted, quality content, whatever platform that's on.'

In a way, fashion is lucky in that it's very suited to the web. 'Online is fashion's natural home,' says the *Guardian*'s Jess Cartner-Morley. 'It ties in with the boom in retail online, too.'

Catwalk shows have been streamed live online since 2009, runway and celebrity pictures are very popular in online galleries, and websites and apps allow monthly and weekly magazines to update their content daily or even hourly.

Content-sharing sites like lookbook.nu and fashion blogs sparked a new interest in street style, which magazines use to drive traffic to their sites.

And magazines and newspapers are able to reconnect with fashion brands online with shopable content. When a reader clicks on a product in a digital magazine, on an app or on a web page and gets redirected to an online store to make a purchase, the publication gets a sum of money in what's called affiliate marketing.

The popularity of fashion online pulls in advertising, too, given that consumers are spending more online. The fashion pages are the most popular part of the *Daily Telegraph*'s online offering with advertisers, for example (Kansara, 2010b).

The websites of national newspapers, in particular, attract a huge audience. By September 2013, the *Daily Mail* had an average of nine million daily browsers, the *Guardian* 4.5 million, and the *Telegraph* three million, according to the ABC (Sweney, 2013).

But the web has left print magazines reconsidering what their purpose is, even the relatively fast-paced weeklies.

'Our readers are so savvy with websites, blogging and Twitter that they hear news about celebrities at the same time as we journalists do,' says Lucy Wood, senior fashion news editor at *Look* magazine.

So we have to think about what we could add to this story, how we could put our journalist spin on this. Otherwise, why would they buy us? We'll speak directly to people, put it in context of a social trend or turn it into more of a feature.

(2012)

Fiona McIntosh, former editor of *Elle* and founding editor-in-chief of *Grazia*, went on to work with Italian *Grazia*'s publishers Mondadori on their digital sites.

'We have endless discussions about what purpose a magazine has, what purpose online has,' she says. 'What we should be doing online is very different to what we should be doing in print. But I don't think anyone is doing it particularly well at the moment.'

As for websites, publications approach them in different ways. Some have a separate web team; some have writers working across platforms. News and features from the print edition are often published online too, but perhaps with added video or a photo gallery. *Telegraph Fashion* online has shopable content, while the *Guardian* launched a network of fashion bloggers in 2013.

Vogue online has a separate web team of seven who sit alongside the print magazine team and work with them. Sometimes they share content, but the online team handles it in a very different way. 'A 2,000-word interview in print might work out online as five contributions to galleries, a guest edit and three news stories – you can chop it up in various ways,' says Jessica Bumpus, online fashion features editor (2013b).

Grazia, on the other hand, used to have a separate web team but now all its writers work across both print and online to ensure both have the same voice and standard. The *Elle* team, too, works across platforms. 'This gives *Elle* content a cohesive tone and keeps it all on brand,' says workflow director Christina Simone (2013).

Given the difficulties in generating money from the web, all eyes were on the 2013 launch of a stand-alone fashion site *Never Underdressed* by Shortlist Media, the publishers of free magazines *Shortlist* and *Stylist*.

The site took on 14 very experienced digital and print fashion journalists from the likes of *Elle*, *Vogue*, the *Independent* and Asos, and aimed to make money through advertising and affiliate schemes.

Harriet Walker, its news editor, said it was trying to resolve the problem of how you translate the luxury experience of a high-end magazine online.

'When you buy a magazine like *Vogue* or *Elle* or *Harper's*, you have this amazing premium product in your hands that's very luxurious and you can really immerse yourself in that high-end glossy world,' she said.

And when you go online and look at their websites, you don't feel that – they're not bad websites but they're very functional. They're sometimes staffed by people who have less experience, who are young and who are therefore hesitant to put their own spin on things.

So the idea was to combine people from a print heritage and people with a digital background and make that incredibly luxurious magazine something that you can find on a computer or phone or iPad.

Sadly, but not surprisingly, the website was closed in July 2014. Its owners said the site had failed to attract a big enough audience to be sustainable. The quest to monetise the Web continues.

Tablet editions

At one point, tablets were being hailed as the saviour of magazines, as publishers saw at last how they could charge money for digital versions of their print products. At £3.99, *Vogue*'s first prototype tablet version launched in 2010 was the same price as the magazine.

It was also a way to keep advertisers happy. A PPA study claimed that 77 per cent of readers engaged with ads they saw in their iPad magazine (PPA, 2012b), while click-and-shop gave retailers direct hits and sales.

And it's certainly where the audience was heading. In the UK, 16 per cent of people owned a tablet in 2012, the highest penetration in Europe (PPA, 2012b), and almost half owned a smartphone.

These tablet versions of magazines gave readers something extra, too. *Grazia* editor Jane Bruton said of the magazine's iPad edition, launched in 2012: 'We introduced functionality which allowed our incredibly responsive readers to shop, share and save. This not only adds value, but really brings the *Grazia* experience to life' (Bruton, 2013).

However, it was already becoming clear that iPad editions of magazines had not taken off as publishers hoped.

A combined circulation chart published by the ABC for January–June 2013 showed that digital downloads were going up but were a tiny fraction of print sales. Digital sales of *Vogue*, for example, grew by 3,898 copies to 7,601 since the second half of 2012 (3.78 per cent of its total circulation) against a fall of 10,349 print copies (to 193,007) at £3.99 each. *Glamour* sold 4,575 tablet editions compared to a print circulation of 400,371.

Rob Lynam, head of display at media buying agency MEC, was quoted by the *Guardian* as saying: 'What we're seeing is marginal growth off an incredibly small base, so it means print sales are even more important to the overall health of the titles' (in Halliday, 2013).

The *Business of Fashion* website speculated that publishers were wrong to think that they had added enough bells and whistles to make their tablet editions different, and that they remained at heart 'paper for the screen'.

It quoted media commentator Jeff Jarvis as saying:

> I think editors and publishers are fooling themselves into believing that the iPad returns to them the control over the experience, content, brand and business models that the web took away.

Sorry, but there is no going back.

(in Kansara, 2011b)

By 2013, magazines were experimenting with smaller-scale weekly or even daily apps, like Vogue Today, Company Weekly Edit and Cosmo Shopping Genie.

These apps kept text to a minimum, often repurposed from web content, were more obviously interactive than their digital magazines, and made money through click-to-buy affiliate schemes, advertising and, in some cases, charging to download.

The importance of brand

When your content is appearing across so many touchpoints – a magazine, various apps, a street-style supplement, a website, even an event like *Elle*'s Style Awards – you have to have a very clear idea of what your 'brand' is so you can be consistent.

A brand is literally a company name, but in publishing it's more what the brand stands for that counts – what identity or image it has, what positive values it connotes, its tone of voice and its relationship with its audience.

If a publisher gets a brand right, then it can go for 'brand extensions', other ways of reaching the audience and making money.

Spin-off events like the *Vogue* Festival and Condé Nast's College of Fashion & Design helped the magazine have its most profitable year ever in 2013, according to Nicholas Coleridge, president of Condé Nast international. 'Brand *Vogue* has never enjoyed a wider reach,' he told the *Guardian* (in Halliday, 2013).

Victoria White, editor of *Company*, says:

> By far the most important part of my job is creating the brand entity, because without the brand, you can't do anything else.
>
> So as print declines, the successful brands will make sure that everything else will grow. It's not just words, it's events, it's thinking of ways to keep consumers consuming you.

It's something she'd like to see applicants think about when they're trying to get into fashion journalism – what they could do for the brand. 'Yes, it's a fantastic career, but we are doing this for a company that needs to make money,' she stresses.

Company's High-Street Edit spin-off makes almost as much money as the main magazine; advertisers pay more, and it's produced by existing staff so there are few additional costs.

The *Company* brand also has Style Blogger Awards and has launched an online shop, promoted through its Office Style Spy section, where members of staff wear the products available.

In fact, as retailers increasingly turn to publishing, magazines would actually like to become retailers, says Victoria. Instead of stimulating desire for another brand's clothes, they could complete the circle by selling their own products.

Melanie Rickey, consultant and Fashion Editor at Large blogger, also gets excited at this thought. 'If *Grazia* or *Vogue* were a shop and everything they put in them was in the shop, they'd be loaded. But they're not – they're a shopfront for lots of other people.'

As a voice of authority in a certain industry, trade magazines are in an even better position to extend their brand. *Drapers*, for example, has an annual awards event it calls the 'biggest night in the fashion business calendar', where prizes are sponsored, and tickets cost from £500 a seat to £6,000 a table (Drapers Awards website, 2013).

The importance of audience

The audience shapes everything a newspaper or magazine does, and a fashion journalist should have a clear vision of whom they're addressing, how they're addressing them and what they want.

This is not just so the writing hits the right tone, and the fashion is at the right price point and style, but also so advertisers will come on board knowing their message will be getting to the right people.

That's why publications will put out media kits or packs – a series of PDFs or slides normally available on their publisher's website – summing up who the reader is and what their habits are (primarily their spending habits), as well as giving their advertising 'ratecard' spelling out how much it costs to take out a single- or double-page ad.

Look magazine, for example, says its reader is average age 26 who works hard and socialises hard. And – this bit for the advertisers – 'She loves fashion and shopping! 97 per cent of *Look* readers have purchased or plan to purchase fashion after seeing it in *Look*' (*Look* Media Kit, 2012).

LOVE's reader is older – between 18 and 40 – and richer, with an average income of £78,000. 'She loves luxury as she loves irreverence, which is why she identifies with *LOVE*,' the media pack states (*LOVE* Media Kit, 2012).

Newspapers and magazines spend a lot of money doing market research to find out more about their readers, and *Company* has a Facebook 'collective' of 1,500 members who it puts questions to regularly.

Speak to any fashion journalist and he or she knows who they're writing for and why. Amber Graafland says:

> We do a lot of reader focus groups. The *Mirror* woman is a mum; she works part-time; she's got two children; she largely controls the purse strings especially where clothes are concerned.
>
> She's dressing herself, her kids and probably her husband; she doesn't have a lot of disposable income. We build up a profile of who she is and what she would like to know.

So our fashion coverage is useful, and we try not to have anything on the page over £100.

Siobhan Mallen, head of womenswear and international content at Asos, talks about her audience as 'our girl':

> Our girl is not interested in investment buys: she wants to wear it then. She's in her twenties, she loves fashion, but she's got a life; she's got a story; she's complex. She loves newness, but she needs her hand held in a sense; she needs guidance. We try to do that in a cool but not an alienating way.
>
> (2012)

Stylist Madeleine Bowden found a big change when she went from *Elle* to assisting at the *Daily Telegraph*. The fashion had to be more suited to an older person, less extreme, no vintage and also no foreign brands that were unavailable in the UK because readers were less likely to shop online.

Journalists at both *Look* and *Fabulous* say their coverage is complicated by the fact that their magazine gets passed round the family, between young women, their mothers and even grandmothers.

'You have to not alienate people, and realise that not everyone is going to want to wear a bright pink dress just because it's fashionable, so the balance of articles has to be right,' says Lucy Wood of *Look*.

And it's not just about tone and content, says Loraine Davies, training director of the Professional Publishers Association. It's also about knowing when and how to reach that person.

'You should have a clear picture of what your audience is doing at the time you send out your newsletter or your web link or special offer,' Loraine says.

> If you have a picture of me in the office at 1pm wanting a brief respite from work, I might want something light-hearted and funny or something lovely to look at.
>
> If you know what it is I want, when, it's much easier to engage with me. Every student on any journalism course needs to be thinking about the audience in this way.

So audience needs will affect what kind of coverage fashion gets, how useful or inspirational it is, what kind of style icons are featured, how expensive the clothes are, where items can be bought and when content will drop – all to fit round the audience's perceived lifestyle.

It works the other way round, as well. Designers and retailers might refuse to work with a certain newspaper or magazine because its audience doesn't match their market or image, and they want to protect the brand.

Before a new publication launches, therefore, it has to have identified a ready and willing market whose needs are not currently being met and that advertisers want to reach.

This is where journalism students often go wrong, says *Company*'s Victoria White.

> Student magazines are often really personal and they're done from the point of view of 'me and my friends all think this'. But it's not personal: it's business.
>
> Also, there's a tendency for them to focus on high-fashion biannual-type magazines. Coming up with something less cool and less edgy that maybe people want is a far greater challenge. It could be something really simple that we haven't thought of. It could be that a young person somewhere could do it.

The importance of advertising, and how it affects magazines

It's hard to exaggerate how crucial advertising is to magazines, and the lengths to which they'll go to keep the advertisers happy.

There are euphemisms like 'showing support' for advertisers, which means the editor turning up to a designer's shows and lunching with publicists, journalists going to launches and parties organised by brands, and fashion editors turning up to retailers' press days where new-season collections are on display.

And then there's 'looking after your advertisers' when it comes to putting fashion shoots and shopping pages together. This means making sure they include items from the brands that advertise with your magazine.

In fact, someone like the executive fashion editor or director, or market editor, on a glossy will have the specific role of tallying up how many 'editorial mentions' its advertisers have had, and ensuring that they're in line with how much that advertiser spends with the magazine.

Elizabeth Walker did that role at *Marie Claire*. 'The influence of advertisers has got stronger and stronger in the last 10–15 years. When I started out, we never had to have lunch with advertisers, and what we photographed was entirely an editorial decision. But that all changed,' she says (2012).

> Latterly, I had this chart, listing all the advertisers and all the non-advertisers in alphabetical order, and how many pages of advertising they'd taken out.
>
> And then it was my unfortunate task to have to tell the editors that I needed, say, four pages out of them somehow over the season on such-and-such an advertiser.
>
> The brands all wanted to be in the main fashion issues, but not everything can be in the main fashion pages. They had to be in X number of times, though.
>
> I'd try to help the editors do it, to ease the pain. You can't put Armani in a bright-coloured story, for example. It's like a business jigsaw puzzle.

Like all journalists, Elizabeth recognises that magazines can't survive without advertising – their cover prices would have to more than double to cover the costs of printing, and readers wouldn't buy them.

But she regrets the effects:

> Only with very great difficulty does any new designer come through. It also has an effect on what magazines look like – I can tell when I look at them what designers they've got. But it's the reality of life.

The novel *Fashion Babylon* (2007) has stories of clothes from non-advertisers being swapped for advertisers' clothes just ahead of fashion shoots, of magazines only using advertisers' clothes for covers, and doling out perfume credits on covers to please brands.

If a brand doesn't get the right amount or type of mentions, they might ring the magazine to complain and threaten to pull their advertising.

The obvious downside to this is that some products in a magazine are selected because they're from an advertiser, not necessarily because they're the best out there. And non-advertisers – including young or even mid-range designers, who don't have the budget to spend on advertising – will have difficulty getting mentioned and noticed.

French designer Isabel Marant complained: 'To be well known in fashion today, you have to be in the women's press. But, without buying advertising, it's almost impossible. Fashion journalists, rain or shine, are in the grip of their advertising departments' (in Tungate, 2012: 116).

Not only that, but the tone of fashion coverage tends to be uncritical, even gushing. Unlike, say, a car magazine where new products will be assessed and rated, in fashion magazines products are featured only to be praised and recommended.

This is exacerbated by the fact that a disgruntled designer or brand can also stop sending you tickets for their runway shows, restrict access to their samples and refuse interviews if you upset them with an untoward comment.

Caryn Franklin, ex-fashion editor of *i-D* and presenter of the BBC TV programme *The Clothes Show*, says she knows beauty journalists who insert code words into their copy to show whether or not they like a product.

'Is a journalist really free to make choices about what they will feature, and what they say about the products they feature?' Caryn asks. 'I certainly question that, because of the pressure they're under to retain advertisers. If magazines were upfront about it, maybe their readers wouldn't feel that they were buying into some sort of magic.'

This is not the case on newspapers, which do not rely so much on fashion and beauty advertising, and so don't have the same constraints.

Charlie Porter was deputy fashion editor of the *Guardian* when he wrote a feature counting up editorial mentions of brands and comparing them to those brands' advertisements in various magazines (Porter, 2002).

Sure enough, when Charlie left the *Guardian* to go to *GQ*, he says he found a huge change. 'When you're on a newspaper, a lot of fashion remains hidden from you because it's known that you could write a story which could expose it,' he says.

'There's no great conspiracy, but a lot of fashion is quite opaque, how it works. If you work on a magazine that openly deals with advertising, then everything about fashion is revealed to you.'

Liz Jones went the other way, from editing *Marie Claire* to fashion editor on the *Daily Mail*, and wrote of her relief: 'Not reliant on advertising revenue and immune from freebies, I was now free to speak my mind' (Jones, 2012).

Polly Vernon also enjoyed her freedom as a fashion writer at the *Observer* newspaper. When she interviewed Roberto Cavalli, she described in hilarious detail how the designer wouldn't answer any of her questions and tried to kiss her and a model (Vernon, 2003).

She says: 'At the time, everyone who'd interviewed him came from a glossy magazine which had advertising, so they were especially careful. I wrote it absolutely as it happened and they were gobsmacked, because nobody ever had.'

Working with brands

Publications won't just carry advertising for a brand: they will also work with them in other, less obvious ways that affect their content.

For example, high-street brands might sponsor a fashion shoot in a magazine – paying for the team to go abroad for a shoot, in return for editorial coverage (Bigger, 2012). Or a brand might fund a fashion journalist's trip to Paris fashion week (Wood, 2012).

Lucy Wood of *Look* describes how she was sponsored by jeans brand Guess to go to the Coachella festival in 2012. 'They asked me what celebrity I would take out there for a diary feature, so we took (model) Tali Lennox out, which was brilliant.' Photos of Lennox in the latest Guess line subsequently appeared in *Look* and other magazines.

Sometimes a brand will piggyback on an already successful part of a magazine's format to create 'advertorial' – a feature that looks like the magazine's normal editorial and is designed as such, but that is sponsored by a brand and normally has 'advertorial' or 'special feature' or 'promotion' at the top of the page.

Grazia's street-style section, Style Hunter, is an example. Brands like Toni & Guy have paid to send fashion editor Hannah Almassi or her assistant round the UK to find and feature the best looks – something they would not have had the budget to do otherwise.

If you read celebrity interviews closely, too, you'll spot that some are arranged by a brand's PR to publicise a fashion or beauty line that the actress/model/musician has a contract with.

'These companies pay a vast amount of money to get the celeb on board, and they need their money's worth in the form of PR, so they always have a publicity clause in the celeb's contract,' says celebrity interviewer Louise Gannon (2013).

'Where these celebrities become harder to get hold of for what they do themselves – acting or music or whatever – the fashion and cosmetics people have become the easier route of getting access.'

It's tricky, she says, because you get a maximum of 20 minutes with the celebrity, the PR asks for your questions beforehand and you have to fight to insert a question about something other than the brand.

So the interview becomes a tussle between the journalist – who needs a new angle about the celebrity's personal life or tastes to get a story that will satisfy his or her editor – and the brand, which just wants the celebrity to extol the merits of its products.

The product will normally get a guaranteed mention in a credit box at the bottom of the interview, and often a couple of mentions stitched into the piece itself.

Providing the right environment for advertisers

Even in news and features that aren't sponsored or lined up by brands, magazine editors have to be careful they provide the right 'environment' for advertisements.

Anything too shocking, controversial or downmarket would make a brand think twice about placing their advertisements in that publication.

Fiona McIntosh, former editor of *Elle* and founding editor-in-chief of *Grazia*, said the only time advertisers would question her was for using a news story or celebrity that wasn't considered appropriate or upscale enough.

At *Grazia* in the early days, they had what they called a 'Chav Line' to decide whether a celebrity was upmarket enough to feature. 'Victoria Beckham was always oscillating between the two, but now of course she's gone way beyond the Chav Line,' Fiona says.

'Cheryl Cole is up and down; she's marginal. We made a big mistake in the beginning with Coleen Rooney – we thought she was all right, but she was wrong.'

Fiona found it even more difficult to tone down her journalistic instincts for a good story.

'The twin pressures of copy sales and maintaining a premium environment for advertisers is the single biggest struggle, because they don't complement each other at all,' she says.

'How far can you push a story or a red line? My journalism side wants to do that, but I have to check it against whether it's going to offend important advertisers.'

What journalists say about working with advertisers

The simplest response to accusations that glossies are too close to advertisers is that they would not survive without the cash.

As *Vogue* editor Alexandra Shulman said in an interview with the *Observer's* Lynn Barber:

> *Vogue* makes most of its money out of advertising – and it does make an awful lot of money – so we've got to have a good relationship with our advertisers.
>
> They're not going to place £100,000 a year and then say, 'Feel free not to use any of our goods' – life's not like that. So although there is this feeling sometimes that creatively it's not pure, well – magazines are a business, you're not sitting there writing poetry.
>
> (in Barber, 2008)

Jeremy Langmead, former editor of *Esquire*, argued that the more ads there were, the more editorial pages a magazine had. 'Magazines are a business, not an art form, and if the adverts enable the staff to be paid and the magazine to be filled with enticing content, what's the problem?' he wrote (Langmead, 2013).

Another point that editors make is that their advertisers are generally the large, successful brands that make up a critical part of the fashion landscape. So it's natural to feature their goods, where relevant.

And they also argue that there's more give and take than critics suppose. Carine Roitfeld, former editor of French *Vogue*, said advertisers need a cool, forward-looking environment to appear in, so it's in their best interests that a magazine retains that. 'It can best be described as a sort of mutual understanding,' she said (in Tungate, 2010: 132).

Polly Vernon, who writes for the *Times* and *Grazia*, agrees. 'Just because you have to promote X, it doesn't mean you can't also say "Look at Y: it's really good." You need the right environment and credibility.'

Those at the coalface of fashion journalism back this up, saying they make sure they are not compromised by the constraints of using advertisers' products. There are generally enough new and exciting things in every new collection to focus on, they say, and they wouldn't use anything they didn't like.

Hannah Almassi, fashion editor at *Grazia*, talks about balance:

> Say you're doing a denim special – which is, for example, a ten-page hose-down of all the latest brands, trends and styling – you need to be aware of who your key denim advertisers are and make every effort to get them in, but if something isn't right, like a skinny jean in a flared jean story, you can't include it just to keep someone happy.
>
> It's striking that balance between respecting your advertisers and keeping your editorial content really strong and reliable. People look to us as a source and you need to be telling them the truth.

Stylist Madeleine Bowden says she had to include several products from advertisers for *Elle* shopping pages but would always select the best pieces that would enhance the page. Other products she would select herself.

Harriet Walker, of *Never Underdressed*, says critics exaggerate the amount of product pushing that goes on. 'It's because they don't understand what the role of the fashion editor is, which is to say, "This is nice; I would buy it if I had the money."'

Harriet's comment also takes us to the nub of the argument over the positive nature of much fashion journalism, which critics describe as gushing and blame on the need to keep advertisers happy.

Many magazine journalists are genuinely baffled at the thought that they'd include something poor on their pages so they could criticise it. That's not how they see their role, which is to highlight what's great that season.

'I don't know if there's really a relevant place in the magazine for readers to know if something's really bad; why not show them something that's really good instead?' says *Grazia*'s Hannah Almassi. 'There's so much out there.'

Fashion is such a personal thing, too, she says, that to criticise certain pieces or looks would be unfair – not to mention the fact that the pace of what's 'in' and what's 'out' is faster than ever.

How advertising is changing

Digital media, as well as the recession, have had an impact on advertising and could potentially change the relationship between publishers and brands.

Brands were spending less on print advertising (8 per cent less with UK newspapers and 11.6 per cent less with magazines in the first quarter of 2013 – Advertising Association, 2013), though luxury titles like *Vogue* were still attracting record amounts.

While brands were spending more on Internet advertising, only a small proportion of this was going to the websites or apps of traditional publishers.

Another headache for magazines or newspapers is that online advertising is measurable; retailers know exactly how many people click on their links, make a purchase, play their videos or read their emails.

'Gone are the days where magazines could charge certain fees for retailers but not necessarily be able to back it up with real figures about what they could sell,' says fashion commentator Caryn Franklin. 'The boot's going to be on the other foot with advertisers.'

Bloggers and digital-only magazines that have to make all their money online can rarely survive on advertising alone, anyway. Instead, they diversify with sponsored content and e-commerce, in a model that traditional publications were already adopting.

In a sign of the times, multiplatform media company *Vice* bought out *i-D* magazine in 2012, planning to use the magazine's fashion credibility to build a fashion video channel online.

Instead of traditional ads, 'we will work with appropriate brand partners on content and other special campaigns,' *Vice* president Andrew Creighton said (in Sweney, 2012).

As we've seen, most magazines and some newspapers had already introduced click-and-buy, where the reader can click on or scan a product and be taken straight through to the retailer's website to buy it, earning commission for the publisher.

This blending of editorial content and advertising/sponsorship is disturbing for some print journalists and editors who believe in a 'church and state' separation between the two.

But they're going to have to get over their distaste, their digital colleagues say, arguing that it's more transparent than the traditional business model where advertisers had more of a say than readers were ever aware of.

Jeremy Langmead, editor-in-chief at Mr Porter, declared on the *Business of Fashion* website: 'This is the publishing model of the future: a blend of content and commerce talking in realtime to a highly-engaged audience with a finger primed to purchase' (2013).

Customer magazines and e-tailer websites

The argument about whether editorial is credible when it's in the service of a brand also rages over e-tailer and customer magazines.

As we saw in Chapter 1, customer magazines *John Lewis Edition* (published by contract publishers John Brown) and *Asos* (published in-house) took two of the top three spots in the chart of biggest-circulating women's lifestyle magazines in the first half of 2013.

Harrods magazine was a member of the Professional Publishers Association, along with venerable titles like *Vogue*, *Elle* and *Harper's Bazaar*.

Meanwhile, e-tailers compile their own digital magazines – like Net-a-Porter's weekly *The Edit* and Mr Porter's *The Journal* – and put other editorial content like runway reports and trend pieces on their websites along with the commerce.

Net-a-Porter even launched a print version in February 2014, created by former *Harper's Bazaar* editor Lucy Yeomans.

The benefits for the retailer are clear. They can use their products in traditional fashion articles like trend reports and shopping pages, but in a magazine entirely in their control. Customers reportedly spend an average of 25 minutes reading them, and they lead to an 8 per cent rise in sales without looking like hard sell (Greene, 2010).

It also allows e-tailers to act as a destination for customers when they don't have a physical shop floor. Jeremy Langmead, editor-in-chief of Mr Porter, describes content as 'the fixtures and fittings of an online store' (in Rousselle, 2012).

And it gives an online brand identity. Siobhan Mallen, head of womenswear and international content at Asos, says: 'The magazine is the only physical manifestation of the brand. It says, "This is who we are," and it gives us fashion credibility – we work with amazing photographers.'

Audiences, too, appreciate the editing and guidance that branded editorial gives, says Fiona McIntosh, former *Elle* editor who worked with My-wardrobe.com on its website. 'There is so much out there and you have to edit it and place it in context for the reader', she says.

Net-a-Porter's new magazine is sold on news stands, but most other brand magazines are free. They are funded through a brand's marketing budget, but can also attract external advertising – *John Lewis Edition*, for example, claims to get 9 per cent more beauty advertising than the market average, while 80 per cent of Mr Porter's ad revenue comes from brands it doesn't stock.

Because of generous budgets, and without the pressure of selling at a news stand, brand magazines are often in a better position to innovate than their traditional counterparts.

'They are the competition for us, no doubt,' says Jess Cartner-Morley, *Guardian* fashion editor. 'A lot of the more interesting ideas are coming from them. They are attracting people that have taken the leap ahead into the digital future more quickly than those on print publications.'

Siobhan Mallen at Asos says content can be more adventurous too, pointing out that she used Lena Dunham as a cover star before her TV series *Girls* even aired in the UK. She says she also has bigger budgets for fashion shoots than many consumer magazines.

Siobhan used to be associate fashion director at *Grazia* and believes she has made the right move to Asos. 'I feel I've future-proofed my career. Girls don't read magazines any more. They don't actually need to read anything more than Asos.'

Her statement gets the backs up of some consumer magazine editors, who say that branded editorial does not yet have the credibility that their publications have.

Lucy Wood, senior fashion news editor at *Look*, says the big difference is that customer magazines only write about the brands they stock. 'We don't work like that – we look at the whole picture and give what we think is the best,' she says.

Others say it's not only selection, but the whole purpose of the magazines that matters. Harriet Walker, of *Never Underdressed*, says of customer magazines: 'It's never truly editorial: it all goes back to them having to shift something.'

But e-tailers insist they're not so different from consumer magazines, not least because the glossies work so closely with advertisers (see above).

Jeremy Langmead, editor-in-chief of Mr Porter, says:

> Everything we sell we have bought ourselves; and we've bought these items to sell because we like them and we think our customers will like them too.
>
> None of the merchandise has been bought by us because an advertiser has asked us to do so ... In fact, the set-up is a lot more transparent than it is with our traditional counterparts.

(2013)

The future of fashion journalism

At the time of writing, the publishing world was in turmoil. The traditional print model of magazines, funded mostly by advertising and partly by sales, was in sharp decline as readers disappeared online and advertising shrank.

After a stuttering start, newspapers and magazines began to pour resources into their own websites and apps, hoping to make up lost ground. But because website content was largely free, digital subscriptions had not yet taken off as hoped, and online advertising generated nothing like as much revenue as print ads, this model did not look immediately sustainable either.

By 2013, it was clear that publishers' digital offerings, as innovative and appealing as they might be, were only being propped up by the profits of print, for the time being at least. The content – expensive to produce, if cheap to publish – was still often being provided by journalists paid for by the print product.

So what does the future hold? Will magazines and newspapers still be around in 50, 20 or even 10 years' time, and how will they be paid for?

Some believe that the luxury appeal of a glossy magazine will never die out, even though they may become a niche product rather than a mass-market medium.

'Our women love print,' says Lucy Yeomans, explaining Net-a-Porter's decision to launch a print magazine. 'There's something incredibly luxurious about it' (in Kansara, 2013a).

Fiona McIntosh, ex-editor of *Elle* who consults for websites, believes monthlies still have their place. 'It will be a smaller place, though. Monthlies are a quieter and more reflective experience than the hard and fast online experience.'

Young journalists, too, who grew up with and work in digital, can still understand the appeal of print, even though they see it from a different perspective. Alex Murphy, of My-wardrobe.com, says: 'It's almost like things have spun on their head, and the print product has to be seen as an extension of the online content, a distilled, beautiful version of it.'

But others are not so sanguine. Sasha Wilkins, who blogs as Liberty-LondonGirl and worked on a number of glossies, says print has already lost the battle.

'Magazines won't exist in five years, because of a lack of advertisers not readers,' she declares, insisting that the big bloggers are better value with cheaper ad rates, bigger digital audiences and much more engaged readers (2013b).

Unsurprisingly, those on the e-tailer side also see traditional print being usurped – this time by brands themselves. 'As long as brands are trusted, they're better placed digitally to satisfy people's hunger for inspiration, validation and knowledge of the new,' says Duncan Edwards, design and editorial director at *Asos* magazine (in Smith, 2012b).

But it could be that traditional magazines will meet them in the middle, opening their own online stores and developing their click-to-buy offerings via a variety of access points (see, for example, showbusiness stories in the *Daily Mail* online which invite you to buy a bikini similar to that of a celebrity snapped on a beach, or a party dress just like one on the red carpet).

Jessica Bumpus, of *Vogue* online, says magazines and retailers are already moving closer together, describing it as 'everyone dancing with each other and not being able to find their feet'.

Whatever happens, fashion journalism by its very nature has to embrace it, says Charlie Porter, ex of the *Guardian*, *GQ* and *Fantastic Man*, who now writes for the *Financial Times* and his own website.

'Never assume that the thing that is there at that moment is the way it will always be', he says.

> Fashion itself is about change, so you have to be able to embrace change.
>
> You have to be able to get excited by the idea of change and want to see what the effect of change is, no matter what it is – even if it's your magazine closing and the industry changing.
>
> If you're going to get scared and timid and pretend the world is the way that it was, then you're not writing about fashion.

Recommended reading

The Business of Fashion: www.businessoffashion.com.

Conboy, M. (2004) *Journalism: A Critical History*. London: Sage.

Harcup, T. (2009) *Journalism: Principles and Practice*, 2nd edition. London: Sage.

Johnson, S. and Prijatel, P. (2012) *The Magazine from Cover to Cover*, 3rd edition. Oxford: Oxford University Press.

McKay, J. (2013) *The Magazines Handbook*, 3rd edition. London: Routledge.

McNair, B. (2009) *News & Journalism in the UK*, 5th edition. London: Routledge.

Magforum: www.magforum.co.uk.

Media Guardian: www.theguardian.com/media.

Oliva, A. and Angeletti, N. (2006) *'In Vogue': The Illustrated History of the World's Most Famous Fashion Magazine*. New York: Rizzoli.

Press Gazette: www.pressgazette.co.uk.

Professional Publishers Association: www.ppa.co.uk.

Whittaker, J. (2008) *Magazine Production*. London: Routledge.

4   The fashion industry

Introduction

One of the UK's best-known fashion journalists, Colin McDowell, has said that there's no point even trying to write about fashion if you can't describe the exact construction of a sleeve.

While you don't actually have to know how to put together a blouse to be a reporter, McDowell is right that good journalists should have a strong understanding of their field.

'You wouldn't expect to become an architecture critic without knowing anything about architecture, and it's not enough to say "Well, I live in a house,"' says Harriet Walker, news editor at former style and beauty website *Never Underdressed*.

'That's why you have to make sure that you're not just a person who likes clothes' (2013a).

A good understanding of the fashion industry – how it's financed, how designers work, how clothes are manufactured, how branding operates, how garments are sold and how people wear them – will make you a much more effective and thoughtful journalist.

Of course, the fashion industry and journalists work pretty closely together, as we've already seen in Chapter 3. Fashion journalists work as consultants for brands, and stylists and photographers will simultaneously work for both magazines, for credibility, and on brands' advertising campaigns and lookbooks (shots of their clothes on models), for money.

So they already know a lot about each other – but what's lacking, some commentators say, is critical distance and informed analysis of how the fashion system works.

'It's a money-making industry that is able to harness what is an instinctive and emotional desire to dress up and sell it back to us as a set of seasonal rules,' says Caryn Franklin, ex-presenter of the BBC's *The Clothes Show* and fashion commentator.

'Deconstructing that bit is an important part of being a journalist, being able to question what that's all about' (2013).

Figure 4.1 Liz Lamb feature on fashion students (Liz Lamb/NCJ Media)

Likewise Charlie Porter, formerly of the *Guardian*, *GQ*, *Fantastic Man* and now the *Financial Times*, says a critical eye on the industry is vital to avoid the cliché of fashion writing as product-driven puffery:

> It's a description of a world – it's not about wanting to be part of that world; it's not about trying to convey 'I'm better than you' or 'If only you could have this life.' It's more, 'This is interesting stuff being done by interesting people, and here's what happened.'

(2013b)

There are specialist books about the fashion industry which will give you a good overview of how it all works, along with the excellent *Business of Fashion* website (see the Bibliography).

What this chapter aims to do is set out some basics about the fashion system, discuss some of the issues facing the industry and highlight the points where brands and journalists intersect.

It should be read in conjunction with Chapter 12, Fashion journalism and PR, which is the main way journalists come into contact with brands on a daily basis.

The brands

Haute couture

Haute couture – literally 'high sewing' in French – is a rarified world for the super-rich now, but it's how the fashion industry began in the nineteenth century.

Before the days of fashion retailers or department stores, all clothes for the wealthy were made to measure, run up by dressmakers on the instructions of their clients.

Dressmaking was considered a craft rather than an art, and its practitioners were generally anonymous. That started to change with the flamboyant Charles Frederick Worth, a Lincolnshire draper who moved to Paris and opened his first shop on the Rue de la Paix in 1858.

Worth was the first couturier to sew his own name into clothes, to come up with his own designs, to stage fashion shows at his shop and to dress actresses and other social figures to publicise his gowns. 'He was the prototype celebrity fashion designer,' wrote Mark Tungate in his book, *Fashion Brands* (2012: 7).

He paved the way for other star names, like Paul Poiret and Jacques Doucet, and the trade body that represents couturiers to this day, the Chambre Syndicale de la Haute Couture, was set up in 1868 to consolidate their status.

It also forever tied the fashion system to Paris. Even now, it's up to the French ministry of industry who can be designated as haute couture or not. As well as having to show in Paris twice a year, a fashion house has to have a workshop in the French capital.

Haute couture clothes are bespoke, fitted to a client and handmade using the finest materials and finishing. They're not just the creation of the fashion house itself, but also ateliers (workshops) in Paris like embroiderers Lesage and feather specialists Lemarie (see Jess Cartner-Morley's description at www.theguardian.com/lifeandstyle/2005/jan/28/fashion.hautecoutureshows).

And they are incredibly expensive: roughly 100 times the cost of a ready-to-wear designer garment, Jess estimates, so around £100,000 for one evening dress (Cartner-Morley, 2012).

Unsurprisingly, the number of couture houses has shrunk considerably from 106 in 1946 to around 14 permanent members by 2013, including Chanel, Dior, Givenchy and Jean Paul Gaultier, although non-French houses like Armani, Valentino and Versace are allowed to show as 'correspondent members'.

The number of clients also dipped alarmingly, down to as low as 300 at one point (Tungate, 2012) though it's now reported to be around 2,000 worldwide (Core, 2013).

Fashion houses justify their couture lines as being good for their overall image. Even if hardly anybody can afford the clothes, the shows get a lot of publicity, a designer can go to town creatively, and the result will help sell the brand's cheaper lines like bags and sunglasses. Bernard Arnault, president of the world's largest luxury conglomerate LVMH, said: 'Its impact on all the other lines – clothes, accessories and cosmetics – is enormous' (in Tungate, 2012: 126).

For years, fashion journalists would have to write articles in January and June ahead of the shows justifying couture in this way. 'It's the tax you pay for having found a way to make a career out of talking about dresses and shopping,' wrote the *Guardian*'s Hadley Freeman (2009: 97).

But by 2011 there were signs that haute couture was undergoing something of a renaissance, as the super-wealthy in the new economic superpowers of China, India, Russia and Brazil began to replace long-gone American socialites.

Chanel enjoyed record sales, Armani, Valentino and Givenchy all reported rises on 2010 and Versace decided to mount a haute couture show for the first time in eight years (Cartner-Morley, 2012).

Free from worrying about the death of haute couture, fashion journalists began to lament that some shows were looking a little too commercial and pandering to customer tastes, 'which makes for a whole lot of beaded, floorlength mother-of-the-bride dresses', complained Cartner-Morley.

Ready-to-wear

Ready-to-wear (RTW), known in French as prêt-à-porter, means clothes produced in factories to standard sizes in more or less limited ranges.

Its origins lie in New York, which built up its own fashion industry when France was occupied in the Second World War. But the first ready-to-wear shows took place in Paris in 1960 and Yves Saint Laurent was the first designer to open a ready-to-wear boutique, Rive Gauche, in 1966.

Now, the RTW collections are the primary focus of fashion houses, and are shown twice a year in fashion weeks in New York, London, Milan and Paris.

Any would-be fashion journalist should be familiar with the history and signature styles of the big fashion houses, and key looks from collections in the past – from Dior's New Look in 1947, to the exaggerated femininity of the 1950s, the space-age tunics and shifts of the 1960s, Vivienne Westwood's journey from punk to romanticism in the 1970s and 1980s, the influence of Japanese designers in the 1980s and the so-called 'end of fashion' (Agins, 2001) until Tom Ford shook up Gucci with a series of sex- and money-drenched campaigns in the late 1990s.

Most brands have timelines on their websites, and there is a wealth of coffee-table books about big-name designers. The Victoria and Albert Museum in London has a permanent fashion collection and stages regular exhibitions centred on seminal moments in fashion. Its website at www.vam. ac.uk/page/f/fashion/ is an excellent resource for students.

There are other fashion museums around the UK – from the Bowes Museum in County Durham (www.thebowesmuseum.org.uk) to the Fashion Museum in Bath (www.museumofcostume.co.uk).

Meanwhile you can find galleries of all collections since 1999 on *Style.com* (www.style.com).

It's important also to be familiar with who owns what in the fashion industry. The landscape was revolutionised in the 1990s and 2000s with a wave of buy-ups by a handful of companies, which have now turned into huge multinational conglomerates controlling more than 500 luxury labels.

The biggest is LVMH (Louis Vuitton Moët Hennessy). Apart from the brands of its title, it also runs some of the best-known names in fashion, including Céline, Kenzo, Givenchy, Marc Jacobs, Donna Karan and Fendi. It owns Guerlain and Christian Dior perfumes and BeneFit cosmetics, Bulgari jewellers, TAG Heuer watches, Le Bon Marché store in Paris and a whole host of champagne brands.

Its fierce rival is Kering, formerly known as Pinault-Printemps-Redoute or PPR, which was a retail business before it bought out the Gucci group at the start of the millennium. Its brands now include Gucci, Bottega Veneta, Saint Laurent, McQueen, Balenciaga, Christopher Kane, Stella McCartney and sportswear brand Puma.

A third big player is Richemont, which largely owns hard goods labels like Cartier, Montblanc and Van Cleef & Arpels, but also has Chloé, Azzedine Alaïa and Net-a-Porter in its stable.

Very few big fashion houses are still in private hands. At the time of writing they included Chanel, owned by the family-run Wertheimer company, Dolce & Gabbana, the Prada Group and Lanvin.

For the conglomerates, the mass buying spree allowed them to tap into new talent and markets, and diversify their product ranges. This helped protect them in the post-2007 recession, as did new demand from emerging countries like Brazil, Russia, India and China.

For designers, the financial backing of a big company can be a godsend. It means money for advertising and hence more clout with editors and buyers, it means they can stage lavish catwalk shows – a Marc Jacobs show in 2011 was reported to have cost at least $1 million – and it means manufacturing and distribution is taken care of.

But not everyone celebrates the era of the conglomerate. Former French *Vogue* editor Carine Roitfeld, for one, says fashion has become such a big business, with so much money at stake, that nobody dares take risks any more. 'It's less light-hearted, less spontaneous. Fashion has become an industry, one that increasingly stifles creation' (2011: 46).

It also means that designers are disposable, even at their own brands. Jil Sander and Roland Mouret are two designers who lost the commercial right to their own names after falling out with backers.

Some reporters saw this new commercialism at work in the reshuffle of several major designers in 2012. Raf Simons left Jil Sander, where he'd won the respect of fashion editors but had failed to generate much profit, and acclaimed designer Nicolas Ghesquière was replaced at Balenciaga by the then 29-year-old Alexander Wang, whose own label had a mass appeal to young women and an enviably high profile in China (Cartner-Morley, 2013d).

Meanwhile, California-based Hedi Slimane's first two collections for Saint Laurent were mocked by some critics but proved hugely successful with buyers and customers (Cowles, 2013).

As Tungate wrote, 'Designers are admirably creative people, but they work for an ever-shrinking number of global conglomerates … The clothes a designer sends out on to the runway are worthless unless they increase sales of handbags, sunglasses and perfume' (2012: 3).

British fashion

The British fashion industry has developed differently from other countries', which has been both a blessing and a curse.

Its roots lie in Savile Row tailoring, outerwear brands like Burberry and Aquascutum and couturiers with royal associations like Norman Hartnell and Hardy Amies.

In the 1960s to 1990s, it became more associated with street fashions and popular culture, like the Swinging Sixties, Mods (1960s), Punk (1970s), New Romantics (1980s) and Cool Britannia (1990s).

Unlike France, it had little support from the government, and London Fashion Week wasn't launched to promote its designers to journalists and buyers until 1984. Even then, it struggled for credibility until 2009, when Burberry and Matthew Williamson returned from Milan and New York respectively.

Unlike Italy, it is not built on the back of textile or leather manufacturers. Indeed, fashion manufacturing all but collapsed in the UK, its value plummeting by two-thirds between 1995 and 2010 (BFC, 2010).

And unlike New York, its designers are widely perceived as having little business acumen, apart from exceptions like Paul Smith, and fledgling design businesses have a high failure rate.

Because the UK doesn't have any big couture houses or manufacturers, its budding designers are educated on university fashion courses rather than through apprenticeships. This has left it with an unparalleled reputation for creativity, but means that many of its young stars go abroad for the big jobs.

Past examples have included Alexander McQueen going to Givenchy, John Galliano to Givenchy and Dior, Stella McCartney to Chloé and Phoebe Philo to Chloé and Céline.

Despite this, in its Value of Fashion report in 2010, the British Fashion Council (BFC) estimated that the fashion industry contributed almost £21 billion a year to the British economy and supported more than 816,000 jobs.

This makes fashion not only the biggest creative industry by far, but also twice as big as the more prosaic businesses of car manufacturing or publishing.

Its strength lies in its high-street retail, which the BFC says has 'unrivalled diversity' and is 'unique internationally in terms of its strong direct links with designers'. It points to high-profile collaborations between New Look and Giles Deacon, and Topshop with Christopher Kane, as well as the Designers at Debenhams ranges.

The popularity of British style also draws tourists to the UK who spend a total of £41 million a year, the BFC says. Chinese shoppers blow an average of £605 a trip, especially on luxury goods that can be 30 per cent cheaper than in their own country (Wallop, 2011).

But to develop further, UK fashion badly needs more teaching of business and management skills to designers, new apprenticeships to improve manufacturing know-how, and more support to promote its talent abroad, the BFC said in a Future of Fashion report in 2012.

It also warned that university tuition fees posed a threat to the flow of design talent from colleges like Central Saint Martins in London. 'All the greats of modern British fashion – McQueen, Galliano, Kane – have come from working-class families. That is the story of British fashion,' said Sarah Mower, the BFC's education tsar, at the start of London Fashion Week in September 2013 (in Cartner-Morley, 2013e).

The seasons

The fashion industry has long operated around two main seasons, spring–summer and autumn–winter (or fall, in the United States).

Designers' collections are shown on the runway six months ahead of the season – so the spring–summer collections are shown in September/October, and the autumn–winter collections in February/March.

This gives brands time to sell and manufacture orders before they're delivered to stores from February ahead of spring, and August ahead of winter. It also gives magazines time to call in and shoot their pick of the collections for their main fashion issues in September and March.

The season really begins, though, more than a year before the collections arrive in stores, with a series of yarn and fabric shows like Pitti Immagine Filati in Florence and Première Vision near Paris.

Designers and high-street brands use the fairs to source suppliers of, say, knitwear or tweed, put in orders for fabric and also get an early indication of upcoming trends. Première Vision 'is one of the few trade shows where you can spot designers stalking the aisles', writes Tungate (2012: 69).

Because fabric is being manufactured in bulk a year ahead, it pays both the mills and the designers to tacitly agree on certain colours and fabric trends for that season rather than risk going off message and being left with unwanted stock.

Première Vision organises a preview before it opens, outlining key trends as drawn up by its fashion team and a panel of 65 experts from around Europe (Jackson and Shaw, 2006).

Fashion journalists for newspapers and magazines will not generally report on these textile shows, but they're big news for the trade journalists on the likes of *Drapers* or *Women's Wear Daily*, who will cover them all to give their industry readers the first glimpse of future trends.

How the seasons are changing

There were signs by 2013 that the seasons were beginning to get more complicated.

In a literal sense, climate change had fashion retailers questioning whether it was wise to have huge quantities of, say, summer stock sitting around on shelves through months of cold and rain.

In February 2012, temperatures in the UK ranged from -18C to +18C, while a very wet spring and early summer in 2013 saw retailers having to cut prices of clothing by up to 75 per cent. John Lewis' head of merchandising for womenswear, Christina Slater, said: 'The lines between the seasons are blurring' (in Thomson, 2012).

In a non-literal sense, many commentators had already remarked that fashion cycles were speeding up, thanks in part to the Internet.

The live-streaming of catwalk shows means that fans could see new collections the instant they hit the runway – or even before, thanks to Burberry's behind-the-scenes Twitter pictures – and were less and less willing to wait six months for them to arrive in shops.

Burberry led the way by offering most of its spring–summer 2011 collection for immediate sale online, with a turnaround time of weeks rather than months. Cathy Horyn, former *New York Times* catwalk critic, noticed a concomitant change in the clothes, with a 'blunt emphasis on embellished trench coats and leather jackets' unsuited to the traditional spring season (2010).

Meanwhile, all designers found that previously under-the-radar collections like pre-fall and resort, shown in December/January and May/June, were getting more attention and coverage in weekly magazines and online.

Trend bureau Editd found that these more commercial, quick mid-season collections often sold better than the main lines. 'With seasonality coming into question, and with the drive to fill the buy-it-now demand that brands like Burberry can generate, brands have to become more reactional and produce new product more seamlessly,' it wrote in its blog (Smith, 2012a).

This lesson was already being learned on the high street, where the likes of fast fashion retailer Zara were doing away with the idea of seasons in favour of constant, small drops.

All of Zara's clothes are designed by its in-house 350-strong team, most of them actually during a season rather than months in advance. Many are also manufactured in Spain in Zara's own factories (rather than in China or Morocco in factories whose slots have to be booked well ahead), meaning it could take as little as two weeks for a designer's idea to materialise on a shop shelf (Stevenson, 2012).

All these changes – climate, online, direct access to the audience, technology – led to some commentators predicting a big upheaval in the way fashion is promoted, sold and delivered.

Asked what the next big thing in the fashion industry was, the Sartorialist's Scott Schuman said:

> Smart designers are going to show their collection to a much wider audience online and ship those products closer to the real time.
>
> It will be much more efficient and effective if you're making clothes that fit people and they're ordering and want, rather than what you're guessing they want.
>
> (Big Think, 2012)

Former Jimmy Choo designer Tamara Mellon had something like this in mind when she announced her own line in 2013. She said she would 'break the traditional retail landscape' by swapping runway shows for small presentations and dropping pieces into stores monthly rather than quarterly (Bowe, 2013).

The designers

Knowing who the designers are, where they work and what they're known for is vital for any fashion journalist. You might have to interview or profile a designer, you'd want to know their history and their form before reviewing a show or a collection, and you're always on the lookout for promising new talent.

Melanie Rickey, *Grazia* contributing editor, compares it to covering horse racing. 'You have to know your runners and riders, who's having a good season, who's not and why,' she says (2012).

And fashion is a godsend for interviewers, says the *Daily Telegraph*'s Luke Leitch, because of the personalities involved.

'It's packed to the rafters with individuals who've got brilliant stories and who are naturally idiosyncratic and extreme,' he says. 'These extremities are often amplified by their position and the money and power and grandeur that swirl around them, so there's plenty of material there' (2013c).

Think of a designer, and chances are someone like Karl Lagerfeld pops into your head. Star designers are promoted as lone, artistic geniuses as part of the whole branding of fashion.

But there are various types of designer across the fashion system, and various ways in which they work.

Designers at leading luxury brands are generally surrounded by a big team, and are often called artistic or creative directors responsible for the overall brand image – from stores, to advertising imagery to collections – rather than hands-on creation of clothes.

Lagerfeld, for example, was appointed as artistic director at Chanel, as was Nicolas Ghesquière at Louis Vuitton.

Even when the brand is in their name, a designer might be more of a figurehead than part of the actual design team. When Alexander McQueen died in 2010, for instance, his assistant Sarah Burton took over without the brand breaking stride, completing his unfinished collection and pursuing her own.

'They go to overseas shows and selling events, and people can talk to them, but they'll have others running the different design divisions underneath,' says Mick Dixon, a fashion designer and lecturer, who has worked for all types of companies, from one-man bands to multinationals.

'They'll have a say, but it might be something like a themed idea that other people will execute technically' (2013).

The importance of image-making is evident in the way designers whose technical skills were renowned in their day sank almost without trace, whereas the legends of characters like Coco Chanel reverberate to this day.

Her successor Karl Lagerfeld is particularly adept at both drawing on the Coco Chanel narrative and creating his own memorable image, which has appeared on the side of Diet Coke tins and as dolls.

It's a commercial imperative as well as a creative one, writes Tungate: 'Designers are useful figures because they incarnate their brands; like strokes of shorthand they embody the complex messages and values the brand is asking the public to buy into' (2012: 49).

So when the Sartorialist blogger Scott Schuman faced a backlash after saying few fashion students looked the part, he was unrepentant. 'You have to learn something about how to manage a business, how to articulate your concept and how to personally embody the spirit of the brand you hope to build,' he wrote.

'Do you think Karl ever says "I'm too busy/tired to look like Karl today?"' (Schuman, 2013).

Designers at the top level might work across various brands and many lines. Lagerfeld is creative director at Fendi, as well as Chanel, and also has his own line, Karl. Paul Smith has around 19 lines, across menswear, womenswear, childrenswear, shoes, accessories and soft furnishings.

There might also be collaborations and licence agreements, on top of the main season, mid-season and couture collections. John Galliano blamed work pressure for the public meltdown that led to him losing his job at Dior and his own brand in 2011. 'Dior is a big machine,' he said in the resulting court case (in Diderich and Wynne, 2011).

Other brands like Diesel or Barbour have a faceless team of designers who inspire little interest. 'It's a different way of looking at a brand – they've got a value based on the technical aspects of the product rather than the stylistic aspects of an individual person,' Mick Dixon says.

High-street retailers increasingly employ their own designers, who will work for a certain product category like knits or swimwear and who will interpret trends in a way suitable for their brand. This type of designer will work in tandem with merchandisers, whose job it is to predict what will sell, at what price and when.

At the budget end of the market, the design task might simply be to deliver expectations at a certain price point. 'Some shoppers will just buy what's in front of them if the price is right and it doesn't make them look stupid,' says Mick. 'They don't think, "This is the statement piece I've been looking for;" they'll think, "I'm going on holiday and I need five t-shirts."'

Finally, there are jobbing designers or designers-for-hire. Smaller retailers without their own in-house team will contract these designers to produce designs and technical specifications for products, and might ask them to organise the manufacture as well.

A local fashion journalist might well seek out more anonymous designers who wouldn't normally make it into the glossies but who come from the writer's 'patch' and are thus interesting to local readers.

Liz Lamb, former fashion writer for the *Newcastle Chronicle and Journal*, for example, has written features about North East graduates who work for national high-street chains and local designers like Tallulah Love and the Libertarian.

Useful profiles of designers can be found on www.style.com, as well as the websites for the New York (www.mbfashionweek.com) and the London fashion weeks (www.londonfashionweek.co.uk).

The markets

The finance section of newspapers may not be the first pages a fashion journalism student might turn to, but they are a must-read.

Fashion is not just a cultural industry but a big business, and it's important to know which retailers are booming and which are struggling, which designer has been bought out by whom, who is buying fashion and luxury goods, and how they're buying them.

This can make a feature in itself. Spectacular financial results from Asos in May 2013, for example, prompted a page by *Evening Standard* fashion editor Karen Dacre ('Meet team ASOS'), while *Grazia*'s Zoe Beaty used a financial report about Asian spending in the UK as the springboard for a first-person piece about hitting West End shops with young Chinese women.

Or, a designer's target market or the plight of the economy might form the backdrop to a catwalk review which seeks to go further than simply describing the garments on show – see Melanie Rickey's story about the autumn–winter 2013 collections on the *Guardian* website, for example ('The autumn/winter 2013 fashion weeks showed us clothes we can really love' – Rickey, 2013b).

How fashion retailers fare in recession, the boom in online shopping and the rise of new luxury markets, first in Asia and then in Brazil, Russia and India, have been some of the big stories dominating the past decade.

'New markets are completely changing the fashion industry,' says Charlie Porter, *Financial Times* fashion critic:

> It's fascinating watching companies try to work out how to exploit them. It will also be fascinating to see how design schools in Korea and China shift the balance from the locked pattern of London-Paris-Milan-New York as the alleged centres of design.
>
> (2013b)

Another big change was a rise in menswear, which at the time of writing was growing faster than womenswear in the UK. London Collections: Men launched in 2012, and its early success got fashion journalists excited.

'There is a market change; you can see it from the success of Mr Porter and Harrods,' says Luke Leitch. 'They show that there's a massive international menswear audience, and they engage with the British point of reference at the retail point and the design point.'

Burberry was estimated to get 14 per cent of its total sales from Chinese shoppers alone by 2013 (BBC News, 2013a). The quintessentially English Paul Smith is part-owned by a Japanese licensing company.

But global brands were not just concerned about the luxury end of the market. To maximise their value and because of recession, they were trying to sell across all areas of the market, with cheap licensed goods at the bottom end.

'People used to talk about pyramids, with volume at low prices at the bottom, then luxury brands at the top,' says designer and brand expert Mick Dixon. 'Everyone had their segment and their slot. But now the ones at the top need to be relevant across all market sectors.'

The retailers losing out in all this were the 'squeezed middle', who had neither the value nor the desirability to compete, according to Mick. Hence the woes of Marks & Spencer, avidly followed by fashion journalists, which could not compete for value against the big supermarket chains or Primark but which also struggled to establish design credibility.

The design process

A designer will start by doing research – into the best and worst performers of the previous season, into trends via forecasting services and textile shows, or, if part of a bigger brand, into a brief provided to them linked to marketing and sales targets.

Initial ideas will be sketched by hand or on computer, then filtered to narrow them down before prototypes are made. A big organisation might be able to test fabric at this stage if it's to be developed specially for them by a mill, while smaller organisations might use readily available fabric.

The prototypes are fitted on a model and changes made. If the design is for a retailer, grading for different sizes will take place, samples will be 'sealed' as a benchmark for production, and the technical specifications will be sent to a factory for manufacture. Merchandisers and buyers will decide how many are to be made and in how many colours.

At this stage, a brand will order samples of each piece that they will keep for their showrooms, to lend to fashion editors for shoots and to give to their sales team to take orders on, if relevant.

The process is different for a fashion house that will show its collection on the runway. Samples are made, but the pieces won't go into production until there are orders for them. So some looks you see on the runway or in a fashion shoot are never actually made, or a more commercial version only is produced.

Although buyers attend catwalk shows along with journalists, most collections are sold a month or two beforehand in showroom appointments. The runway show is more for publicity and image than actual selling (see Chapter 7).

Samples

Fashion editors, journalists, buyers, stylists and invited celebrities will get a chance to see a designer's collection close up in a showroom. On the London Fashion Week website (www.londonfashionweek.co.uk) you can see the addresses of the bigger brands' own showrooms around London; smaller designers have space in the British Fashion Council's own showroom.

High-street stores show off samples of their new collections at 'press days', to give journalists the opportunity to write about upcoming trends and stylists a chance to decide which pieces they want to call in and shoot.

All the looks in a new range will also be compiled into lookbooks, where they're photographed on models, and on line sheets where sketches appear with product details. Stylists can use these to call in specific items for shoots later.

Samples are made in one size – generally the size that will fit the catwalk models, in the case of designer samples – and the system is regularly castigated for fuelling the promotion of very thin body types in fashion.

Vogue editor Alexandra Shulman wrote to some designers in 2009 to complain that their samples had become 'minuscule', forcing magazines to hire models that were too thin just so they could wear them in shoots (Nikkhah, 2009).

Caryn Franklin, who heads the diversity campaign group All Walks Beyond the Catwalk (www.allwalks.org), says she sympathises with designers who may not have the time or the budget to fit prototypes on models of differing shapes and sizes.

But she says future designers should be educated to do better. 'Trainee designers need to experience the body and create clothes on a body that can give them feedback,' she says.

'So the immovable bust stand and a model that's paid to be silent are only part of the process in training to make clothes.'

Where clothes are made

Unless you're getting a suit tailor-made for you on Savile Row, it's unlikely that any item of clothing you buy is made by one person or in the same place – or even in the same country – from start to finish.

According to an Oxfam report, 'A company may source fibre from Korea, dye and weave it in Taiwan, buy zips from China and send it all to Thailand for assembly' (2004).

That's why it's virtually impossible to know where your clothes come from, and labels aren't much help either. 'People got round it by having components assembled here so they could say "made in Britain",' says designer Mick Dixon. 'The only sure way of telling is the cost, really.'

From the 1980s onwards, the bulk of clothing manufacture moved overseas, especially to South East Asia and China where the cost of labour was much cheaper and workforces weren't unionised.

Marks & Spencer, where 90 per cent of products were British made, decided in 1997 to source more from overseas. Textile factories run by suppliers Dewhirst and William Baird shut down, and within a few years 90 per cent of M&S products were made abroad (Hines, 2006).

Retailers, and especially designers, didn't like to shout about this, and it only came to public attention when there was a particular scandal, like sweatshop labour (Nike in the early 1990s, Primark in 2008) and factory disasters (fire in Karachi, Pakistan, 2012: 264 deaths; collapse of the Rana Plaza in Bangladesh, 2013: more than 1,100 deaths).

Because clothes prices in the UK have fallen in real terms, and because retailers want quicker turnarounds and smaller orders, pressure has increased on garment factories, with reports of workers being locked in to complete orders and fired when work is complete.

Brands don't want bad publicity and have developed corporate social responsibility departments that report on things like sourcing and sustainability (see the H&M one at http://about.hm.com/content/hm/aboutsection/en/About/Sustainability.html).

But it's very difficult for any designer or brand to know whether factories overseas are complying with legal and ethical standards, says Mick Dixon. Factories might subcontract work and falsify timesheets and payrolls when inspectors visit.

'Unless you're there all the time, it's really hard to know where your stuff's getting made,' Mick says. 'Especially if you're a smaller brand, you might never visit the factory. You can lose the product trail completely.'

But he says the worst thing brands can do is pull out completely, as it would destroy a local economy. Bangladesh, for example, has four million people employed in the garment trade, which accounts for 80 per cent of its exports revenue (Mustafa, 2013).

However, by 2013, there were signs that some brands were moving production back closer to home. Not only were wages and fuel costs in China rising, but costs overseas have always to be offset against the expense of freight and travelling, and loss of control.

Some brands moved manufacturing from Asia to the likes of Eastern Europe, the Middle East and Turkey, while an increasing number talked about manufacturing in the UK again.

In fact, 'Made in Britain' was something of a trend in itself, and it was being used as a marketing tool by firms. Mick Dixon knows a traditional factory in Manchester which has manufactured for Mulberry, Burberry, Barbour, Paul Smith and Rapha. The brands it works with sometimes have a video clip on their websites showing products being made there. 'It's a good story for them; they're supporting British manufacturing,' he says.

'There are lots of blogs about British manufacturing and a lot of networks being set up around it – it's a massive story.'

Some designers like JW Anderson manufacture only in Britain, while Arcadia Group (which owns Topshop) was pushing to use more British factories.

But manufacturing in the UK tended to be for specialist, niche and premium-priced product – and was not always as extensive as people would expect. Mulberry, for example, was often talked about for its factory in Somerset, but only 30 per cent of its products were made there. Burberry made raincoats in Yorkshire, but the rest of its lines were made overseas (Rickey, 2013a).

Branding

One of the most fascinating aspects of the fashion industry is branding. The image of a retailer or fashion house, and the values attached to its products, all come from the story it tells about itself.

As Tungate points out in his book *Fashion Branding*, clothes leave a factory as 'garments' or 'apparel'. 'Only when the marketers get hold of them do they magically become "fashion"' (2012: 1).

Tungate describes branding as 'telling a story' (22). He points to the way Chanel draws on the story of its founder Coco, and the way that Italian leather company Tod's has created an image of classicism and heritage even though it was only created in 1979.

Mick Dixon, who worked as a designer for Nike, sees it as a relationship. 'Brands make you feel a certain way. It's an emotional attachment or a relationship or a conversation,' he explains.

Companies promote their brand through their advertising imagery, stories they put out to the press, catwalk shows, the décor of their stores and – as we saw above – their figurehead designer.

That's why fashion houses tend to create their own advertisements, rather than hire an agency. It's also why Tom Ford redesigned everything from ads to store design to visual display – not just the clothes – when he shook up Gucci in the 1990s. 'A dress does not exist in a void, it exists in a world, and its context can radically alter its effect,' Ford explained (in Tungate, 2012: 64).

Fashion brands also align themselves with celebrities as a way to communicate what they stand for and give them a personality.

A star may be contracted to appear in advertisements or short films about the brand – as Nicole Kidman and Keira Knightley have done for Chanel – appear on the front row at their runway shows, and do interviews with the press where they will promote the brand.

Celebrities are also rounded up to attend events or parties organised by the brand – thus securing a picture and a mention on the diary pages of newspapers and magazines – and will be sent sponsorship offers and free products in the hope they'll be snapped wearing them.

This so-called seeding, the sending out of free products to stylish celebrities, is considered more effective than a straightforward advertisement.

'Celebrity endorsement is worth a lot more than that of a model,' wrote Imogen Edwards-Jones in a newspaper report on seeding (2009):

> When Cameron Diaz wears a dress, or Nicole Kidman carries a bag, it is something like 30 to 40 times more effective than if it were snapped in the hands of, say, supermodel Natalia Vodianova.

The perception is that the model was styled, whereas the actress actually chose to wear it.

It is useful for fashion journalists to know which stars have contracts or associations with which brands – not least to avoid the kind of legal pitfall involving Nicole Kidman and perfume that is explained in Chapter 13.

Also, it's one of a journalist's regular tasks to identify what brand a star is wearing when they step out on the red carpet or in public. 'I spent a year of my life finding out what Cheryl Cole was wearing when the *Daily Mirror* was obsessed with her,' says fashion director Amber Graafland (2013).

'To save you trawling through websites, it's really useful to know who's working with whom.'

With the advent of bloggers as influential trendsetters, it's not just the big labels that seed their products. Smaller organisations might find it a cost-effective way of brand building, says Mick Dixon.

'All the young brands will supply products as readily now to someone who has got a good following on social media as they would to a traditional trade or specialist magazine,' he says.

Rather than pay £12,000 for an ad in a glossy, I could give 100 top-quality jackets away for the same price. Assuming the product is good, the value of that is a lot more – people tend to believe those they identify with on social media, and it crosses more boundaries.

Extensions and collaborations

Once a designer or company has created a strong brand identity, it can be put to use in a whole variety of money-spinning ways.

Art director Thomas Lenthal, who has worked with Dior and Saint Laurent, says: 'Once you understand a brand, you can imagine every element within its specific world. Is there a particular Saint Laurent chair, telephone or lamp? The answer is yes' (in Tungate, 2012: 83).

This is not far off what happens in reality, where designers have lent their name to everything from motorbikes to hotels to crockery.

One way of extending the brand is through a collaboration with a company in a different market. When Karl Lagerfeld collaborated on a range with fashion chain H&M in 2004 it caused a sensation, but now such designer–high-street tie-ups are regular events.

Not only does this garner both sides extra publicity, but it gives the designer extra injections of cash (they will get a percentage of the sales) and increases brand awareness.

For the high-street chain, it enhances their fashion credibility and puts some clear blue water between them and the budget retailers snapping at their heels, while for the customer it allows them a little piece of the designer universe at a price they can afford.

But the most common means of brand extension is producing accessories, cosmetics and perfume, often through a licensing arrangement with another company.

Bags, branded sunglasses, belts, lipsticks, perfumes and moisturiser are where even luxury labels will make most of their money, so high are the profit margins and so broad the customer base.

'Skin care is so huge that it is often the supporting scaffolding of a fashion house, sopping up debts incurred by the unprofitable clothes division,' writes Hadley Freeman (2009: 15).

Unprofitable the clothes may be, but it is they that give the skin care range the cachet that makes people want to buy it. Cosmetics and perfume, Tungate writes, are the 'interface between the general public and the world of luxury' (2012: 135).

Fashion online

Surprisingly, perhaps, the fashion industry was a little slow to make the move online. Designers were wary of catwalk pictures going straight up on the Web, for fear they'd be copied, and luxury brands worried that their air of exclusivity would be compromised online.

Online fashion retail got off to a stuttering start, too, with the collapse of pioneer clothing company boo.com six months after launch in 2000. Some in the business feared customers would always want to feel clothes and try them on, and high customer returns rates of 40 per cent or above seemed to justify this.

Within a decade, though, that had changed. Net-a-Porter, launched in June 2000 and sold to Richemont in 2010, managed to sell luxury online with a website that replicated a glossy magazine. Asos became an online phenomenon, with 23 million visitors a month by 2013, a Sydney office and a planned China operation (Shah, 2013).

Like the media, fashion houses now went to where their audiences were, live-streaming their shows and engaging with fans on social media.

'Fashion has become much more accessible. There's not much left of the closed-door attitude now,' says Peter Henderson, Hapsical blogger and fashion writer for an e-commerce site (2013).

This has had the effect of turning fashion into a global pastime, with the general public much more knowledgeable and engaged.

'*Style.com* and nowfashion.com were down for a weekend because they had so many views for the menswear and couture shows – it's quite extraordinary that so many people watch fashion online,' says Peter Henderson.

This huge surge in interest was a godsend for fashion writers, catering for an ever-widening audience. 'Fashion coverage has absolutely exploded. I find it a privilege to do what I do at the moment,' says Jess Cartner-Morley, fashion editor of the *Guardian* (2011b).

Some worried, though, that it was robbing fashion of what was special about it. 'If you homogenize fashion, if you make it incredibly accessible, then what's special about it any more?' asks Harriet Walker, of *Never Underdressed*. 'If the web means it's all pop-up shops, and no couture, then that's a terrible thing. It's diluted.'

For retailers, it meant a global customer base with the complications that brings. It's almost hypnotic to log on to Net-a-Porter's live global map, and watch the little shopping bags pop up whenever someone in Australia, Russia, New York, Saudi Arabia or anywhere else makes a purchase. Asos sends four jumbo jets' worth of clothes to Australia every week.

Even a regional store, like the Newcastle-based chain of Jules B boutiques, is affected. 'In store, your catchment is a 10-mile radius but online it's endless if you do it well,' says PR and marketing manager Adam Mooney. 'We're looking into creating separate sites for Germany, France and the US.'

This inevitably affects buying patterns. The luxury retailers are reliant on designers producing mid-season collections like resort, to allow their southern hemisphere customers to shop in season.

Jules B has found itself stocking well-known, commercial brands that it wouldn't have in store, like Juicy Couture and Melissa by Vivienne Westwood, because that will pull in customers through searches in a way their speciality – niche brands – would not.

Some journalists have noticed signs of a change in the way clothes are designed, too. Peter Henderson, who writes for an e-commerce site, says: 'Companies like Net-a-Porter are such big players now that designers have in mind how things will look on a screen.'

Some in the industry were predicting more bespoke services online in the years to come, with technology able to show customers what a garment would look like on them, personalised content and increased geo-targeting.

Social media was predicted to become ever more influential, and mobiles were seen as the future of online retail. Already by 2013, 30 per cent of sales on Net-a-Porter were from mobile devices.

Future trends

In his book on the way fashion is branded (2012), Tungate outlined four main developments already underway that would affect fashion brands in the future – the 'search for a soul', authenticity and transparency, cultural content and consumers as their own brands.

It's fascinating to see that already taking shape, especially online, where brands are able to communicate directly to audiences and tell their own stories.

A niche company like high-end menswear firm Private White VC, based in Manchester, was a prime example of this 'search for a soul', a genuine human face. On its website you could tour its factory floor and cutting room, and meet 76-year-old Jean Seddon, who'd worked in the industry all her life (www.privatewhitevc.com/tour-the-factory).

Another was an urban cycling wear company Vulpine, set up by Nick Hussey, who remortgaged his house to start it up and shared it all on Twitter

(@aslongasIcycle). Vulpine also got customers to tweet pictures of their children and pets with the hashtag #cyclistfamily, as part of a safety campaign.

'Because he lives and breathes what he does, people are more likely to be trusting. It's a fantastic story, and it's not faceless – it's changing our perception of things,' says designer Mick Dixon.

It ties in, too, with honesty and transparency. Even huge brands like H&M and Nike began to list all their sources and suppliers on their websites, and the *Business of Fashion* website wrote about design label Honest By that listed not only the manufacturer of each zip and button in the clothes but also broke down the costs, including mark-ups.

'Buying a mystery will be an absurd concept soon,' said its designer Bruno Pieters. 'There's no luxury in riddle' (in Young, 2013).

As for cultural content, we've already seen that brands were becoming their own publishers. Burberry is active across social media, produces short films of up-and-coming British musicians, and has a street style-type website called Art of the Trench featuring pictures of people worldwide wearing the brand.

'Burberry is producing its own original content,' declared Joanna Shields, vice president at Facebook. 'Burberry is no longer just a fashion company – today they are a thriving media enterprise' (in Amed, 2011).

Karl Lagerfeld puts on photography exhibitions and makes short films for Chanel, and LVMH has won plaudits for its website Nowness.com, which showcases films about fashion, culture, art, design and music without any of the hard sell normally associated with branding.

Conclusion

Although it's not necessary to have trained in fashion design yourself before you write about it, it IS vital to be familiar with what designers do and how they do it, and have an understanding of the pressures they are under.

A book like *The Fashion Designer's Directory of Shape and Form* (Travers-Spencer and Zaman, 2008) is a simple guide to cuts, shapes and design that will help build up your vocabulary for describing clothes.

If you get the chance, go into boutiques and big stores like Harvey Nichols, Selfridges and Harrods to see designer clothes close up. Look at them, feel them, try them on and get a feel for what the different brands are doing and how.

Keeping on top of issues in manufacture, sales and retail will throw up a wealth of news and feature ideas and also help inform any profiles or reviews you do.

And knowing who owns the fashion houses, who their chief designers are and what their heritage is are all vital to covering your chosen specialism properly. After all, a football writer would not get away with not knowing who a team's manager was.

If you're at college or university, you should make every effort to know who's who on your own patch – local designers, either working in your area or for a national brand; local boutiques and department stores; photographers and models; buyers, the lot.

And you should make sure you get to know any fashion design students at your institution. Watch how they work, offer to style their shows and get them to take part in test shoots with you. You might get work published, you'll build up your portfolio and you'll get a better understanding of the industry you want to work in.

Recommended reading

Agins, T. (2001) *The End of Fashion: How Marketing Changed the Clothing Business Forever*. London: HarperCollins.

British Fashion Council: www.britishfashioncouncil.com.

The Business of Fashion: www.businessoffashion.com.

Editd Journal: http://editd.com/blog/.

Freeman, H. (2009) *The Meaning of Sunglasses: A Guide to (Almost) All Things Fashionable*. London: Penguin.

Jackson, T. and Shaw, D. (2006) *The Fashion Handbook (Media Practice)*. London: Routledge.

London Fashion Week: www.londonfashionweek.co.uk.

McDowell, C. (1984) *McDowell's Directory of Twentieth Century Fashion*. London: Frederick Muller.

McRobbie, A. (1998) *British Fashion Design: Rag Trade or Image Industry?* London: Routledge.

Mercedes-Benz Fashion Week, New York: www.mbfashionweek.com.

Stevenson, N.J. (2011) *The Chronology of Fashion: From Empire Dress to Ethical Design*. Lewes: Ivy Press.

Travers-Spencer, S. and Zaman, Z. (2008) *The Fashion Designer's Directory of Shape and Form*. London: Quarto.

Tungate, M. (2012) *Fashion Brands: Branding Style from Armani to Zara*, 3rd edition. London: Kogan Page.

Victoria and Albert museum: www.vam.ac.uk/page/f/fashion/.

5   Ideas, sources and interviewing

Introduction

When I go to interview Melanie Rickey, journalist, fashion editor and consultant, at her home for this book, she has a teetering pile of cuttings on her desk.

'Look at this. I've already acted on this for a *Grazia* story about the rise of disco trousers and why it's happening,' she says, waving one of the pages at me.

> Here's another about the hottest young female acts at a festival. A Nicki Minaj interview because I think she's fascinating. A retrospective on the photographer William Klein. Philip Green and Arcadia having a bad time. The England football manager. And that's just a snippet.
>
> (2012)

Melanie is one of the most important and influential fashion journalists in the UK. As well as playing a crucial role in establishing *Grazia*, she writes for the *Guardian*, blogs as Fashion Editor at Large, and consults for luxury and high-street fashion brands. A *Guardian* profile of her and her partner, Mary Portas, referred to them as 'fashion's power couple' (Cartner-Morley, 2011c).

But Melanie is never too busy or important to scour newspapers, magazines, Twitter and blogs on an endless quest for information and ideas.

'Number one rule of fashion journalism: read everything. Absolutely everything – no stone unturned,' she declares. 'You've got to keep up or you're nowhere.'

This hard work, thirst for knowledge and lack of complacency is what got Melanie to the top of fashion journalism – and keeps her there – and it's a lesson for all those hoping to follow in her footsteps.

You can be the best writer or stylist in the world, but if you don't have any ideas of your own and you don't do the research then you are not going to be much use to a newspaper, magazine or website.

Coming up with your own ideas ahead of a placement or internship will also help you stand out, and is far preferable to sitting twiddling your thumbs or looking at your phone when there's nothing else to do.

Figure 5.1 Liz Lamb fashion feature (Liz Lamb/NCJ Media)

Asked to describe their dream candidate for a job, most editors will cite ideas. 'When I'm looking at your CV, I don't care which university you went to or how many A Levels you've got, I want to know what you would bring to the *Grazia* table next week,' says deputy editor Marianne Jones (2012).

This is something that anyone looking to get into fashion journalism should work on, regardless of their age or location. Anyone can keep up with current affairs, and even though you might not yet have the contacts that established journalists have, you are just as capable of coming up with a great story idea that will resonate with other people your age, or another demographic altogether. After all, you may end up working on a magazine aimed at younger or older people or even the opposite sex!

This chapter will look at what makes for a good idea, where they come from and how to research them. It will also give advice on how to carry out effective interviews and explain some of the potential pitfalls.

Journalists in the fashion media will describe how they monitor what's going on, from daily routines to the moments when inspiration strikes out of the blue.

But first – lead times

Fashion journalists produce news, features and shoots in advance of publication – that much is obvious – but how far in advance differs from platform to platform, and is called the 'lead time'.

It's important to know the lead time before you propose ideas for a story or a shoot, as you may have to think months ahead.

A monthly glossy has a lead time of between six weeks and three months for stories, features and shopping pages.

Main fashion and campaigns will be planned six months in advance of the issue, once the editors have seen the spring–summer or autumn–winter runway shows and press days, and know which clothes and stories they want to feature.

It's quite an art to think that far in advance when generating ideas, and it's one of the things interns find most surprising when they first start. Alex Murphy, of *Elle*'s Edited by the Interns issue, says:

> We posed for a shoot for the June issue, and it was freezing cold and hammering it down outside. The poor stylist said it had to be really summery so we were all in flimsy silks and I had to take my tights off.
>
> The *Elle* team are really good at thinking months ahead about when the audience will be reading the issue and in what context – on holiday, at an airport, at festivals.
>
> (2013)

A problem with lengthy lead times is the difficulty of coordinating what's on your pages with what's in the shops. 'It's frustrating with a monthly. You may love that top on page such-and-such, but there's a minimal chance of you ever finding it,' says Fiona McIntosh, former editor of *Elle*, who puts a large part of *Grazia*'s success down to its coverage of what's on the shelves that week (2012).

Newspaper supplements, like *Guardian Weekend* and the *Sun on Sunday's Fabulous*, come out once a week but their fashion sections have longer lead times and are generally compiled two to three weeks ahead, apart from main shoots which may have been longer in the planning.

But weekly glossies like *Look* and *Grazia* are turned round within the week – apart, again, from the main fashion shoots – which gives them their newsy, immediate appeal.

So Hannah Almassi, fashion editor at *Grazia*, will pitch ideas on Monday morning, start work on them in the afternoon and have words and pictures ready for Thursday when the magazine goes to print.

At *Look*, the bigger fashion stories are planned three weeks ahead, with a shoot taking place once a week, and more newsy stories are peppered in every day until the magazine goes to print, again on Thursday night or Friday morning.

On newspapers, more timeless features or shoots can be prepared a week or fortnight ahead, but many stories will be written just a day ahead of publication. In fact, a story or picture could change at the last minute before deadline, if a fantastic photograph comes in or a celebrity suddenly hits the news.

Harriet Walker, who went from *Glamour* to the *Independent*, says:

> When I left the magazine in July we'd just been doing a beauty shoot for the December issue, and I found that difficult in terms of ideas.
>   I like the pace of a newspaper, being able to react to stuff and it feeling immediate.
>
> (2013a)

Harriet went on to work on the *Never Underdressed* website, where turn-around times were even quicker. After a morning conference, the short newsy items went straight out, while feature-style articles were planned for the afternoon, evening and the next morning.

Of course, it's the same for anyone writing for the Web, even if they work at a monthly or weekly magazine. Competition is fierce to be the first to get a Kate Middleton dress identified online, or to post the first looks from a Burberry show, and be the story that everyone clicks on.

Generating ideas

Most journalists do not sit round waiting for stories to be handed to them by their editor, and that's overwhelmingly the case for specialists like fashion journalists.

Instead, they're expected to come up with their own news and features ideas, which they or their section editor will pitch to a twice-daily or weekly news conference (see www.graziadaily.co.uk/fashionissue/archive/2012/02/13/day-1-grazias-fashion-issue-live–the-madness-begins.htm for a short video of a morning news conference).

An intern or assistant will help an editor research or write a story, but they need to come up with their own ideas if they're going to make it as an editor themselves.

Successful fashion journalists are thinking of ideas all the time, not just when they're at work. 'I'll spend all day Sunday researching, reading every newspaper, going through my blog list and websites for both fashion and wider news, so I'm ready for Monday's news conference,' says *Grazia*'s Hannah Almassi (2010).

It's the same for freelancers, who are always on the alert for ideas they can sell. Polly Vernon says: 'It's like a video game of life. Half of you is uncomfortable at seeing your ex-boyfriend at a wedding, but the other half is thinking, "Hang on a minute – this could make 900 words for such-and-such"' (2012).

There's added pressure on those who write fashion news to come up with the 'exclusive' – the first story about a new collaboration, or the only interview with a celebrity or industry figure. That comes from maintaining excellent contacts (see below).

Even if it's not an exclusive as such, a story has to be fresh and original, which is why you need to keep track of what's already out there. 'If you're not on top of the stories, you're behind the stories,' Melanie Rickey says.

'You've got to be thinking what the stories are going to be this week, and second-guessing what editors will do – what story is big, who's wearing what, and where.'

Obviously, then, you have to be aware of what stories your publication and all your rivals have already covered. 'If you ring up someone, and say, "I was thinking of this story" and they say they've done it, you're definitely in the wrong headspace,' Melanie says.

If you're on staff, you might have responsibility for certain pages, like news pages, shopping pages or trend reports, so you know you have to generate regular ideas for them. But you will often find yourself helping out on other sections, doing extra stories for the website or being roped in for first-person features, so the more flexible you are the better.

If you're on a newspaper, you should also be on the lookout for stories for other departments, argues showbiz reporter Louise Gannon. 'You should see your whole industry from a different perspective which will make it part of news as well as fashion,' she says. 'If you hear something's happening in Topshop, go and speak to the business desk and say "I don't know whether this is a story but … ". Be part of the team' (2012b).

Types of story

Story types vary from publication to publication, but here are some of the main categories that they cover:

Fashion news: shorter, snappy stories about what's happening in the world of fashion, like a designer collaborating with a high-street chain, a model caught with drugs, a company posting record profits, or a celebrity starting a new fashion or beauty craze (see Chapter 6).

Trend report: a piece explaining either a big catwalk trend or a micro-trend spotted in shops and on the street, who's wearing it, where you can buy it, and how to wear it, accompanied by pictures of product and people in the trend (see Chapter 8).

Shopping page: picture-heavy pages showing products grouped around a certain theme, with accompanying short blurb (see Chapter 8).

Profile: an interview with a single person of interest to your target reader, like a celebrity or a designer (see Chapter 6).

Catwalk report or round-up: a review of a runway show, setting it in context and giving a verdict (see Chapter 7). Websites will cover all the main shows, quality newspapers might cover the very biggest ones, weeklies might do a round-up from a fashion capital, while a glossy will feature the collections in its own shoots or in a series of trend reports.

Street style: went out of fashion in the late 1990s and 2000s as celebrities became the main focus of magazines, but crept back thanks to the street-style blogger phenomenon (see Chapter 10).

Jury pieces: round-ups that give short verdicts on what celebrities and style-setters have been wearing, especially prevalent after the Golden Globes or

Oscar ceremonies. Verdicts can be given by the fashion editor, by readers or by industry experts.

Features: longer articles exploring some aspect of fashion in a colourful, humorous, informative or investigatory way. Often revolve around the point at which fashion meets real life (see Chapter 6).

Main fashion, or photoshoots: picture spreads based on a theme or trend, either in a studio or on location (see Chapter 9).

What makes a good story?

The rock-bottom definition of news is something that is new (either in itself, or in its revelation), factual and of interest to the target reader. Features are less instant than news, but will often have a 'peg' or hook that is tied to a current event or talking point.

Journalists often talk about 'gathering' news, as if it's out there already, waiting to be collected. But it's rather the journalists themselves who select, shape and create the type of stories they know will resonate with their audience.

The ground rules they use to do that are called 'news values', and are end-lessly discussed in journalism studies and textbooks. For a good explanation, see Tony Harcup's *Journalism: Principles and Practice* (2009).

Here are some of the main news values that are relevant to fashion journalism:

- Surprise, or incongruity. This is a story that grabs your attention and gets you talking. A quaint definition from a nineteenth-century American editor is 'anything that makes the reader say "gee whiz!"' A cruder version from our own era, credited to a tabloid editor, is 'f*** me, Doris!' – 'that moment when you take a breath and think, "Wow, that's extraordinary",' says Rachel Richardson, award-winning editor at *Fabulous*.

  An experienced journalist can help this along. When *Grazia* got hold of a pattern of Victoria Beckham's jeans, they asked Louise Gannon, showbiz reporter, to help turn it into a story. She had the brainwave of getting a friend to measure her seven-year-old daughter's jeans, and comparing them. 'The child's jeans were slightly bigger than Victoria's. So it came out as "Victoria Beckham wears seven-year-old's jeans" and it went all round the world,' Louise says. 'It was a "f*** me, Doris" story. Women were sitting in their size 14 trousers spitting their cornflakes out over that one.'
- Relevance to reader. The importance of the audience is discussed in Chapter 3, and the best stories will almost talk to the reader. Rachel Richardson says that at *Fabulous* they referred to 'people like us, or PLU. If we're all talking about it, and we're interested in it, then it's an issue,'
- People. People like to talk about people and read about people, and as a result most stories will be hung around people rather than issues.

Sometimes fashion journalists can lose sight of this, focusing instead on product. For example, the late designer L'Wren Scott asked a fashion journalist if they wanted to do a piece on her designing clothes for her boyfriend Mick Jagger. The idea was rejected because the journalist pitched it as a product piece, with stills images of the clothes. But when Louise Gannon got hold of it, she turned it into a human story. 'I asked L'Wren for lots of funny anecdotes about Mick, and it worked well. I sold it to *Grazia*,' she says. 'Fashion journalists need to think more like journalists.'

Luke Leitch adopts this approach at the *Daily Telegraph*, helped in part by the fact he was a news and features writer before moving to fashion. He says: 'It's very difficult to write compelling material about … material! Some people are brilliant at that. But I'm constantly grateful for all these great personalities and the relationships between fashion and the wider world' (2013c).

- Good news/bad news. This is probably where fashion journalism diverges most from news journalism, where bad news is considered to be more compelling than happy stories. Fashion, as we saw in Chapter 3, mostly edits out the bad and focuses on the good – partly because of advertising, but also partly because it's a genuine news value in fashion journalism. 'Yes, you're in bed with advertisers,' says ex-*Elle* and *Grazia* editor-in-chief Fiona McIntosh. 'But there's genuine enthusiasm and interest in what's new and exciting – that's what makes a good fashion story.'

- Timeliness. The latest twist, a new revelation, an upcoming collaboration or trend – what's new makes the news, and nowhere more so than in fashion journalism, where change is fundamental to the system. Fashion editors will forever be looking for whatever is new or unique in a collection, new designers or models on the block, new trends and new ways to wear things, and their ability to spot these is a major part of their professional *raison d'être*.

  Tied to this is the importance of the exclusive in fashion journalism. The best type of story is not only new, but it is being revealed exclusively by one publication. 'It's an amazing opportunity to say to your readers, "This is the place that you come to for these amazing stories, these are the things you're going to want to buy, and we've got it first,"' says *Grazia*'s Hannah Almassi.

  One of the biggest exclusives of recent years was the identity of Kate Middleton's dress designer ahead of her wedding to Prince William in April 2011. After months of speculation and mistaken 'scoops', it wasn't until Sarah Burton was identified by her silver belt as she tried to sneak into the Middletons' hotel on the eve of the wedding that journalists had a definite name.

- Magnitude. The bigger the impact of an event, the more likely it is to be covered. So the deaths of 1,100 people in the collapse of a garment factory in Bangladesh in 2013 got coverage when other smaller-scale disasters were overlooked. But it's all relative, of course – the death of one well-known figure in the UK would overshadow all that. The suicide of Alexander McQueen in 2010 was big news for fashion journalists, who were expected to be able to pick up the phone to their contacts and get the inside track on the story, explaining both the personal tragedy and McQueen's importance to fashion.

- Pictures. Visuals are hugely important to any branch of journalism, but especially so for fashion. A good picture can make a story; having no picture can break one. When you're pitching a story, you should always think about how it will look on a page or screen, and how it can be illustrated. Polly Vernon, freelancer, once wrote a whole feature on the politics of body hair after being struck by a French Connection advert showing a woman getting her legs shaved in a barber's shop. 'The cover was a photograph of me with hairy legs, getting them wet-shaved. It's so much of journalism, marrying your words with pictures,' she says.

  Often, a story idea will spring from a picture, which is why good editors and journalists will trawl through agency photographs first thing in the morning. In 2004, the then *News of the World* features editor Carole Watson spotted Victoria Beckham wearing a red string bracelet in several such pictures, and, after contacting her spokeswoman, ran a page-three exclusive on her possible interest in the Kabbalah religion.

Where ideas come from

Because journalists have to come up with a steady flow of ideas, they have regular routines each day or week that will be guaranteed to generate copy.

But they are also always on the lookout for more offbeat stories tied to real life, and that's something any would-be writer can do, whether or not they have access to industry events.

Below are the main sources of story ideas for fashion journalists.

Contacts

One of a journalist's most valuable resources is their contacts – people in fashion or in other walks of life who they can ring for facts, comment or analysis on a story they are already working on, or who will tip them off about a story they hadn't heard about. Good contacts are so important that some job adverts will specify 'bulging contacts book' as part of the requirements.

Any would-be journalist should start building up their contacts, keeping phone numbers and email addresses of everyone they've ever talked to for a story, noting down names of people who are regularly quoted in fashion articles they read, and going out to cultivate new contacts.

Melanie Rickey, fashion editor at large, says she impresses this on all her young assistants. 'They must build up their own contacts book with their own generation, so when they go to a press day they've already met their own people and can make sure they give a good impression to the older people.'

A journalist will meet important contacts face-to-face as regularly as they can, to build up trust and cooperation (Chapter 12 describes how they do this with PRs). Melanie says a big part of her role as editor is teaching young journalists how to behave with contacts and at events: 'Your social life stays outside work, for one, and you don't get your head turned by the drugs, drink or socialising that goes on.'

Other media

Fashion journalists relentlessly monitor what's going on. They're on top of Twitter and Instagram, they read both mainstream and niche blogs, they look at news, fashion and celebrity websites and follow the trade press like *Drapers* and *WWD*.

But it's also important that they pick up newspapers and magazines too, says Melanie Rickey. 'Online it's easy to miss things. With a newspaper, you turn every single page and see things you weren't even looking for. I'm talking sport, I'm talking business, every page.'

They do this at weekends, ready for Monday, and every morning before they start work. It's hard work, but it's better than looking foolish when their editor throws a name or talking point at them in the morning conference that they haven't read about.

Fashion journalists will never simply copy a news story that's somewhere else. They might check the facts with a PR, and they'll always put their own spin on it. 'You adapt it to be right for your own publication,' says *Grazia*'s Hannah Almassi.

A news story can also be put in a little more context for a quick trend-type piece (at the time of writing, TV journalist Jeremy Paxman's beard was the inspiration for a gallery of stylish news anchors on *Never Underdressed*).

A simple story could also be the jumping-off point for a bigger feature, like the story about Asian spending in the UK that prompted *Grazia*'s Zoe Beaty to spend a day shopping with some young Chinese women (Beaty, 2012).

It could also raise a talking point that a feature could explore; when the *Daily Mail* did a news story about a woman being banned from nightclubs because of her skimpy outfits (Enoch, 2012), *The Sun*'s features team were straight on it to ask women around the country what they wore on nights out (Watkins, 2012) while the *Daily Mirror* gave her a makeover (Bletchly, 2012).

It's not just stories that spark inspiration – covers of the new issues of glossies, especially British and US *Vogue*, can be news in themselves, as will be new-season advertising campaigns by the big brands. (The *Guardian* once declared smiling was back in after happy-faced covers on *Vogue*, *Tatler* and *Marie Claire* coincided with laughing models in Mulberry and Bally campaigns – Cocozza, 2012.)

To keep on top of what's going on in the fashion media, it's worth setting up an online reader, which will pull through new posts and stories from selected websites and blogs so you can see them all in one place. The BBC guide to RSS feeds is at http://news.bbc.co.uk/1/hi/help/rss/default.stm.

You can also sign up for email alerts and newsletters from the likes of the *Business of Fashion* and *Style.com*, as well as newspaper and magazine websites, so they arrive in your inbox each day. Liking brands and media on Facebook, and following them on Twitter and Instagram, will also help you keep track of new stories.

PRs and press days

PRs and journalists work closely together and this relationship is described in detail in Chapter 12.

Not only do journalists meet regularly with PRs for breakfasts, coffee or a drink, speak to them by phone, swap emails and receive press releases, they also go to press days organised by brands' PRs to show off a new season collection before it drops in the shops.

Press days are a useful way to monitor trends and what the various brands are doing, and attending is also vital to keep advertisers happy. Fashion news editors also try to go if they can, because they need to keep in with the PRs to get exclusive news of new ranges and tie-ups.

They can also secure useful introductions to other people through PRs, whose job it is to network and know people in the industry. Liz Lamb, former features writer for the *Newcastle Chronicle and Journal*, interviewed Geri Halliwell through a PR contact at Next (when Geri did a swimwear range for them), and catwalk photographer Chris Moore, who was friends with a PR she knew and who had a house in nearby Northumberland.

Events and seasons

A lot of fashion journalism is pegged to regular events in the social, cultural and even sporting calendar as a way of making it relevant to the regular reader. Festivals have become a big fashion event, as have TV and film awards ceremonies.

Zoe Beaty at *Grazia* got dressed up and spray-tanned with women race-goers at Aintree, while Wimbledon sparked a top ten tennis fashion moments piece in the *Daily Mirror*. The *Mirror*'s Amber Graafland says: 'Something like Wimbledon is great for us – it combines sport, it's a very British thing that everyone loves, lots of celebrities go. It ticks all the boxes' (2013).

A change of seasons, too, always brings forward a slew of regular stories, like finding a bikini to suit your body shape, or why the British are so bad at dressing on holiday.

High and low culture

Another useful peg for fashion journalists is anything going on in the world of the arts – an exhibition like the V&A's *David Bowie is* in summer 2013, a film with a strong fashion element like *The Great Gatsby* or a TV show that inspires a micro-trend, like *Gossip Girl*, *Mad Men* or *The Only Way is Essex*. Again, it's a point at which fashion touches their readers' lives. 'It has to go beyond the catwalks for us,' says Jess Cartner-Morley, *Guardian* fashion editor (2011b).

Celebrities

Celebrities have become part and parcel of the fashion world, dominating magazine covers, appearing on front rows and in adverts, and snapped carrying the latest 'It bag' or wearing a designer gown on the red carpet. Some in the media resent this – Grace Coddington at US *Vogue* is a well-known refusenik – while some welcome it. 'Celebs – good copy!' chirps Jess at the *Guardian*.

Readers tend to identify more with walking, talking celebrities than silent models, and so stars are seen as an accessible way into fashion. 'Not a lot of my readers will be saying "Oh my god, what happened on the Chanel couture catwalk today?" but it's interesting when Rihanna suddenly turns up in a see-through top, so I've written about that,' says Amber Graafland at the *Daily Mirror*.

Securing a celebrity for a cover or an interview can be a very long drawn-out process involving PRs and agents, and difficult even for the top glossies. But many stories revolve around celebrities without ever speaking to them.

A lot of newspaper and website stories, for example, are based on identifying what a celebrity has been spotted wearing. Journalists go through images from photo agencies like Splash, Rex and Getty every day for eye-catching pictures, then ring round celebrity and designer PRs and trawl through Net-a-Porter and other websites to pin down the label.

Longer features can be concocted from a trend or a talking point that the celebrity has provoked. Gwyneth Paltrow got journalists talking about side-bottoms being the new cleavage after she wore a sheer-panelled gown to the *Iron Man 3* premiere in April 2013. A spate of pictures posted by bare-faced celebrities on Twitter prompted writers to ditch make-up themselves for the sake of a feature.

Publications are very careful about which celebrities they write about, as the wrong ones may put off their readers and advertisers. *Look*, for example, has a constantly updated list of ten celebrities right for the magazine, based on readers' focus groups and Web analytics.

What you and your friends are talking about

This may sound trite, but it's true. If something has got you talking, then chances are your readers will be talking about it too. The sweet spot is landing on a subject or thought that has just started to surface but hasn't really been formulated until now.

Experienced journalists and editors are always looking out for these moments. 'The good editors are always the ones, when you're slightly drunk somewhere and you say something, their first response is, "Is that an article?"' says freelancer Polly Vernon.

> I texted my editor when I was in New York on holiday, and said, 'I'm wearing hotpants, I'm 35 years old, I think I might have jumped the shark.' She texted back, 'I will have a photographer with you in half an hour.' I was on holiday! But she could see the image and the story.

The daily newslist at *Never Underdressed* contains many talking-point stories – 'Hot outside but freezing in the office? You need an air-con cover up' was one; 'Kim Sears is probably lovely but don't you miss "proper" wags?' was another on the same day (9 July 2013).

This kind of story is why many journalists say their biggest inspiration is their own colleagues. 'My main source is my desk – we'll rabbit on about what we have seen and heard, and that's how we pick up on things, batting ideas about, establishing connections,' says Jess Cartner-Morley of the *Guardian*.

Jane Bruton, *Grazia* editor, puts it at the heart of her editorial philosophy. She told a PPA conference in 2013:

> For 90 minutes every day, we have conference with 20 or so women between 20 and 50 years of age, sitting, discussing, debating, ranting about the issues of the week, and the magazine is a direct result of that.
> When the magazine is at its best, it is a diary of those heated debates that get your blood pumping – a gut reaction to modern life.

If you don't yet work in an office, how do you come up with these instinctive, zeitgeist type of stories? Social media is a good way of monitoring what people are talking about at any given moment, and what is capturing their imaginations.

But there's no substitute for just talking to people, and finding out what they think. A former editor once told me he made it his mission to ask four questions of everyone he met during the day – from colleagues to shopkeepers to taxi drivers – to plug in to what people were talking about.

Polly Vernon is almost evangelical about it. 'Ideas come from being as engaged as possible with everything – with what's going on in the world, with your friends, with your family, being out there, experiencing things, enjoying things,' she says.

'The best thing a journalist can be is curious and interested in everything and everybody. Don't write anybody off. If you do you're an idiot. Talk to people all the time; listen to them carefully; follow things up.'

Observation

Fashion is not just about what's in the shops or on the catwalk. Sometimes it's about what's happening on the street or in clubs – a new way of wearing something or a new type of product – and a good journalist will be on the lookout for that.

Hannah Almassi, who often writes about street style at *Grazia*, says: 'You have to keep your eyes open, to look at everything around you, to do things you wouldn't normally do and meet people you wouldn't normally meet.'

A story based on observation might be completely ahead of the curve; Hannah was the first person to clock a new craze for clog boots, and she's covered niche things like backpacks and single earrings.

But if your audience is less likely to be fashion-forward, then an observation story could focus on what the broad mass of people wear that normally goes under the fashion editor radar. The *Guardian*, for example, has written features on the emergence of quilted and waxed jackets on city streets (Fox, 2010) and the ubiquity of skinny jeans year after year (Cocozza, 2013).

Researching your ideas

Each section editor will put together a list of ideas that they'll pitch at the news conference, drawn up from talking to their staff. In conference, ideas will be batted about, some will be put together with others, some will be saved until later, some will be dropped for lack of originality or relevance, and some will get the go-ahead.

'It's frank and forthright, because by the time the 10 Hot list [the news and fashion stories at the front of *Grazia*] gets through to everybody, it's Monday afternoon and we go to print on Thursday evening so there's no time for faffing,' says fashion editor Hannah Almassi.

Immediately, journalists set about researching their stories, to 'stand them up' – find facts and pictures to back up their angle – and make them as interesting and informative as possible. Stories can fall through or be dropped for lack of information, because there's breaking news or to ensure balance in a publication.

Research is a vital task in journalism, and is what will make one story much better than another. A mistake student journalists sometimes make is to write a whole story from their own head, without making the effort to get extra facts and comments to illustrate it.

A proper story or feature MUST have research. As Polly Vernon says: 'You've got to ground them in hard facts – otherwise they just float away; they don't mean anything.'

And Melanie Rickey tells her assistants: 'Don't just look at *Wikipedia* and write something. That's a cardinal rule – it would get you kicked out of my door in seconds.'

For a fashion story, like a trend piece, often the right pictures are key. First of all, the fashion editor or assistant would have to source the correct products to fit the trend. This would involve looking on websites and in lookbooks and contacting brand PRs. On a daily or weekly, high-resolution pictures of the products would be sourced either from the brand's website or PR, while a monthly might call in the products to be shot.

But the research doesn't stop there. The page needs pictures of people wearing the trend to bring it to life, so the editor needs to locate photographs of celebrities or catwalk pictures. This is where going through agency pictures and celebrity websites every day pays off, as does being familiar with what all the fashion houses have done each season.

Even then, sometimes, the story falls through. 'You will have a week where it just isn't happening,' says Hannah. 'You know that everyone's wearing it but you can't find the right imagery or products to represent it, and you need something to hold the page other than just the idea.'

For news and features, there are two kinds of research: primary research, where you talk to real people and put specific questions to them, and secondary research, where you dig out facts and figures from reports, press releases, websites and previous stories.

Longer stories need both – facts to anchor them, and direct quotes to add colour, anecdotes and opinion.

Polly Vernon describes research she did for a 3,000-word story on how shoe heels were getting higher. 'The only way that would work was with shedloads of voices, shedloads of facts and a lot of statistics,' she says.

> I talked to Net-a-Porter to find out the average height of a shoe; I talked to a shoe historian in Toronto; I talked to Mariella Frostrup and Caitlin Moran about what they thought about the politics of wearing high-heeled shoes, and I talked to a couple of doctors about how it affects us physically.
>
> And that's the only way that piece would work. If it was just me saying 'Shoes used to be tall, then they were short, and now they're tall again,' who gives a shit?

The moment her piece fell into place was when someone told her shoes were 3.5–4 inches tall until Christian Louboutin and the late 1990s, when suddenly they went up to 4.5–5.5 inches. That was the hard idea at the heart of her story.

A mistake inexperienced journalists sometimes make is contacting one source, then waiting for a response. If you need to speak to a doctor, contact ten in the hope that one will get back to you before deadline.

The research stage is where your contacts book is worth its weight in gold. The types of sources that will be useful to you are:

- PRs. Newspaper and magazine offices will have a list of contacts for all the designer and high-street PRs, and the more you've tried to get to know them, the more helpful they'll be. If you're a student, start compiling your own PR contacts. (A list of designer PRs is up on the www.londonfashionweek.co.uk website.)
- People in the fashion industry, like designers, models and photographers. Get to know up-and-coming designers and models in your local area; they'll be good for profiles and shoots, and you never know where they'll end up.
- People in the retail industry, who can tell you about buying patterns, trends and challenges. Fashion directors at the big retailers like Harvey Nichols, Selfridges, Net-a-Porter and My-wardrobe.com are very credible sources. Buyers, merchandisers and managers are also very useful people to know. If you're a student, try to make contact with retailers in your own area.
- Trade bodies and associations linked to fashion and retail are good for analysis and overview. There's the British Fashion Council, but also less well-known bodies like the British Footwear Association, Glove Association and Hat Guild. The trade union Equity has a models committee. On the retail side, there are the British Retail Consortium, the Charity Retail Association and the Independent Retailers Association at a national level, and regional chambers of commerce at a local level.
- Campaigners can make good sources, as long as you give the other side, too. Examples are the Ethical Fashion Forum, Caryn Franklin's All Walks Beyond the Catwalk, and PETA (People for the Ethical Treatment of Animals).
- Fashion experts, for context and history. Fashion academics, curators at museums, historians, authors and bloggers can add interesting insight on a topic.
- Other journalists. In a specialism like fashion, other journalists can be considered experts, especially one from a trade publication like *Drapers*. Remember, though, that they're often extremely busy chasing up stories of their own.
- Real people. Some of the best stories will seek the opinions of people at the sharp end of fashion, i.e. those that wear it. They are not a substitute for officials and experts, but are the icing on the cake. The more effort you put into questioning relevant people, the better your story will be, so never just ask your friends or fellow students. A vox pop is when you go out on a street and put a question to random members of the public, getting their

details and either photographing, videoing or recording them. It can lead to a lively sidebar (accompanying panel) to a piece, but should not be the be-all-and-end-all of your research.

Using yourself

It's often a no-no in news journalism, but in features you can construct a story around yourself – you trying out a new trend or range or a whole new look, you undergoing a new beauty treatment, or you behind the scenes of an industry event.

It means you can write the piece in the first person, describing your own experiences and feelings with lots of lively detail, anecdotes and humour. Not only does this inject colour and personality into a feature, it can also strike a chord with readers who identify more with a fashion writer who shows her face.

This is especially important now that fashion editors are fighting for influence online with bloggers, whose USP is accessibility and identification.

Grazia's Hannah Almassi said the biggest response she got to one of her stories was when she wrote about the difficulty of being curvy and wearing fashionable clothes. 'I was really scared about writing this piece, because I wasn't used to putting myself out there, but I got a lot of really nice letters afterwards,' she says.

Later, that became a bigger part of her job as *Grazia*'s coverage became more personalised – she was photographed trying to wear some of *Vogue* Japan's editor-at-large Anna Dello Russo's outré accessories collection for H&M in the street, for example ('Queen of bling hits H&M!' 2012a). 'It's good for connecting with our readers,' Hannah acknowledges, 'because I'm just a normal girl who happens to work in fashion.'

Polly Vernon has used herself as a prop for various features, including one for *Grazia* where she tried to get snapped by street-style bloggers outside London Fashion Week. She can send herself up like this, she says, because she's freelance and not dependent on the fashion industry. 'You can't do that and ask to be taken desperately seriously by advertisers. But I've stayed slightly outside fashion and haven't played the game.'

Interviewing

For most stories and features, a fashion journalist will interview people as part of their research. They need direct quotes, for different voices, colour, opinion and emotion, and they need facts to back up and explain their stories.

So it's important to learn how to interview effectively. A lot of it comes down to experience, learning how to read people and how to draw information out of them without being intimidated. But below are some tips from journalists who make their living out of interviewing, as well as guidance on how to avoid some of the most common pitfalls.

Face-to-face, telephone or email?

Some interviews are for information only – you need facts and figures about, say, a new collection, and perhaps a few quick comments from a PR or an official. These are the types of interviews that can be done by telephone.

Other interviews are more in-depth, where you are writing a profile of someone or you're delving into their personal style. You need lots of quotes and anecdotes from the subject, as well as facts. These interviews need to be carried out face-to-face so you can establish human contact with the subject as well as observe their mannerisms and their looks. Journalists will ideally go to their home, or meet them in a pre-arranged setting like their office, a restaurant or a hotel.

It is easy to track people down by email, and sometimes it's the only way to contact someone abroad, but email interviews are not recommended for anything but the driest facts. People NEVER write as they speak, and direct quotes lifted from an email stand out like a sore thumb in stories because they sound flat, rehearsed and stilted. If at all possible, contact people by email or social media (without giving away your story to rivals who follow you) but arrange to ring them for an interview.

The same goes for statements and news releases put out by a brand or a well-known figure. A PR might offer to email you a statement or press release in response to a question, but resist if you can and ask to speak to someone – you'll get more specific and relevant answers, and they will be less formal and jargon-filled.

Research before you go

A journalist will always look at past stories ('cuts') about their subject, research their website, listen to their music or watch their show before they go to interview them. This will prevent them wasting time with obvious questions, and throw up possible avenues to explore. 'Also, if you drop in a mention of their film/book/show/CD, this will make your subject realise you are genuinely interested in them, and make them trust/like you more and therefore be more open to talking to you,' says celebrity interviewer Louise Gannon (2012a).

Plan some questions in advance

Jot down, say, ten questions or areas to cover at the back of your notebook just in case your mind goes blank or you get so sidetracked during the interview you forget to ask something important. Check them at the end to make sure you've covered everything. Julie McCaffrey, former feature writer at the *Daily Mirror*, says:

> I've heard other journalists do interviews that go nowhere because they're too busy blethering on and trying to be the subject's friend. When they

listen back to their tape, they realise they've got no good lines and gave the interviewee an easy ride.

(2012)

But above all, listen!

Be prepared to veer off your planned questions if your interviewee says or hints at something more interesting. Listen carefully to what they have to say and pursue that line of questioning – you can always return to your planned list later.

Louise Gannon says:

> The single most important point in an interview is to LISTEN to what the interviewee is saying. Questions that arise from what your subject has just told you will be invariably more pertinent or emotive than the questions you have written down.
>
> (2012a)

Put your subject at ease

I have watched many a student slap down a notebook, hit 'record' on their Dictaphone or phone and start grilling a subject as though they're in a police interview room. Don't.

You'll get much more out of someone if they're relaxed, they warm to you and it seems more like a conversation than an interrogation. If they're not used to the media, they may be more nervous than you and will need to be put at ease.

'It's your job to create an atmosphere that is relaxed,' says Louise Gannon, who scopes out an interview venue in advance if she can and decides which would be the quietest corner of a room for an intimate chat.

Hannah Almassi, of *Grazia*, sometimes goes to people's homes to do features on their personal style and is very careful to respect their space:

> I was with a designer and another magazine had done a shoot in her home the day before. They'd taken everything out of her wardrobe, made themselves whatever they wanted in the kitchen and her house was ran-sacked by the end of it. So understandably she was worried about me being there.
>
> You have to make people feel comfortable, and be sensitive to their things and their feelings. You have to be as calm and easy as possible.
>
> (2012b)

That includes being polite and friendly to everyone who's there – the security man, the bodyguard, the hairdresser, the friend – and starting off the interview with a few easy icebreakers, even if you don't intend to use the answers.

Ask simple, clear questions

When you're nervous, it's easy to ramble on and on when you ask a question. But you'll only confuse your subject, and they'll only answer the last part of the question they heard. Legendary interviewer Lyn Barber says: 'I find the most effective question is normally "why?"'

Charlie Porter, who has interviewed many designers for his newspaper and magazine work, says he likes to catch them off guard by treating them as humans rather than fashion gurus.

'They are so trained to say particular things to particular questions that if you ask them a normal question like "How are you feeling?" rather than "What's the colour of the season?" or whatever, they're so thrown by it they start telling you stuff,' he says (2013b).

Ask closed questions – ones that can be answered by 'yes' or 'no' – to pin someone down on a fact. Ask open questions ('How did you feel?' 'What did you do then?') to draw out new facts and to get interesting quotes.

Don't be afraid to look stupid if you don't understand something. Ask again in a different way, or paraphrase it back to them ('So what you mean is … ?') to check you've got it right.

And hunt for specific anecdotes and examples, which will bring your story to life. So instead of asking 'Do you enjoy being a stylist?' ask 'What do you like most/least about being a stylist?'

Asking awkward questions

Sometimes there will be a difficult question that your editor wants you to ask, but the PR definitely doesn't. Many journalists will wait until the subject has relaxed and they've already got most of the interview in the bag before they put the killer question, just in case it all ends there.

They look at previous interviews for clues to the best approach, couch the question sympathetically and hope for the best.

If the subject refuses to answer, an uncomfortable silence sometimes does the trick, as does moving on to another topic and returning to the difficult question later under a different guise.

Whatever happens, 'Battle through it – always remain calm, polite and keep the moral high ground,' says *Fabulous* celebrity editor Beth Neil. 'If they're being a complete prat, take revenge with the pen.' Julie McCaffrey recommends the same, if your publication is up for it: 'Interviewee really rude? Tell the reader. Bolshie PR terminate the interview? Describe the situation.'

Observe as well as listen

If you're interviewing someone for an in-depth profile, do more than jot down their words – look at how they present themselves and how they behave.

'Don't just listen to the words, listen out for the patterns of their speech and then directly quote them, because then you will catch their voice in your interview,' says Louise Gannon.

> Sounds weird, but say what someone smells like – it's your job to get that sense of actually being with that person and painting a picture. For example, Jack Nicholson's skin smelled like expensive leather car seats and cheap cigarettes.
>
> Look out for bitten nails and body language, and describe it. Sometimes people give more away by how they are than what they say.

Recording the interview

You need an accurate record of the interview for facts, quotes and legal protection. If you use a recorder, make sure you've got a spare tape or SD card and lots of spare batteries. Take notes too, so you can note down the date, figures, spellings and any observations or descriptions.

You can never be too careful, says Louise Gannon. 'Have a tape back-up, learn shorthand, keep spare batteries on you at all times, carry a pencil as well as a pen. Tapes sometimes don't work; pens run out.'

If you're interviewing someone by telephone, some mobile phones have inbuilt recorders you can use. If not, an easy method to use is a telephone pick-up microphone, with an earpiece at one end and a jack to plug into a recorder at the other. It will then pick up both sides of a phone conversation and record them.

On and off the record; copy approval

Many magazines and newspapers agree to copy and picture approval in order to secure a celebrity interview, which means the subject or their agent gets to vet a story before it goes to print.

Don't agree to copy approval for a lesser-known subject if you can possibly help it, because they don't stick to fact-checking; they often want to rephrase quotes or anything they think doesn't make them look good, even if it's factually correct or based on your impressions of them. It can also hold up your story and make you miss a deadline.

If somebody asks for an interview to be 'off the record', you should clarify what that means. Sometimes it means you can quote them without naming them (the so-called 'friends said ... '), and sometimes it means you can't quote them at all but can just use the facts as deep background to check with another source.

If you agree to go off the record, stick to it. But if someone asks for it AFTER the interview, when perhaps they're regretting what they said, you're not obliged to agree. You'd have to weigh up whether it's worth keeping on the right side of this particular source or not.

The celebrity-promoting-a-brand interview

As discussed in Chapter 4, fashion and beauty brands are now keen to secure celebrity endorsements as a way to reach more customers.

The contract with the celebrity generally has a publicity clause, so the star ends up doing interviews with the media on the brand's behalf.

Even though the interviews are aimed at publicising a particular product, journalists play along with it because it's often the easiest way of getting access to a celebrity.

It's not something that a young journalist just starting out is likely to do, because editors will want a big hitter who is guaranteed to get a good angle out of the interview, but it's interesting to be aware of how these interviews work, even so.

Louise Gannon is a freelance celebrity writer whom many editors trust, and she's interviewed the likes of Madonna, Lady Gaga, Cheryl Cole and Jennifer Lopez for newspapers and magazines.

But even she finds it tricky:

> The brand PRs are not used to dealing with celebrities and they're very controlling about the questions you can ask, and they demand your questions upfront.
>
> They also don't understand how long you need. The maximum time you get is 20–25 minutes, even if you have to fly all the way to New York to do it, like I did with Lady Gaga when she did a lipstick for MAC.
>
> The PRs want all your questions to be about the lipstick, so you have to argue beforehand with the PR for, say, two questions about something else.
> (2013)

Because the Viva Glam lipstick raised money for HIV and Aids, Louise had her opening. She began with standard questions about why it was such a great lipstick, and then led onto safe sex, which led onto sex in general. 'Lady Gaga told me she had been celibate for two years which is a good line,' she says.

Louise normally tries to convince the PR beforehand that the better angle she gets, the better coverage the story will get. If that fails, she tries to slide her extra questions into the interview and hope the PR won't stop her, or ask an open-ended question and hope the star themselves will go off track.

She says all beauty and fashion journalists have to learn to think on their feet like her:

> A few journalists were flown to New York for 15 minutes with Courteney Cox who was promoting Avon. There was one girl from a beauty magazine who got literally nothing from her after 15 minutes.

Her editor wouldn't have been happy with her coming back from New York without a single line.

The best line was actually one that involved the product, like multi-millionaire Courteney Cox saying she swears by a £2.99 face cream.

Interviews like these normally stipulate how many times you have to mention the fashion line or beauty product in your story, and how high up, so the journalist has to work out how to do it cleverly rather than insert a blatant plug.

What to do with your story ideas

Even if you're still a student at college or university, you should keep a notebook of saleable ideas, and a file of tears (pages torn from newspapers or magazines) that you could develop.

Be ambitious, too. Dolly Jones, editor of *Vogue*'s website, was told to interview someone at the top of their game when she did a periodical journalism course at the London College of Communications.

'I was completely flummoxed, but I plucked up courage to ask Alexandra Shulman thinking there was no chance at all she'd agree to it. She did, and 10 years later I'm here doing my perfect job' (in Lafferty, 2010).

If you have an excellent idea for a feature, and you've secured the sources, it's worth thinking about pitching it to a publication to get published.

Some publications pay by the word, some fix a sum in advance, and some will ask for the first piece free, and then pay for any further articles.

To pitch an idea, choose a publication it would be suitable for, and make sure you know that title well and where your feature would fit. Email the commissioning editor or features editor and explain what your topic and angle are, why readers would be interested now, what treatment you'd use (see Chapter 6) and who you'd talk to. If you can suggest an eye-grabbing headline, and ideas for sidebars and visuals, so much the better.

A word of warning from freelancer Polly Vernon:

Know the title, and know you're right for it. Don't come up with a good idea and scattergun it out to 17 different people. Make sure you address the right person.

If it works, great. You could be a bit of an average writer but you'd have a hell of a career if you had lots of ideas, because that's what is in the shortest supply of all.

Recommended reading

Adams, S. and Hicks, W. (2009) *Interviewing for Journalists*, 2nd edition. London: Routledge.
Barber, L. (1999) *Demon Barber*. London: Penguin.

Hennessy, B. (2005) *Writing Feature Articles*, 4th edition. London: Focal Press.

McKane, A. (2006) *Newswriting*. London: Sage.

Pape, S. and Featherstone, S. (2006) *Feature Writing*. London: Sage.

Quinn, S. and Lamble, S. (2008) *Online Newsgathering: Research and Reporting for Journalism*. London: Focal Press.

Randall, D. (2007) *The Universal Journalist*, 3rd edition. London: Pluto.

6 Writing fashion news and features

Introduction

Some people say they are born writers who have been scribbling words down all their lives – poems, diaries, letters and stories. Other people have to learn to write, painstakingly, on the job.

But both can make excellent fashion journalists as long as they bear certain ground rules of writing in mind.

Number one is that you're writing for the reader: not to indulge yourself, or to please the person you're writing about, but to inform and entertain the reader.

Second, fashion may ostensibly be about product, but fashion journalism is based on telling stories just like any other kind of journalism. You're writing about the fantastic personalities in the fashion industry, what fashion can mean to people and how fashion fits in with our everyday lives. The product slots into those stories.

And third, you must be accurate with your use of language, in terms of facts, spelling and grammar. It's what separates the professionals from the amateurs, and is especially important if you are uploading content online without the sort of editorial and legal checks that traditionally happen in print.

One magazine editor said that she turned down a writer for a senior job because there was a single spelling mistake in the first paragraph of a rewrite she was asked to do. Imagine, then, what would happen to a student's CV if it had mistakes in it.

This chapter will outline the basics of good journalistic writing, for print and online. It will discuss the different structures used for news stories and features, and will give tips on how to develop your writing skills.

Good journalists say they are always looking to improve, and are never complacent about writing.

Louise Gannon, showbiz freelancer, says: 'I'm not confident about writing even now. If you felt confident about how you wrote, you wouldn't write well' (2012b).

Grazia's Hannah Almassi says the same. She keeps a blog so she can practise outside of work. 'I'll always be learning to write, forever and ever. I learn something new with each story' (2010).

Figure 6.1 Zoe Beaty feature on 'A day at the races' (Grazia/Bauer Media)

Ground rules for good writing

Good journalistic writing is not the same as good creative writing or good essay writing, so everyone is on a level playing field when they start to write journalism whether or not they did English A Levels.

While news and features are structured very differently, as we'll see in the next section, there are certain basic rules that run across all types of journalism and which are outlined here.

As always, there are whole books on this subject, so for further reading, see the recommendations at the end of the chapter.

Write for the reader

Good journalists act as a bridge between the specialist world they're writing about – fashion, in this case – and the reader. They do not show off about how much they know about it, they do not make it out to be more complex than it is, and they do not try to inflate their own importance.

'I try to involve some sort of self-deprecation or puncturing of an idea to make it clear I'm not attempting to talk from a position of "I'm better than you" or "Fashion is better than you,"' says Charlie Porter, the *Financial Times'* menswear critic (2013b).

Polly Vernon, freelancer, says her main aim is to convey the 'sheer, unmitigated joy' of fashion:

A lot of the reason people sneer is because they feel excluded from fashion – which is partly their problem, but partly fashion's problem, because it is an excluding environment. So I hope I operate as a bit of a bridge.

(2012)

What does this mean in practice? It means avoiding fashion jargon that might alienate or confuse your reader. It's almost always possible to explain an industry practice or a garment or a colour in simple, descriptive language that will mean something to everyone.

For example, Jess Cartner-Morley, in a review of Christopher Kane's autumn–winter 2013 catwalk show, describes 'coats with silky feathers sprouting along the seams, so that the models looked like very slender teddy bears spilling their couture stuffing' (2013c), and you can picture exactly what she means.

For all types of writing, you should use simple words and straightforward sentence construction, rather than pretentious or overly complex language.

Long words and lots of subordinate clauses stand in the way of the reader's understanding, especially if there are other distractions and claims on their attention. If you lose them, they're not going to keep rereading to try to follow your thinking. They'll turn the page or click on something else instead.

A paragraph should express one thought only. In newspapers, many paragraphs are one sentence long, especially in a news story. For features they can be longer, but are often no more than three or four sentences.

Punctuation is kept to a minimum. Parentheses are considered distracting and are avoided, semi-colons are rarely used, and exclamation marks are kept to a minimum.

This doesn't mean dumbing down. Complex images and thoughts can be conveyed by simple words and sentences, and are all the more effective for it.

Get used to proof reading your own work once you've finished writing, and try very hard to see it through a reader's eyes to check it all makes sense, leaves no unanswered questions and is interesting.

While you reread it, constantly think, 'Would I say this?' If you wouldn't, don't write it.

Write to the tone of the publication

Different publications have different audiences and different aims, and this affects their tone of voice.

That's why the coverlines of *Vogue*, the self-styled fashion bible, are authoritative and formal – 'Ultra violet – the colour of now' or 'The trouser suit takes centre stage' (August 2012) – while those of *Company* magazine address the reader like an excitable best friend, 'Dear High Street, we would like … ' or 'The skirt suit, your new bestie' (spring summer 2013).

For more on this, Linda McLoughlin's *The Language of Magazines* (2000) is a useful introduction.

When *Grazia* launched in 2005, it deliberately set out to democratise high fashion and introduced a whole new writing style designed to be fun and accessible, full of made-up words like jeggings (jeans and leggings), skort (skirt shorts), WAGs (wives and girlfriends of sports stars) and FROW (front row at fashion show).

'It was a fashion writing style that was easy to read but you could see there was information and knowledge behind it,' says Melanie Rickey, who was fashion news and features editor at the magazine (2012).

For someone coming out of school or university, used to writing in the formal, theoretical style of essays or dissertations, the kind of lively, conversational language used on many magazines and websites can be very difficult to grasp.

Hannah Almassi, who started as Melanie Rickey's assistant on *Grazia*, says:

> It took me a long time to work out the Grazia tone and be peppy and upbeat, rather than explain everything in a very serious, academic way.
>
> I asked another journalist there for advice, and she said, 'Hannah, you need to stop thinking about it, you just need to do it in under five minutes and then go back to it later.'
>
> That actually helped. Because of the pace of the magazine, I don't have time to think 'Should I use this word or that word?' It's just 'bam-bam-bam-bam', and that almost gives it the energy and speed and excitement it needs.
>
> (2010)

Freelancers have to adjust their writing depending on which publication they're aiming at. Polly Vernon writes for the Saturday *Times* and *Grazia*, for example. '*Grazia* is more breathless and excitable and giddy and fun. *The Times* is still fun, but my writing persona is more grown-up when I write for them.'

Show, don't tell

Journalism is concrete and precise. If you know a name or a specific number or a fact, you give it, so you don't leave any questions hanging in the reader's mind.

On the whole, you keep your feelings out of it. Certainly in news stories, you would not insert comment, even little references like the use of 'luckily' or 'fortunately', and you would not refer to yourself at all.

And even in features, good writers tend to *show* you what something or someone is like, rather than *tell* you. If they tell you a dress is beautiful, or someone is very loud and bossy, what does that mean, at the end of the day? You've only got their word for it, and their standards might be different from yours anyway.

But if they describe someone's actions in the way that Jess Cartner-Morley of the *Guardian* does for Mary Portas, you know what they're talking about.

Jess describes listening back to her tape of an interview with Mary's partner Melanie Rickey:

> Suddenly in the background there is the unmistakable clack-clack-clack of someone hurrying in high heels and the noise of a door bursting open – all so exaggerated and theatrical it sounds, on the machine, like a radio play – and then Mary's booming, head-girl tones as she cuts off our conversation, shouting, 'Lies! It's all lies! Don't listen to her!' while whipping off her jacket with a flourish that would shame a matador, laughing, hugging me, kissing Melanie and, basically, taking over.
>
> (2011c)

The reader can picture the scene and know exactly what it's like to meet that person.

Or when she describes the 'liquid slink of a bias-cut velvet gown in poison green' in an Oscar de la Renta show (2013b), again her words paint a picture, even if you hadn't seen the catwalk photos to go with it.

So try to use active verbs, precise description, quotes and anecdotes to convey impressions in your writing, rather than meaningless adjectives, clichés and woolly phrases.

Make sure your spelling and grammar are perfect

You are competing against many other people when you try for a job in the fashion media, so your writing has to be flawless.

If your editor can't trust you to know the difference between 'your' and 'you're', or to spell Cara Delevingne's surname, then how can they trust you to get your facts right?

Common mistakes are misuse of commas, full stops and apostrophes, lapses into text-speak, random capital letters and homophones ('phased' and 'fazed', for example, or 'compliment' and 'complement').

It's important. 'I get lots of letters from people asking about internships, but when someone's spelling and grammar are bad – which is most of the time – I tell them to sort that out, then get back to me,' says Polly Vernon.

Harriet Walker, former style editor at the *Independent* and news editor at *Never Underdressed*, insists it's the best way to give yourself a fair chance of getting a fashion job when you haven't had a privileged background and very formal education. She says:

> If you haven't learned grammar rules at school, learn them yourself. If you're coming out of university now, you're going for jobs in places that either can't afford or are about to sack their subeditors.

So if you can't write perfectly, you won't get that job because someone else will be able to, and it will be someone who went to private school and that's terrible.

(2013a)

It goes without saying that accuracy applies to facts, too. Double-check everything against your notes as you write – people's names, addresses, numbers and figures – even if you think you've got it in your head.

Lucy Wood, senior fashion news editor at *Look*, says there is nothing more frustrating than getting an exclusive on a launch, interviewing people, shooting products and designing a great page ... then someone getting the launch date wrong. 'It annoys the readers who are so shopping-hungry; it annoys the PRs; it annoys me as an editor,' she says (2012).

Develop your own voice

Good writers with a point of view and a distinctive tone of voice are worth their weight in gold in fashion. It may sound like this contradicts the earlier injunction to match your tone to the publication, but it's possible to have a strong, well-honed voice that fits with the style of a newspaper, magazine or website.

'Find your own voice,' urges Polly Vernon. 'It's your own way of looking at the world. It's the persona through which you write. That's what will make you different.'

It's why journalists are sometimes wary of recommending that students have favourite fashion writers that they follow, because they can end up parroting their style. 'There's nothing more cringey when we get people on placements and you can tell who they want to be – it's one of three people, and it's hideous,' says Harriet Walker of *Never Underdressed*.

'You think, "Why do you want to become a writer?" because copying someone else is not how it works.'

Harriet recommends that students read all sorts of journalism, not just fashion, to mix things up a bit, and experiment with bringing new vocabulary into their speech so they work out what sounds right and what doesn't.

What you should avoid is clichés, the sort of hackneyed phrases that people associate with fashion journalism when they haven't read much of it. Phrases like 'bang on trend,' 'fashionista' and a 'pop of colour' are easy to insert into a fashion piece but will make your reader switch off.

Writing news

News stories have a style and structure all of their own, developed over the years to convey information in the quickest, clearest and most attention-grabbing way possible.

The very idea of news writing can terrify student journalists, who insist that they want to write features for magazines and will never need to get their heads round the 'inverted pyramid' theory of news structure.

But who knows what their first job in journalism will be? Some, like *Elle* editors past and present Fiona McIntosh and Lorraine Candy, might start on news before moving over to features and magazine writing.

Moreover, news writing has become more relevant than ever with the rise of digital media. Short, snappy stories with the main facts at the start are the bread and butter of online writing.

And news happens in fashion, whether you like it or not. New collaborations are announced, brands can go bankrupt, adverts get banned, designers appear in court, supermodels can launch campaigns and public figures die in accidents, suicides or attacks. You can't refuse to cover these things.

Besides, news writing is nothing to be scared of. The basic structure is very formulaic and can be learned, and the writing should be as clear and simple as possible.

The news angle

A news story does not follow a conventional narrative. It puts the most important or interesting facts right at the beginning, and works its way down to the extra detail and background at the end.

A good description of how this works comes from Lynette Sheridan Burns in her book *Understanding Journalism* (2002), and it's worth quoting in full:

> News writing always starts with the most important fact. When you report on a football game, you do not start with the kick-off, you begin with the final score.
>
> If someone were to blow up the building across the street from where you work, when you got home you wouldn't start the story by saying 'today seemed an ordinary sort of day, little did I know how it would turn out.' You would say, 'someone blew up the building across the street.'
>
> In other forms of journalism, it's fine for your story to have a beginning, a middle and an end. News stories, in contrast, blurt out something and then explain themselves.
>
> (2002: 112)

The same holds true for all types of fashion news stories. If Karl Lagerfeld were to give an interview during which he criticised a public figure's face, body or dress sense – as he has been known to do – the news story would begin with the gist of the controversial comment.

The second paragraph might give more detail, perhaps with a direct quote, and it might not be until the third paragraph that we learn to whom he gave the interview, and when.

Further down the story, we'd get more quotes, more background on other times the designer has been less than flattering about people, other things he said in the interview, perhaps some angry reaction from fans and a right of reply for balance.

What the story would NOT do is explain the story from the beginning – Karl Lagerfeld gave an interview to such-and-such a magazine, he said this, he said that, and then he criticised the public figure.

The most important or interesting fact at the start is called the *angle*. All stories and reviews are reported from an angle; it highlights what's new or interesting or important about the story, and why we should read it.

The angle is selected according to news values (see Chapter 5). Any aspect of the story that is surprising or unusual, is about people, affects the reader, is the latest twist or is exclusive to the publication is likely to become the focus of the write-up.

But the angle can be contested. Everyone from PRs to politicians disputes some of the angles that journalists choose, accusing them of misrepresenting a story or sensationalising an issue.

But it's the publication's prerogative to angle the story whichever way they choose, as long as they are doing it in good faith and they are sure the facts back it up. They certainly should not let the angle be dictated by a PR, whose job it is to portray a brand or a celebrity in the best light possible.

The news intro

Journalists will often say that the intro – the introduction, or first paragraph – is the hardest part of the story to write. Once they've got that down, the rest of the story will flow easily.

That's because the intro has to give the most interesting part of the story, the angle, in a nutshell and grab the reader's attention at the same time. The idea is that the reader can stop after the intro, and know basically what the story is about, even if they don't know all the details.

For example, a *Daily Mail* intro reads: 'Karl Lagerfeld has provoked fury by labelling pop superstar Adele "fat"' (Sparks and Todd, 2012).

It names the two protagonists, gets straight to the heart of the row and hints at the reaction, all in 11 words.

A *Sun* report on another story has this intro: 'Controversial fashion brand American Apparel has been told to remove a series of images from its website – after a watchdog ruled they were "overtly sexual"' (Sayer, 2013).

It sums up the most important point of the story – the ban – while adding the 'sexual' angle, which is guaranteed to get the reader's attention. It names the brand, with a short description in case its readers aren't familiar with it, but does not name the watchdog until the second paragraph.

Even straightforward interviews with models, designers or celebrities are reported from an angle – the aspect of the interview that was the most timely, or unexpected, or attention-grabbing.

For example, a *Vogue* online interview with French actress Marion Cotillard begins: 'Marion Cotillard's BAFTA red carpet look took just an hour and a half to create' (Alexander, 2013). Another with Donatella Versace began with a quote from her saying she'd like to dress the Queen in black leather (Jones, 2012).

It can be difficult to identify the best angle and intro, especially if you have a notebook full of quotes, claims and counter-claims. The best thing to do is to think about news values (see Chapter 5) and how you can highlight them.

What's surprising about this story? What's new? Why should your readers be interested? How does it affect them? Is there any telling detail or twist that will lift the story out of the ordinary?

Jessica Bumpus, of *Vogue* online, says she always remembers this advice: 'When you interview someone, use the quotes you remember. You remember them for a reason: they were interesting' (2013b).

Other journalists recommend you imagine your mum, friend or even a stranger on a train asking you what story you're working on. What's the first thing you'd tell them? That's your intro.

Some general rules of intro writing are:

- Keep it to one sentence, especially for a newspaper or website, normally under 25 words. Magazine intros are sometimes longer.
- Don't start your intro with a subordinate clause or the time element (for example, 'Yesterday afternoon, Rihanna gave us a sneak peek of her second collection for River Island ... '). It slows the story down.
- Don't clutter up the intro with too much detail, and don't use names that your reader won't instantly recognise. Explain later.
- Don't make the mistake of writing it like a headline: 'Rihanna launches second collection with River Island ... '. It should be a proper sentence like any other, with articles ('the' and 'a'), a verb and proper use of tense.

The inverted pyramid

The inverted pyramid of news simply means that the important details and angles are at the start of a story, narrowing down to minor details and side issues by the end.

Readers aren't thought to get much beyond the first three paragraphs of a story before moving on, so the inverted pyramid ensures they can stop reading at any point and won't have missed anything important.

With the simplest story structure, the intro gives the main gist of the story, uncluttered by too much detail.

The next couple of paragraphs explain and expand upon the intro, giving key detail like numbers, times and people's names but keeping the pace of the story up. That's the news story 'blurting things out', in Sheridan Burns's words (see above).

Then, typically, the writer can relax and perhaps wrap the first section up with the strongest quote from a person central to the story, backing up the angle.

Thereafter, they will either retell the story with more detail, colour and quotes. Or they will go into secondary angles, like reaction to the story.

Finally, if there is room, they will give background on the story – previous cases, context and background detail on a brand or a person.

Paragraphs are kept short and are linked smoothly with 'transition' words and phrases, like 'but', 'however', 'he/she added', and even 'and' at the start of sentences.

Writing features

Features have been described as the beating heart of a publication, the stories that give it personality, imagination and a voice.

Although they are usually topical, features are less tied to the news agenda than news stories, and can explore any topic under the sun so long as it's interesting to the target reader.

They can entertain as well as inform, argue a point as well as investigate. They can be written in the first person and can be set out like diaries, letters, question and answers, and mini-interviews, as well as a straightforward block of text.

On newspapers and magazines, lots of things come under the features remit – not just features themselves, but profiles, listings, reviews, readers' letters, book serialisations, personal columns and agony aunts.

What journalists call features proper – generally longer articles exploring an issue or talking point – are in short supply in fashion journalism, in general magazines at least. The fashion desk often have their hands full with shoots, trends and shopping pages, while feature writers tend to be allocated to more general interest topics.

But newspapers run many more fashion features, as do more specialist fashion magazines like *Grazia*, *Vogue* and *Elle*. Freelancers like Polly Vernon also specialise in longer fashion features.

They often home in on the point where fashion meets real life. At their best, they can add a welcome dose of human interest, insight, analysis and humour to the fashion world.

What features need

Features vary in length according to publication. *Company* editor Victoria White says readers rarely want more than two pages these days, but Charlie Porter – writing for an older and more specialised audience at the biannual *Fantastic Man* – put together features that ran for 8,000 words.

> If we interviewed someone, we met them two or three times and became part of their lives until we understood them. I did a super long, complex piece about the relationship between men and colour, talking to someone who studied colour and how we see it and engage with it.

The magazine had the space to allow you to do things you wouldn't be able to do elsewhere – they wanted to celebrate text.

Other features will be picture-led, with an introductory blurb and short captions. So features vary in length, in complexity and in aim, depending very much on the target audience. But what they all need is:

- A point. Yes, the feature is on a certain topic, but it should address a particular angle or question about that topic. For example, Polly Vernon did a big feature for the Saturday *Times* magazine about Alexa Chung, but the point was how influential Chung is, as summed up in the standfirst or sell (a sentence just below the headline, introducing the feature): 'She's the ultimate trendsetter and can create waiting lists for new products with a single tweet' (Vernon, 2013).

  In her book *Good Writing for Journalists*, Angela Phillips describes this as a controlling idea or coat hanger from which all the feature material is hung. If you can't sum up the idea in a sentence, she says, then you don't have a story but 'a rag-bag of ideas vaguely connected to one another with no over-arching dynamic to keep your readers' interest going until the end' (2007: 42).

  It's an important point. A feature can't just be you writing about everything you know or have found out about a topic or issue. It needs an overarching idea.
- A peg. Features may not come out the same day as a news story or event – though they can do if they're planned in advance, to coincide with something like London Fashion Week or the end of John Galliano's court case. But they will still have some sort of topical peg to impress upon the reader *why* they should be interested in this issue *now*. The peg could be an event, a report, a new book or collaboration, something that somebody important has said or done or worn, and a talking point raised by a story (it doesn't even have to be real life: many a feature has been spun out of a storyline in a TV show).

  The peg will be mentioned fairly high up in the feature. Polly Vernon mentions in the third paragraph of her feature that Chung was about to publish her first book and launch her first clothing line.
- A treatment. One of the joys of feature writing is that you can approach it any way you want; indeed, sometimes the whole point of a feature is its treatment. You can write it like a news story, in the impersonal third person with lots of quotes from sources, or you can write it as a series of composite interviews, telling the story through the words of others. Or, you insert yourself in the story, experiencing something and writing about it from the first person. Sometimes, the treatment isn't decided until all the information is gathered.

  When Zoe Beaty wrote a feature for *Grazia* about how much women spend on getting ready for Aintree Ladies' Day, she went up to Liverpool and joined a group of four women getting spray-tanned and primped before going to the races with them ('A day at the races, Scouse style', 2013). Not only does this bring the topic alive, with lots of colourful detail and anecdotes, it also helps the writer get close to the subjects and avoid the tendency of some London-based media to get sniffy about so-called Northern tackiness. 'We're not all as clichéd as the newspapers like to make out,' Zoe quotes one of the women telling her.

- Research. Rather than being an excuse to pour out all your own innermost thoughts and feelings about a subject, features contain more primary and secondary research than most news stories. For the Alexa Chung feature, Polly Vernon spoke to the editor of a trend forecasting agency, a stylist, a buyer at Selfridges and the chief executive of Whistles, and dug out lots of secondary research about how quickly things sell when Chung endorses them. Even though Zoe Beaty wrote her 'day at the races' piece in the first person, with description and observations, she quotes four Liverpool race-goers and speaks to the owner of designer boutique Cricket. Her secondary reseach includes how much money is spent at Aintree, how much the average outfit costs, the cost of all the beauty treatments, the percentage rise in sales at local shops, how many litres of fake tan are used, and how many stilettos and clutch bags are sold.

Writing up a feature

Feature writing is much less formulaic than news, and writers can have fun with them as long as they don't lose the reader.

But they do have certain conventions, and if you read enough of them (which you should), you can start to discern rules of structure that will help you when you put together your own features.

A feature won't normally start with a news-style intro, summing up the story. Neither, though, will it begin with something really vague – a general thought, or a string of rhetorical questions – that inexperienced writers sometimes indulge in.

Instead, they often start with an extended description, almost narrative in style, that has two aims ... to lure the reader in, and to start building up to the point.

This kind of features intro is almost cinematic. You're plunged straight into a close-up of a scene, a conversation or an observation, before the camera pans out and you start to realise what this is all about.

So they will start with either:

- A personal memory or anecdote. Zoe Beaty's Aintree piece, above, begins: It's 5am and I'm freezing on a windy street in Liverpool's city centre. In just a few hours, the city's social event of the year – Ladies' Day at Aintree – begins. Ten minutes ago, a fire alarm went off in our hotel, and so I wait on the street in my pyjamas, bleary eyed and sporting bed-head hair. Next to me, a group of five girls are standing in heels and skinny jeans. I spot a sweep of bronzer and mascara. The Swarovski-crystal rollers are in, the make-up and outfits are in tow. Fire or no fire, these girls aren't taking any chances.

It's written like a story to pull the reader in, but it's designed to lead up to the point that Liverpool women go to huge lengths with their appearance for Ladies' Day, so much so that Zoe and an eight-year-old girl are the only evacuees who didn't get dressed before fleeing the hotel.

- An anecdote about someone else, normally the subject of your piece. Polly Vernon's feature about Alexa Chung recounts how she once posted a picture of her manicure on Twitter wearing a still-to-be-released enamel that looked like leather. By the next day there was an 800-strong waiting list for the enamel, which sold out in two seconds when it came out three weeks later. It's the first in a series of anecdotes that hammer home just how well Chung can sell things.
- A description of a person, especially at the start of a profile, which has the effect of whooshing the reader straight into the scene. 'Joanna Coles is perched on an arm of a purple velour sofa in her glass-walled Manhattan office, and talking, without a blush, about sex', begins a *Mail on Sunday* profile of the new editor-in-chief at US *Cosmopolitan* (McMahon and Churcher, 2012), introducing the twin themes of power and sex.
- A description of a scene. How else could a profile of this particular super-model begin? 'Inside a large studio in east London, photographers, assistants, stylists and make-up artists are waiting, and waiting, for Naomi Campbell. Some are very anxious. Others – the more experienced, I presume – are more resigned as time ticks slowly by' (Gannon, 2010).

All of these types of feature get straight into the action. Polly Vernon, freelance feature writer, says her one rule of writing is: 'Look at your first paragraph. You almost certainly don't need it. Hit the ground running really hard. I can't bear musing and waffling and wondering.'

The feature will build the description for one, two or maybe three paragraphs, before getting to what's sometimes known as the 'nub paragraph', where the writer explains what the feature is about and why the reader should be interested.

So the third paragraph of the Joanna Coles feature reads:

> Coles, born and brought up in a village outside Leeds, is the newly-appointed editor-in-chief of *Cosmopolitan*, the world's largest women's magazine and it is one of the most talked-about magazine appointments in America for years … What it says about sex is hugely influential in shaping the attitudes of a whole generation of young women.

That pushes us off into the rest of the feature, duly hooked and informed.

The rest of a feature will be made up of lots of quotes, colour, anecdotes and facts, woven in skilfully so they don't bog the story down. The material is organised into themes, linked smoothly and signposted to the reader, and sections like a potted biography of a profile subject would be relegated to, say, the middle part of a feature once the reader is well and truly interested.

Unlike a news story, a feature can be written in the present tense to make it sound more immediate – 'she says' and 'It's 5am and I'm freezing.' A common mistake is to switch tenses during the feature. Make sure they stay consistent.

Also unlike news stories, features don't stop dead but try to end with a satisfying pay-off line, often echoing the theme of the start so the story is 'top and tailed'. The Joanna Coles profile, which started with a description of her in her office, ends with her getting her picture taken for the piece. 'She looks directly into the camera. "Make me look younger, thinner, richer, blonder!", she tells the photographer as Manhattan glimmers behind her.'

Sells and sidebars

The reason features can get away with a descriptive start is because there are plenty of other clues on the page or the screen as to what the story is about.

There are the pictures, for starters, which are generally used bigger and more frequently than on news stories. There might also be a 'pull quote', where a particularly telling direct quote from the story is enlarged, highlighted and used as a design feature on the page.

Then there's the 'standfirst' or 'sell', a short blurb of one or two sentences, which appears in smaller type under a headline or in a panel near the start of the story.

The sell is an extra step designed to ease you into the piece once you've read the headline and looked at the picture, by giving a little extra information before you make the investment of plunging into the text or gallery.

So the sell on Polly Vernon's Alexa Chung piece is: 'She's the ultimate trendsetter and creates waiting lists for new products with a single tweet. Polly Vernon on the selling power of Alexa Chung.'

A sell normally invokes some kind of emotion, be it sadness, envy, curiosity or guilt ('the story every parent must read').

It also sets the feature up factually, and is a useful tool for inserting ages, jobs and home towns that would slow the start of the story down, especially if the feature is written in the first person. It also sometimes includes the writer's byline ('Polly Vernon on … ').

It doesn't repeat any words from the headline or intro, and doesn't give the full story away, but it frees the feature up from having to tell you what it's all about right from the start.

It can also be a slick piece of writing in itself. For example, a *Guardian* online gallery on punk fashion, starts:

> Punk style, the subject of the spring fashion show at New York's Metropolitan Museum of Art, is all over the high street at brands ranging

from Topshop to Asos and Zara (where even the kids' sandals have studs on them). So if you are a fan of tartan, rips, zips and PVC, here's how to dress with a rebel yell.

(*Guardian online*, 2013)

There you have it – the topic, why now, why you should care, a bit of word play and intertextuality, all in the two-sentence sell.

Even though sells are often written by subeditors rather than the writers, that's not always the case, especially online. So student journalists should get in the habit of writing sells at the top of their features, not only to master the art but also as a useful wake-up call when their story idea is too unfocused to lend itself to a summary.

Sidebars, or box-outs, are another design device for pages and screens that makes the job of the feature writer easier. They are a panel or box containing extra information like a series of pictures plus captions, a mini-interview (often a reaction to or commentary on the subject of the feature), a series of bullet-point facts, useful addresses or contact numbers, or background – anything that gives extra value to the reader.

They're useful because the writer can use the sidebar for information that would clog up the feature. Sometimes, the sidebars can be more entertaining or interesting than the main article itself, and they are certainly easier and quicker to read.

Writing for online

Online writing style is evolving all the time, as improved analytics allow publishers to see what their audience is reading and how and when they are reading it.

For example, the initial orthodoxy was that people did not like to scroll down through several screens and so articles should be kept short. By 2013 that had changed – perhaps because we all got used to reading blogs – and some newspapers and magazines were happy to use lengthy articles online interspersed with copious photographs, especially on fashion and celebrity stories.

But it's not all long stories. One thing an online writer quickly gets used to is how material can be handled differently on a website from in print. Jessica Bumpus, fashion features editor for *Vogue* online, says that galleries work well online as a way to turn a 2,000-word print feature into something more digestible (and something that racks up page impressions, too).

So instead of a long feature, an online writer might write a shorter piece introducing the topic, leading into an embedded gallery of photographs with captions on each. The initial feature might also give rise to a couple of shorter news stories, too, based on angles or lines dug out of the original piece.

Standing content is important to many websites – that is, evergreen content that is of particular use or interest to the audience and can be updated all the time. On Vogue.co.uk, for example, there is an archive of fashion show galleries dating back to 2001, and every British *Vogue* magazine cover since the first one in September 1916 – a fantastic resource.

When she's interviewing fashion figures for news content, Jessica will also ask them specific questions for evergreen galleries she is responsible for. 'One of mine is, "What's your first memory of *Vogue*?" So I will ask that question along with others, and use the information for different things,' she says.

Searches and speed

Two things Jessica and anyone else writing for the Web have to bear in mind are searchability and speed.

Most online articles are accessed through searches rather than somebody going deliberately to the home page, so writers have to ensure their stories are as visible and as high in search engine rankings as possible.

This is called search engine optimisation (SEO), and it basically involves labelling your story with the kinds of words that people search for online. Some of this labelling takes place at the back end of a website, with keywords present in the title bar and in the HTML code that created the page.

But online journalists will also fill in an SEO box with keywords when they input their stories onto a content management system, and will also try to pack those keywords in the headline, subhead and high up in the story. 'It also means getting the story into the first sentence, like news', says Jessica Bumpus.

To get a good idea of what words people use when searching for information online, go to Google Trends (www.google.co.uk/trends) where you compare two or more different search terms to see which one is most used, when people search for it and where they are in the world.

You can also see the most searched-for keywords at the current time, which is useful if you intend to put out related content that will pull in readers through searches. For example, newspaper and magazine websites regularly uploaded stories about what an *X Factor* judge was wearing at the start of the show on Saturday nights.

Another great resource is the portal NewsNow (www.newsnow.co.uk), which aggregates articles on specific topics like fashion minute by minute, so you can see all the stories going up on the Web and find out which ones are the most read.

Searchability on the Web also means that writers have to bear in mind the fact that most of their readers won't be dedicated *Vogue/Grazia/Daily Mail* followers but will have landed on their story via a search.

They won't have the context that a print reader will have – knowing the publication, knowing which section of the newspaper or magazine they are looking at, even knowing which country or date they're looking at – so the story has to be much more self-explanatory than a print article.

'We're not just writing for followers of *Vogue* online: we're also writing for a more general online audience,' says Jessica Bumpus:

So we have to get the news in the first sentence – it has to be succinct, and tell the story directly and clearly.

People use the content for information gathering and don't spend as much time reading. So our content is shorter and punchier – news stories are 200 words.

Headlines on the web are much more specific than in print, using those all-important keywords, locations and place names, and will often appear with a short subhead on the home page to add context.

Another important factor online is speed. If your story goes up first, more people will click on it, your search rankings will go up, you'll hit your targets for visit statistics that month, you attract more advertising … 'It's a domino effect, and it's very competitive,' says *Grazia*'s Hannah Almassi. 'It's like tweeting from shows: everyone is trying to be the first as well as the most accurate, the most insightful, and all while maintaining a house tone' (2012b).

As Hannah says, the rush to publish should not compromise accuracy and legally safe copy. The *Sun*, *Daily Mail*, *Sky News* and a *Guardian* live blog all mistakenly announced Amanda Knox had lost her appeal against her conviction for the murder of British student Meredith Kercher (3 October 2011). She had in fact been cleared of murder; the news outlets had reacted too quickly to the judge first turning down her appeal against another conviction for slander.

Writing style

Online stories are often written in a more conversational, informal style than news and features in print, especially on magazine and stand-alone websites.

So a story will use more colloquial language, more humour, more asides, more rhetorical questions and a more direct address to the audience than it would in print.

Harriet Walker, who went from the *Independent* newspaper to stand-alone fashion website *Never Underdressed*, said the tone they were aiming at online was informed and authoritative without being patronising, and irreverent and cynical without being moany.

'When you write a proper news story for a newspaper, there's a formal structure you stick to, a certain language and a certain mood or tone', she said.

> You don't necessarily have to stick to that in digital writing. We try to do so for news, because we want readers to feel we are credible, but it's interesting how much you can mix things in so it doesn't have to be as flat as newspapers.
>
> And for more lifestyle stories, it's more like a conversation – it's almost like writing an email to someone you know gets you. It can be jokey.
>
> We stay away from daft Internet speak like LOL, but it doesn't mean it has to be serious. People react really well to humour in fashion writing

because it's very easy to get a bit up yourself when you write about fashion. People want it to be funny because they want some kind of escape.

So a story about Sarah Ferguson and Kate Moss being snapped together starts:

> It's one of those strange things about the world of famouses: that everyone in it seems to be friends with everyone else, by sheer dint of them all being in it together in terms of knowing what life is beyond our own mere civilian existence. Sigh.
>
> (Walker, 2013b)

Charlie Porter, who has worked for the *Guardian*, *GQ* and *Fantastic Man*, believes that online writing can be pushed much further to change the way we read about fashion.

Charlie quit magazines in 2012 to set up his own website at charlieporter. net and relishes the freedom it gives him. 'It's the best thing I've ever done,' he says.

> It completely changes the way I write, and deal with thought.
>
> Going to online changes boring things like paragraph structure or process of ideas. You don't have to get the basic information and a hook in the first paragraph, then make people follow you through to the end of the story, like you do in print.
>
> You can work line by line following an idea through, and you can be really specific and then completely lead an argument somewhere else without worrying about breaking the structure or losing the reader, because you can make them follow you in a much more intuitive way.

In fact, Charlie believes some of the most interesting writing is probably going on in private emails between friends rather than the more formal language of magazines, and this is the way he'd like to see journalism going.

> Emails go in a much more linear way – you don't write emails like a feature, you write it like 'oh my god this, oh my god then that, that, that and that'.
>
> It seems really weird that we are living in this world where all these amazing things are written, probably by people who don't see themselves as writers, but because it's nothing to do with the traditional way of writing then it's seen as irrelevant.
>
> I actually see it as very valid. People should look at the way they're writing their own language, and see how it could be used in a more formal context.

Writing for e-tail

Writing for a retailer might involve contributing articles to a print or digital magazine, which involves much of the type of writing discussed earlier in this chapter.

It can also involve writing for the website directly – short pieces on the home page, like trend reports or hero pieces, as well as copy to go with each product and emails out to customers.

'The job is to describe garments in a really concise way that is not just editorial in nature but also with Google keywords built in,' says Adam Mooney, of the Newcastle-based Jules B boutiques. 'You have to get in certain things, but also make it fresh and unique' (2013).

An important part of the job is awareness of search engine optimisation. Retailers have an even greater commercial interest than publishers in topping the search rankings for terms like 'Marc Jacobs' or 'Barbour'.

Alex Murphy, who wrote for My-wardrobe.com, said at the time: 'A simple thing that you pick up very quickly is repeating key phrases that customers will Google, so if you can put something like "Marc Jacobs bag" in the copy, it will push your Google rankings up.'

But it's not just about brand names: it's also garment types that you know customers will be searching for. 'Writing "shoes" isn't going to push the product up as high as using "kitten heels", because it's a more specific search term,' said Alex.

> We have endless debates over the editorial, holding up a shoe and saying, 'What would you call this? Is it a shoe or a pump? Is it a heeled pump? Is that a stiletto heel?' Today we had a very lively debate over backpack versus rucksack.

Alex then wrote two sentences, or 30–50 words, to go with each product on the website. She had to describe the item, dropping in snippets of information about the brand or the inspiration. She tried to anticipate the customers' questions, explain how to wear the item, and why they should buy it.

'You really learn how to make those two sentences really creative, and you have to make every word count,' she said.

'I'll write about 30 in a day, and the last item I write has to be just as engaging as the first. It was really difficult at first but now I relish the challenge.'

Having the garment in front of her helps Alex describe it in a vivid way. 'I have it on my desk. I can play with it, try it on, see what it's made out of, feel it, see how heavy it is,' she said.

A product copywriter also puts together the description of item details and care, specifying the shape, cut, fabric and washing instructions. It's basic, but important legally and to cut down on the number of returns.

Alex also wrote product titles for the emails that went out to subscribers twice a week showcasing what was new in, based on products that merchandisers selected.

And she wrote copy for the 'inspirations' section of the website, using the eye for a trend that any fashion journalist would have and employing the language of the magazine shopping page.

Click reports and heat maps help the company see what customers are looking at and how they navigate the site. The editorial team work closely with merchandisers to react to what they find out and boost sales.

To help set products in context, Alex watched designer fashion shows and went on *Style.com* and Voguepedia (www.vogue.com/voguepedia/) as well as brands' own websites.

When he started at Jules B, Adam Mooney drew up his own terminology glossary whenever he learnt a new word, for use another day. 'I never had formal fashion training, so it's the way I learned,' said Adam.

'I did a journalism degree, and that was really useful for learning how to edit down a long piece of text. I use that all the time.'

Now he's PR and marketing manager for the company, he writes and sends out emails four times a week to its customer database. One is trends-based, two are specially targeted based on the customer's buying habits, and one on a Sunday is more editorial in nature, containing entertaining stories to suit the weekend but still with links to push sales.

Writing for men

Any journalist has to consider their audience, and some editors and e-tailers say that male readers need a different approach from women when it comes to fashion.

Jeremy Langmead, former editor of *Esquire* and now editor-in-chief at Mr Porter, says men require a lot of information about a product because they are not as spontaneous as women (Gabrillo, 2012).

He says they're less trend-driven than women – 'With women you can say, this is the handbag of the season – and they love it. Men prefer a softer sell' – and like to see editorial about non-fashion figures they admire mixed in with their fashion content.

He also believes they're attracted to brands with credibility (see Mick Dixon's comments in Chapter 4). 'Men like a brand where they feel there's truth to it, whether it's a tailoring brand that's been going for 300 years on Savile Row or some cool dudes in New York who have set up shop.'

This carries through to the Mr Porter website, where writers have to follow a very gentlemanly, British and self-deprecating style, with names prefaced with Mr or Ms and other very formal flourishes.

To add credibility and a human face to the brands they stock, Mr Porter's video style editor Aaron Christian goes to factories and films how the products are made. This particular series took him to 14 different countries in a year.

'For men, when they see the technicalities of it, that hits home. Video does the educational aspect really well and that helps with the way men consume,' Aaron says (2013).

Aaron is also editor-in-chief of men's style website Individualism, and says he deliberately tries to make fashion less daunting for men. It stages its own social events in London, where members of his team meet their readers, and has a series called Sins of Style, where they all talk about their fashion mistakes. 'For us, being approachable is one of the biggest brand values I'd like to grow,' he says.

Luke Leitch, deputy fashion editor at the *Daily Telegraph*, also believes that pure fashion can be daunting for many men. 'I've just been listening to the cricket, and Geoffrey Boycott was teasing Jonathan Agnew about his shirt. It's a great subject for banter, fashion, but once you start being literal about it, they can get uncomfortable,' he says.

> But I don't think you have to be apologetic when you write about men's fashion or compensate for that fear of derision by doing that formal, throwback thing.
>
> I think part of the problem is that fashion is a terrible word in the context of menswear. The broad conception is that fashion is aimed at a very mainstream level, at younger guys, so I think it can be a barrier rather than a catalyst.

Instead of writing about trends for trends' sake, Luke is more interested in the stories around menswear – why a new type of garment arose, little-known stories behind brands, stories about personalities and links between menswear and sport. That's what his weekly column Mencyclopaedia focuses on.

'It's for a man who might not necessarily tend to want to read about shoes, is pulled in because of a picture or headline and comes out thinking "I was quite interested in that." It doesn't mean they have to go off and pick up a selection of loafers,' he says.

'I can't believe I've done two years' worth of columns on menswear and I'm still overwhelmed by the amount of little stories that are out there.' He says he gets brilliant letters from readers in response, giving him other obscure facts he hadn't known. That's how men – *Telegraph* men, at least – engage in fashion.

Charlie Porter, who covers menswear shows for the *Financial Times*, says he doesn't adopt any deliberate writing style for men but always tries to pitch fashion at a realistic level to appeal to them. He says:

> At the end of the review I wrote about the Paris shows, I ended up saying 'Trousers will always be trousers, and shirts will always be shirts,' rather than get too involved in the hyperbole of the whole world about to change.
>
> It's an attempt to be comforting to the reader, to let them know it's safe to be interested in fashion, it's not scary, and they could themselves get pleasure from it without it feeling like a judgement or an attack. With men I'm aware of that – hopefully it's not visible in the text.

Charlie enjoys writing about the radical and important changes he sees in menswear, like the disappearance of the tie and the suit as the uniform of power.

And he believes that menswear journalism is more forward-thinking and realistic than a lot of fashion writing for women in this respect.

'Womenswear is getting stuck in a bit of a cul-de-sac. It's become very much about cocktail dresses and looking pretty and correct; yet nobody I know dresses like that', he says.

'It would be super-interesting if you were a journalist in womenswear to try to effect change, and push it somewhere else. There's a space for a new group in womenswear to really grab it and talk about reality.'

Developing your writing

Writing is a tool, so if you want to be a professional writer you should practise and master it.

Whereas journalists used to recommend you kept a diary, the easiest way to practise writing now is via a blog on a relevant topic.

A blog will help you develop your style, will allow you to voice your opinions about fashion and will demonstrate to future employers that you are interested and engaged in the subject.

'It's a discipline,' says freelancer Hattie Crisell. 'Even if nobody sees your blog, it's really good practice to be writing all the time so you become better at self-editing and being self-critical in a more useful way' (2012).

But some journalists worry that blogging will make you too self-conscious as a young writer. Polly Vernon, freelancer, says:

> The problem is you're thinking about being read and having an audience, when what you should be doing is getting so comfortable and relaxed with writing stuff down that it's just not an issue.
>
> It's like that thing, 'Dance like nobody's watching you'. When you write, think, 'Would it make my friends laugh?' Don't think beyond that.

Polly recommends you also write letters, stories and poems, anything to get good at writing. 'Make writing your first language; get as fluent as you possibly can. I've never looked at an empty page and not known where to start, and I know damn well it's because I've always been writing.'

She also highly recommends developing a sense of humour when you write. She was taught to do that in her first staff job on a young woman's magazine called *Minx*, but believes it's not normally encouraged in young female writers, and should be.

Other tips are to read all types of journalism, not just fashion journalism, and lots of fiction, too. Try to develop your vocabulary while you speak, so you can get a feel for how new words sound and how they're used.

And the main thing – develop that voice. As editor of *Fabulous*, Rachel Richardson could recognise the writing of any of her team because their style and personality shone through. 'Some people manage by aping other people's style, but having your own tone of voice is what makes you a superstar writer,' she says.

Recommended reading

Carroll, B. (2010) *Writing for Digital Media*. London: Routledge.

Hennessy, B. (2005) *Writing Feature Articles*, 4th edition. London: Focal Press.

Hicks, W. (2008) *Writing for Journalists*, 2nd edition. London: Routledge.

——(2013) *English for Journalists*, 4th edition. London: Routledge.

McKane, A. (2006) *Newswriting*. London: Sage.

Phillips, A. (2007) *Good Writing for Journalists*. London: Sage.

Watt, J. (ed.) (1999) *The Penguin Book of Twentieth-Century Fashion Writing*. London: Penguin.

Wheeler, S. (2009) *Feature Writing for Journalists*. London: Routledge.

7   Reporting the catwalk

Introduction

In her memoir, the veteran US *Vogue* creative director Grace Coddington describes the catwalk shows of her early career.

Editors sat in deep sofas, others on gilt chairs, with ashtrays on tall stands next to them. Stately models came out holding cards with the number of their outfit on.

'They continued walking very, very slowly, leaving enough time halfway to execute plenty of twirls so the audience could absorb all the details,' Coddington writes. 'And that's how the whole show went. There was no music, no scenario, and no drama to distract you from examining the clothes. It was one hundred percent about the clothes' (2012: 99).

When *Grace: A Memoir* was published in 2012, Coddington was still a familiar sight at the shows, her cloud of red hair bent over her notebook as she absorbed and sketched every look.

But how things had changed. Models marched out at a furious pace in extravagantly produced shows that lasted around ten minutes – Marc Jacobs got it down to five minutes in September 2012.

Models, designers, celebrities and journalists posted instant pictures and comments on social media, and thousands of fans worldwide joined in as they watched the shows live-streamed online.

Coddington wasn't a fan. 'There are no secrets anymore,' she lamented. 'I can't stand it' (2012: 324).

But the fashion journalists themselves loved it, many describing the shows as their favourite part of the job. They relish the excitement of seeing the new collections and the sheer spectacle going on in front of them.

'Some of the great catwalk shows I've seen will stay with me forever,' says Jess Cartner-Morley, fashion editor of the *Guardian* (in Roy, 2010). 'When a catwalk show is really incredible, you just can't beat it.'

This chapter will look at what is involved in covering a catwalk show, and how journalists manage to turn these '11-minute puffs of smoke' (as the *Telegraph*'s Luke Leitch puts it) into something that makes sense and is relevant to their audience.

Figure 7.1 Chanel runway show (CN/Fairchild)

It will also look at why fashion houses choose to show their new collections this way, when it would apparently make more financial and environmental sense to show them only online.

The shows – who, where and when

Haute couture

Haute couture shows first take place in Paris, in January (spring–summer) and July (autumn–winter) – much closer to the actual seasons than ready-to-wear, as the collections don't have to go into production.

Now that an increasing number of couture clients come from the emerging economies rather than the United States or Europe, some couture shows are also repeated elsewhere. Since 2009, Chanel has visited China twice a year to cater to private clients, and Dior repeated its couture show in Shanghai in March 2012 and 2013.

At the time of writing, 14 fashion houses had full haute couture accreditation (see Chapter 4), including long-established members like Chanel, Dior and Jean Paul Gaultier and newcomers like Maison Martin Margiela. There were five correspondent members, including Armani and Alaïa, and 11 guest members.

Couture shows are reported in quality newspapers like *The Times*, *Independent*, *Daily Telegraph* and *Guardian*, and on the websites of glossies like *Vogue*, *Grazia* and *Elle*.

Tabloid newspapers and weekly magazines are more likely to cover them from the point of view of which celebrities show up in the front row, rather than send a reporter out to review them. The Chanel autumn–winter 2013 show, for instance, got widespread coverage when not only Rihanna but film star Kristen Stewart turned up.

Women's ready-to-wear

The ready-to-wear, or prêt-à-porter, shows take place twice a year – in February/March for the autumn–winter collections, and September/October for the spring–summer collections.

Traditionally, the four big fashion capitals that get the lion's share of coverage are New York, London, Milan and Paris, but specialist fashion publications might also report on other fashion weeks in the likes of Shanghai, Copenhagen, Sydney and São Paulo.

Covering the four main capitals means a frantic month or so for fashion editors, journalists and buyers, who will travel from city to city and see up to 50 shows. On top of that, they have showroom appointments, interviews and parties to attend.

'It's the same bunch of people who show up in every city, and towards the end of it they're looking more tired than they did, and it's nice; it's like a community,' says Harriet Walker, formerly style editor of the *Independent* and news editor of *Never Underdressed* (2013a).

The first in the calendar is *New York* (www.mbfashionweek.com) – home to giants like Calvin Klein, Ralph Lauren, Marc Jacobs, Diane von Fürstenberg, Donna Karan and Michael Kors. Victoria Beckham also chose to show her collections here. New York has the reputation of being the most commercial and conservative of the four big fashion capitals.

Second up is *London* Fashion Week (www.londonfashionweek.co.uk). It has struggled for credibility in the past and some predicted its demise in 2002 after big-name designers like Stella McCartney, Alexander McQueen and Matthew Williamson chose to show abroad. Stung by accusations that London fashion was creative but irrelevant, the British Fashion Council launched schemes like NewGen, sponsored by Topshop, to foster young talent.

Burberry's decision to return in 2009, after eight years of showing in Milan, boosted London Fashion Week enormously, bringing a host of celebrities to the front row and luring US *Vogue*'s Anna Wintour back to Britain for the first time in several years. Other returnees in 2009 included Matthew Williamson, Jonathan Saunders and Amanda Wakeley.

By 2013, its place in the big four seemed assured. A new generation of designers like Christopher Kane and Mary Katrantzou stayed instead of beating the well-trodden path to New York or Paris when they achieved success, and American designer Tom Ford chose to show his eponymous womenswear collection in London.

Figure 7.2 Cara Delevingne on runway (CN/Fairchild)

After London comes *Milan* (www.cameramoda.it/en/). Italian fashion has been built on the back of the wealthy manufacturing companies, and its collections are described as a 'roll-call of the fashion powerhouses, the gods of glossy advertising – Armani, Gucci, Versace, Dolce & Gabbana, Prada' (Fox, 2011).

The biggest of all, though, is *Paris* (www.modeaparis.com/en), the home of the luxury conglomerates LVMH and Kering. The brands that show here include Chanel, Dior, Saint Laurent, Louis Vuitton, Givenchy, Valentino, Balenciaga, Lanvin and Céline.

Showing in Paris represents the pinnacle of achievement for designers. The head of the French federation that runs the Paris collections, Didier Grumbach, says: 'You can be a genius in London, but to gain true international status, you must eventually show in Paris' (in Tungate, 2012: 121).

British designers who have made it to the hallowed ground are Alexander McQueen, Vivienne Westwood, Stella McCartney, Gareth Pugh and Hussein Chalayan, who either had the financial backing or artistic credibility to get noticed in the French capital.

Mid-season collections, like cruise/resort and pre-fall, have no set slots for shows, part of the reason they have been traditionally overlooked by the media. Some fashion houses stage shows outside the four fashion capitals – Chanel, for example, has shown everywhere from a plane hangar in Santa Monica to the old port in St Tropez – or dispense with shows in favour of less costly presentations.

Men's ready-to-wear

The men's ready-to-wear shows take place in January for autumn–winter, and June for spring–summer, in London, Milan and Paris.

New York does not have a separate men's fashion week, so its designers either slot into the women's shows (several months later than the other menswear shows, putting them at a disadvantage) or show overseas. Calvin Klein Collection and Marc Jacobs, for instance, show in Milan.

Traditionally overlooked in favour of women's ready-to-wear, the men's shows and menswear in general were the subject of much excitement by 2013. Men's clothing represented 50 per cent of the luxury market (BFC Future of Fashion report 2012) – fuelled by demand in Asia, where traditional British style was much admired – and Burberry reported that men's accessories were the fastest growing part of its business in 2012.

It certainly helped put London Collections: Men on the map when the men's shows launched in June 2012 to instant acclaim. Burberry moved its men's collections back to London from Milan in 2013, following other big hitters like Alexander McQueen and Tom Ford.

Who attends the shows

As many as 5,000 people attend London Fashion Week, according to the British Fashion Council, but they're not all from the media.

At least a quarter are buyers, from 39 countries, representing everyone from the big department stores to e-tailers to independent boutiques. Between them, they put in around £100 million of orders, the BFC says.

The other big contingent is the press, both from the UK and 42 other countries. They are not all there for the same reason, though.

Magazine editors are expected to go to the big shows to court advertisers, and keep big account-holders happy. 'When I arrived to work on a glossy, *Marie Claire*, I was shocked to learn I not only had to attend each and every fashion show, in case any of the designers became offended at my empty chair, but give each and every collection a glowing mention,' wrote Liz Jones (2012).

Fashion directors, editors and stylists from the monthly glossies mainly go to the shows to see the collections and start the process of coming up with the next season's big trend edits and fashion stories. They look for new silhouettes, proportions, colours and fabrics, and take note of which pieces they'd like to call in for shoots.

Other journalists, staff or freelancers for websites, newspapers and weekly magazines are there to write reviews of the shows. How they do this, and what they include, will be described later in this chapter.

Not all publications will send a reporter to every fashion capital. While practically every magazine, newspaper and website in the UK will have someone at London Fashion Week, some weekly magazines might only send someone to Paris, Milan or New York if there's sponsorship money involved (a brand paying, for example, to cover a launch while they are there).

Amber Graafland, fashion director at the *Daily Mirror*, says she can just as easily cover shows from the web and from agency copy and pictures. 'I did something on the Chanel couture show today,' she says. 'The show was at 11 a.m. and I'd written it by 1 p.m.' (2013).

As well as the shows themselves, the fashion weeks are crammed with parties and launches staged by the big brands. They can be eye-wateringly glamorous – Luke Leitch describes catching a water taxi in Venice with Anna Dello Russo on their way to a Dolce & Gabbana masked ball, and watching Verdi-choreographed fireworks over Mount Etna after another D&G launch – but are sometimes just too much for writers on tight deadlines and under no compulsion to keep advertisers happy.

'I was really looking forward to the amazing parties at London Fashion Week but in reality there was no way I could get there, I had so much work to do,' says freelancer Hattie Crisell, who covered the shows for *New York Magazine*'s The Cut website. 'I was like fashion's Cinderella, heading home to write and swap emails with my editor in New York until midnight' (2012).

A journalist might have associated jobs to do during the shows, too, like street-style round-ups, interviews with designers, showroom appointments and even video reports. Hannah Almassi, covering London Fashion Week for *Grazia* in 2012, did back-stage interviews with designers and front-row chats with celebrities on camera for an associated YouTube channel called Fashtag.

What you need to know before a show

Fashion vocabulary

One of the biggest difficulties a junior or trainee journalist has when first writing up show reports is finding the words to describe the clothes on the catwalk.

We'll discuss the structure of a catwalk report below, but what you'll also need is a good fashion vocabulary, so you can bring the clothes to life with vivid descriptive flourishes but also pin them down with authoritative detail.

Take a look at the references in any catwalk report on, say, *Style.com*, and you'll see the wealth of knowledge at the fingertips of the writers. A Tim Blanks review of an Alexander McQueen show, for instance, has the cultural references of Madame Grès (early twentieth-century French couturier), Fortuny (early twentieth-century Spanish designer), Gaudí (Spanish architect), Gaia (Ancient Greek goddess) and the trademarks of earlier McQueen shows.

It refers to fabrics like matelassé jacquard, silk chiffon, lace and organza, embellishments like appliqué, pleating and ruffles, and cuts like trapeze and the Empire line.

On top of that, it has linguistic flourishes that convey what the clothes look like – the glossy black leather appliqué that looked like an 'oil slick', a colour palette 'as translucent as the inside of a shell' and ruffles that 'undulated as the models walked' (Blanks, 2011).

Not many people write like Blanks, a very experienced critic with a fairly specialised audience. But you do need the vocabulary to describe fabrics, cuts, colours, prints and decoration in an authoritative and credible way.

Fabrics come in and out of fashion, so you may find yourself having to talk about a particular type in any given season. The previously obscure guipure, a kind of thick lace, was the story of spring–summer 2012, for example.

It's worth venturing into fashion design departments at your college or university and literally getting a feel for the types of fabrics used. Fashion books (like *Fabric for Fashion: The Swatch Book*, 2010, by Clive Hallett and Amanda Johnston) can help. Browse the haberdashery departments or shops in your local area, and take every chance you can to see designer clothes up close, looking at the labels to see what they're made of.

Cuts and shapes, too, might be the story of a season – things like sunray pleats, paper-bag waists, scalloped hems and leg o' mutton sleeves. Again, simple fashion design books, like *The Fashion Designer's Directory of Shape and Form* (Travers-Spencer and Zaman, 2008), can help you learn to spot and name different cuts.

Colours may seem simple in comparison, but rarely do fashion writers simply refer to blue, green or red. 'Madder carmine' was the colour of autumn–winter 2013, apparently, though writers had to explain it was burgundy. To be able to recognise the difference between cobalt, azure and air force blue, look at the website for Pantone (www.pantone.co.uk), the colour-matching company that does its own trend research and nominates a 'colour of the year'.

Also, use your imagination to pinpoint colours with real-world references. When Jess Cartner-Morley talks about the 'heady shades of lipstick, tobacco and turquoise' that gave a Diane von Fürstenberg collection a 1970s sheen, you can picture it more clearly than if she'd used more technical references (2013a).

Finally, you will have to comment on decoration and embellishment, too, like studs, fringing, embroidery, sequins, spangles or paillettes.

Context

Just about every catwalk review is taken up mostly with context – what the designer is known for, how they've developed since the previous season, what their inspiration is for this season, the broader cultural context that they're tapping into, the economic situation, their financial backing … the list goes on.

Readers would soon be lost if each catwalk report was a stand-alone description of 50 or so individual looks. The only way runway shows make sense is if they're set in some sort of narrative, with themes for each season or strands for each designer.

For the journalist, that means having a clear idea before a show of what the designer or brand is known for, and how it fared in previous seasons. It's not difficult to research – the London Fashion Week website (www.londonfashionweek.co.uk) has quick profiles of each designer, detailing their background, signatures and ideal client, together with galleries of previous shows.

A designer's show notes, given out to guests attending a catwalk show, often detail their particular inspiration that season. Inspiration can range from high culture – Givenchy cited the 1927 film *Metropolis* as its starting point for its spring 2012 couture line, while Diane von Fürstenberg referenced surrealist art the same season – to the more popular or bizarre, like Christopher Kane's 'Princess Margaret on acid' spring–summer 2011 collection and Marc Jacobs's 'Cat in the Hat meets Kurt Cobain' for autumn–winter 2012.

What many catwalk critics like to do is interview the designer either before or immediately after a show, so they can add direct quotes about the context to their reports.

'I like to hear what designers have to say, so I can quote them on their inspiration rather than it just be me saying it,' says *Vogue* online's Jessica Bumpus. 'I'll either go to their showroom and do a preview ahead of the show, or speak to them by telephone' (2013b).

Charlie Porter, menswear critic for the *Financial Times*, says it will vary from designer to designer.

> Tom Ford is a very good raconteur, so when he invites you to his show-room to talk you through his collection I find myself taking down everything he says, because I know I can make some jokes about it.
>
> Kim Jones at Louis Vuitton talks to journalists before his show, which is great because there are complex procedures that have gone into the making of the collection.
>
> LVMH are investing millions at the moment in Berluti, and they want the message to get across about the quality and the make and the fit, so they invite you to speak to the designer and get a sense of that story.
>
> (2013b)

Other more unpredictable and complex shows, though, like Prada, dictate a more focused look at the garments, he says, rather than looking for an underlying human or financial narrative.

Other journalists – especially those on a quick turnaround time, like newspaper and website reporters – will speak to the designer backstage after a show, to get some immediate quotes to add to their reports.

That can be hectic, says freelancer Hattie Crisell. 'There's a fight to get backstage, your name has to be on a list and it can get quite aggressive,' she says.

> You do your interview surrounded by other journalists who are waiting for their slot, and usually the designer's PR will be standing there watching you like a hawk and tapping their watch.
>
> But it's worth it because having a few good quotes from a designer that you can weave into your report brings it to life. The more perspectives you can get, the better.
>
> (2012)

As well as the immediate context, a catwalk reviewer should have a strong sense of fashion history. They can go away and look up references to Gaudí, Grès or Gaia, but they need to be able to spot something that's gone before when they watch a collection, rather than write everything up as brand new.

Only sustained interest and research can equip a journalist with this kind of knowledge. Long before she worked in the fashion media, Harriet Walker, of *Never Underdressed*, would buy old copies of *Elle* and *Vogue* from charity shops and online, and has always read history and academic books about fashion.

At the shows

To attend the shows, a journalist has to have accreditation from the official organisation running them, like the British Fashion Council in London or the Camera Nazionale della Moda Italiana in Milan.

They also need an invite for each individual show, which is sent out by the PR acting on behalf of the fashion house or designer.

The bigger the publication, the more invitations they are able to secure for a show, so a glossy might have the editor and several of its staff there.

It's a common complaint that the show schedules are increasingly packed. For spring–summer 2014, there were 60 shows over five days on the official schedule at London Fashion Week, another 45 off-schedule shows, and 30 presentations and salon shows (BFC).

Some journalists have drivers and cars at their disposal to get them from show to show, but others are on foot and public transport. With the best will in the world, there is a limit to the amount of shows they can attend, especially when they have to write and file their reports throughout the day, too.

Once in a show venue, the next issue is seating. There have been screeds written about where people sit and what it means, and certainly PRs have to be mindful they do not upset any powerful editors.

The front row is normally taken by any celebrities (see below), the editors of the big glossies and occasionally their fashion director, critics from major newspapers and buyers from major international stores.

In the second and third rows will be other fashion directors, magazine fashion editors, assistants, stylists, other buyers and journalists, and standing at the back will be students, friends and hangers-on.

It's seen as a declaration of status. *Grazia* editor Jane Bruton says: 'It doesn't matter in the grand scheme of life. But it's seen as a public reflection of your magazine's overall status and how important you are to the designer' (in Drew, 2009).

Seating became more complex still after Dolce & Gabbana caused a sensation in 2009 when they put bloggers Scott Schuman and Bryanboy on the front row, next to a disgruntled-looking Anna Wintour.

Four years later, bloggers with the highest profiles and largest followings regularly command front-row seats, with some insiders complaining that it had gone too far and important critics were being sidelined.

Elizabeth Walker, who covered the shows for years for *Marie Claire*, says: 'What's happening now is certain magazines haven't been given any tickets, or maybe one instead of three or four, because there are so many more people trying to get into shows' (2012).

Other front-row regulars are celebrities – actors, models, singers and sports stars invited by the fashion house to give a show extra glamour and sought-after media attention. 'A tiny paparazzi photo of a celebrity in the front row will do more for a designer's career than a front-page headline proclaiming his brilliance,' writes Hadley Freeman (2009: 70).

So brands go to considerable lengths to get the celebrity there, providing air tickets, hotels, the pick of the new collection and, in some cases, payments. They will style and escort the star to the show, giving journalists the chance to interview them beforehand and photographers the opportunity to snap them on the front row.

Shows often start late because PRs are waiting either for a celebrity to arrive or for influential editors delayed by an over-running show beforehand.

When they do eventually begin, newcomers are often astonished at how quickly they go by. Luke Leitch, deputy fashion editor of the *Telegraph*, was sent to cover fashion weeks within a week or two of moving over to fashion from the features desk.

He wrote in a piece for *Vogue*:

> From New York right through to Paris, that first month of shows was, frankly, befuddling ... The shows were 11-minute puffs of smoke through which I'd make frenzied notes but then emerge thinking 'Mostly black', 'Quite short' or 'When's lunch?'.
>
> (Leitch, 2012: 125–6)

To keep track of what they're seeing on the catwalk, and to record their initial reactions, editors and journalists take pictures, make sketches and take notes while they are watching the show.

While it may be tempting just to take pictures to jog your memory, some seasoned veterans warn against it. For starters, it's hard to take a non-blurry picture when you are holding your phone or iPad above or in front of you and the models are moving at a swift pace, as many a fashion editor's Instagram feed will testify.

Second, some think it is harder to remember looks that you have passively snapped rather than sketched or described in words. Moreover, experienced editors say they are mentally editing and reviewing as they watch a show and take notes, making their jobs a lot quicker and easier.

Charlie Porter, who reviews menswear shows for the *Financial Times*, says:

> In one show you can see 40 looks, over 100 bits of clothing, so you have to write down very specific details so you can remember it.

I write a succinct description of the clothes, with details of the colour and cloth, and a brief note of what I thought about it.

If I've just written 'the coat was horrible', and not written that it was a red wool coat which didn't work because the collar was too wide or the balance wasn't right or the buttons were wrong, then I won't remember what it was that was horrible.

After a show, website or newspaper journalists will often have to write and file their report very quickly. Jessica Bumpus, who covers shows for *Vogue* online, says: 'I write the report up on my Blackberry, send it back to the office and it's posted within the hour.'

Even if a report doesn't have to be filed immediately, journalists will have only small windows of opportunity to write up their reviews during a day of shows.

To avoid having to stay up all night, many will look for a café with Wi-Fi or even a park bench if they have time between shows to start writing their reviews. Elizabeth Walker, who covered the catwalk for *Marie Claire*, says she used to watch in wonder as newspaper critics sat typing up perfect reports of a show they had just watched before the next one started, demonstrating the value of news training.

What you're looking for in a show

It's neither possible nor desirable to describe every single look in a catwalk show when you come to write it up. Instead, as we'll see below, you will select a main angle, with the rest of the report a blend of sub-themes and detail.

So what you should be looking out for when you take notes of a show are:

- Themes, and key pieces. There are anything upwards of 30 looks in a show, but there will be two or three themes coming through that you should be able to spot and describe. That makes the write-up far easier, as you will be able to pick out some key examples of each theme and describe them in detail, rather than home in on random looks or try to describe every one. For example, in a review of Anna Sui's autumn–winter 2013 show, Jessica Bumpus identified Parisian chic and 1960s retro, and described how each strand came through in the collection. Garment types can also be a theme. A show might focus heavily on evening wear or daywear, biker jackets or sweatshirts, suits or separates.
- Silhouette. When there's a major new direction in fashion, it's generally the silhouette and the proportion of the clothes that change. That's easier to see when you are outside an era – the shoulder pads and boxy shapes of the 1980s, for example, or nipped-in waists of the 1950s – but it's something you should look out for in new collections to identify the first signs of a changeover. A silhouette might be anything from angular to rounded, slouchy to structured, bodycon to cocoon, while the emphasis

shifts from the shoulders to the legs, waist or back. Magazine editors saw a major new shift in autumn–winter 2011, for example. 'It's all about the changing silhouette,' *Grazia*'s editor, Jane Bruton, told the *Guardian*. 'From rock-chick narrow, it is moving towards rounded shoulders, full trousers and balloon sleeves' (in Cartner-Morley, 2011a).

- Colour and print. Often a couple of colours emerge as the key looks of a season, or you might want to comment on a designer's characteristic use of colour. Prints and how they are put together – clashing or matching – also emerge as key trends on the catwalk. Improvements in digital printing led to an explosion of hyper-real, layered images on fabric, which was one of the key trends of 2012. Animal prints come and go, as do checks, stripes, florals, polka dots and dip-dye.
- Fabric. Developments in textiles mean designers can do much more with lightweight tweed, for example, or laser-cut leather, and these can become catwalk trends in themselves. From the offbeat, like Perspex and vinyl, to the traditional like wool or silk, fabrics will be part of any write-up of a runway show. Show notes can help a journalist identify fabrics, as can a quick call to a PR or seeing the collection close up in the designer's showroom.
- Texture and decoration. Sometimes texture might be the story of a catwalk collection, be it gauzy, diaphanous, sheer or multilayered. Decoration and embellishment are important, too – studs, beads, sequins, fringing and rips emerge and disappear, according to the season.
- Production. It's not all about the clothes. Fashion brands spend hundreds of thousands of pounds on models, lighting, music and effects in order to stand out from other shows and increasingly to make an impact online and on video. When that's combined with a designer's unique vision – like Alexander McQueen's big glass asylum in spring–summer 2001, or his hologram of Kate Moss in autumn–winter 2006 – the result is unforgettable.
- Styling. Hair, make-up, accessories and shoes are important parts of a runway show and are often mentioned in a report, especially if they add to the theatricality of the presentation.
- Celebrities. In runway reports aimed at the general reader who is not necessarily interested in fashion, the celebrities in the front row are often the main point of the article. Not just in the front row, either – when Giles Deacon cast TV presenter Kelly Brook and footballer's wife Abbey Clancy as models in his spring–summer 2011 show, he guaranteed media coverage far beyond the fashion pages. Similarly, actors Gary Oldman, Adrien Brody, Willem Dafoe, Tim Roth and Jamie Bell stole the show on Prada's autumn–winter 2012 catwalk.

How to write up a catwalk report

As with any news or feature, a catwalk report does not start at the beginning of the show and guide the reader chronologically through the looks to the end. That would be extremely dull, as well as confusing.

Instead, the writer chooses an angle to write it from, which will then be backed up and explained through the report, with other issues and themes brought in later if needed.

The angle is selected on the grounds of news values (see Chapter 5) – something unexpected, something shocking, a new twist, a star name – and also what will make the report relevant to the reader.

The most common angles used in catwalk reports are:

- The designer's inspiration, if it's not too esoteric. Starting this way can help bring a human story to a report, and make the clothes understandable to the reader. When Victoria Beckham said that her autumn–winter 2012 collection was inspired by her son Romeo and husband David's sportswear, hundreds of catwalk reporters must have sent up a silent prayer of thanks.
- Context. A new designer, a designer's performance, his or her business situation and where they show will often be used as an angle for a catwalk report. When Burberry brought its menswear collection back to London in June 2013, most reports started with that fact and commented that the return home had had a positive effect on the brand's clothes. When Christopher Kane presented his first collection after he sold 51 per cent of his company to Kering, reviewers were agog to see his reaction on the catwalk. 'This is what grace under pressure looks like,' was how the *Guardian*'s report began (Cartner-Morley, 2013c).
- A key look or theme. This is surprisingly rare in catwalk reports, but if a collection throws up an interesting theme, then that might make the angle. Charlie Porter, of the *Financial Times*, is interested in the changing role of the suit in menswear, so when it cropped up in Prada for spring–summer 2014, it was worthy of mention. His report starts:

> In a season where the lack of business tailoring is becoming something of an issue, trust Miuccia Prada to take the opposite approach – from the get-go: pinstriped double-breasted high rise suit jackets worn over florid shirts with mismatched baggy tailored pants and assorted varia-tions of trainers. The net impression was of young men playing business dress-up; the message: in a fashion sense at least, the business suit is now just a styling toy.
>
> (2013a)

- Production. If the staging of a show is particularly striking or lavish, then that will often be the angle of a piece. When Karl Lagerfeld imported an iceberg from Sweden as the centrepiece of Chanel's autumn–winter 2010 show, that was the first thing that reviewers mentioned. Three years later, when he had models walk round a 50ft high globe with all of Chanel's 310 stores marked on it, that again caught the journalists' attention. 'Walking into Chanel's show-refitted Grand Palais this morning felt like entering the no-expense-spared lair of some old-school, James Bond, megalomaniacal villain', wrote the *Telegraph*'s Luke Leitch (2013a).

Sometimes, however, writers try to resist focusing on the production. Charlie Porter, catwalk critic for the *Financial Times*, says: 'I try not to review the set. I find that very distracting … unless it's a video being used as a way of making you do everything but look at the clothes.'

- Celebrity. If a front row is particularly starry – Victoria Beckham clinched it again, when she persuaded husband David to sit next to Anna Wintour – or if celebrities appear on the catwalk itself, then a report will often start with this before going into the clothes. For general-interest magazines or tabloid newspapers, whose readers might not be interested in the shows, the celebrity is often the whole point. The *Daily Mirror* only wrote about Chanel's spring–summer 2014 couture show because Rihanna turned up apparently naked under a long cardigan.
- Verdict. If a collection was scintillatingly brilliant, or especially awful, that can form the angle of the piece. Because a bad review is far less common than a good one, a negative verdict is particularly newsworthy. Jess Cartner-Morley started her review of Tom Ford's spring–summer 2012 show like this:

> I'm going to come straight out with it. Deep breath: I didn't think Tom Ford's show was all that. Not that it was awful, by any means, but despite the beautiful tailoring and the immaculate execution, it fell a little flat. It felt too self-referential.
>
> (2011d)

- An anecdote. Personal anecdotes are the way in to all sorts of features, and catwalk reviews are no different, especially if they are aimed at a non-specialist audience. Hattie Crisell lures the reader in to a review for *New York Magazine*'s website thus:

> If I hadn't known the Tom Ford menswear presentation was today, I'd have guessed it anyway. A friend whose office happens to be in the same building as Ford's texted me at 9am: 'There are two hot models opening the front doors for everyone. I'm going to be smoking *a lot* today.'
>
> (2013)

The second paragraph explains that this is a trademark move of the designer, thus tying the angle to the main body of the review.

It is striking how many catwalk reports start with people, rather than the technical aspects of the clothes. 'It's all about knowing how to write a story; it's always story-based journalism', says the *Guardian*'s Jess Cartner-Morley (2011b).

Once the journalist has set up the theme in the first paragraph or two, they link it to the main body of the review. For example, when Victoria Beckham cited her family as the inspiration for her autumn–winter 2012 collection (see above), the *Guardian* reviewer duly quoted her before commenting: 'Beckham is a woman who knows how to reel in her audience with an anecdote almost as expertly as she knows how to execute a faultless collection' (Fox, 2012). That then led into a discussion about the strengths of the collection.

The body of the review is a balance of generalisation and detail. While the reviewer identifies key themes, like military or evening wear or a 1960s feel, they will always highlight one or two looks which they will describe in detail to explain what they mean. Without this detail, a review will be too vague for the reader to be able to picture it.

Like any feature (see Chapter 6), a review is grouped into topics with each new section carefully linked and signposted so the reader can follow the angle or argument through to the end. It should not be a series of unconnected observations, nor should it follow a simple chronology ('the next look on the catwalk was … before it finished with … ' or 'the models wore' or 'the models looked fabulous in … ').

And like any review, a catwalk report must explain why something worked or didn't work. Again, it's a question of showing the reader something, with description and explanation, rather than simply telling them something.

As Charlie Porter says:

> You have to unpick what's desirable about the clothing – it's often someone's sense of colour, of cuts, some sense of balance or often tension in the way things sit together that creates this attractive piece.
>
> Conversely sometimes there's no tension, the colours are bad, the fit's terrible, you can see the seams aren't working, and so there's nothing desirable about it at all.

How critical can you be?

Magazines cannot be critical of advertisers in print, as we saw in Chapter 3. That, together with publication dates, means their catwalk coverage is more likely to be of the round-up variety (in weeklies), trend reports (in weeklies and monthlies) and shoots.

If a collection is judged to be poor, it will simply get fewer mentions, or none at all. As Elizabeth Walker, former executive fashion editor at *Marie Claire*, says: 'Magazines comment by omission. If one show is dreadful, you might use one picture because they did show, but that's all.'

Magazine websites, however, do post instant catwalk reviews. They aren't always glowing, either, though any criticism will be very much tempered.

Jessica Bumpus, who writes for *Vogue* online, says: 'You can be critical but it has to be relevant, and you have to do it in a way that's constructive. For example, you could say the jumpers were great but another part of the collection didn't work.'

Newspapers, which are not reliant on fashion and beauty advertising, can publish outright criticism. It's no surprise that the big names in runway reporting – Hilary Alexander, Cathy Horyn, Suzy Menkes, Tim Blanks and Lisa Armstrong – all made their names writing for newspapers or websites.

Fashion houses may not be able to threaten to pull their advertising, but they can still wreak revenge for a bad review by banning a journalist from their shows or allocating them a humiliatingly poor seat.

Some journalists wear these bans as a badge of honour. Liz Jones, fashion editor of the *Daily Mail*, says she was banned from Marc Jacobs for saying she'd stab him if she ever saw another polka dot prom, and from Chanel for complaining about the smell of wet fur in the audience (2012).

Suzy Menkes was banned from all LVMH shows on a single day in October 2001 after a critical review of Dior, while the *Guardian*'s Hadley Freeman has written about being banned by Paul Smith and Jean Paul Gaultier: 'It seems pretty ridiculous to invite critics to a show, but only on the understanding that they will write gushing hyperbole,' she concluded (Freeman, 2008).

Armani, a powerful advertiser in fashion magazines, has banned both the *Sunday Times'* Colin McDowell and the *New York Times'* Cathy Horyn for things they said in reviews.

Horyn found herself at the centre of another storm in 2012 when Saint Laurent designer Hedi Slimane posted an open letter to her on Twitter calling her a 'bully' and a 'publicist in disguise'.

Colin McDowell responded by writing ferociously about the sensitivity of fashion brands and the effect it has on critical journalism. In a column for the *Business of Fashion*, he wrote that there were fewer than half a dozen writers who were prepared to voice an opinion: 'And that's because the sanctions for speaking truth are severe, because if they are not, the entire self-congratulatory, smoke and mirrors, candy floss edifice of fashion could collapse into an unedifying goo,' he added (2013).

Moreover, he said it was doing the fashion industry a disservice. 'Whereas most art forms are kept on their toes by informed commentary, the fashion world has virtually none.'

Charlie Porter, who was himself banned by Balenciaga briefly in 2003, says that as long as the criticism is well informed and honest, the reviewer should be allowed to get on with their job (see Chapter 13 for the legal defence of honest opinion).

'I try to approach each show without prejudice, though I do know the back story – it has to be an instinctive reaction to what you see,' he says.

> If I were to meet that designer, I have to be able to stand in front of them and justify any criticism I had made, so the criticism doesn't become name-calling or knocking and running. There's responsibility to it.

Do we still need the shows?

Fashion shows have changed immeasurably since Grace Coddington's early days, and not just in their presentation and choreography.

Once they were mainly trade shows, aimed at selling and publicising the clothes under strict conditions and embargos. Journalists were not allowed to sketch or take pictures, so concerned were the fashion houses about copying, and the glossies were allowed to borrow the clothes to photograph overnight in the knowledge the shoots wouldn't be published for months.

In 1972 a couple of designers broke their own embargoes to televise their collections. By 2010, the Internet enabled London Fashion Week to start live-streaming shows online. Several years later, most shows were shown live on the likes of Facebook, YouTube, magazine websites and the brands' own sites.

From 2011, the website NOWFASHION (www.nowfashion.com) also posted photographs from runway shows and presentations almost in real time.

So fashion followers at home were getting a good view of the collections at the same time as the journalists, editors and buyers in the audience, and were taking to social media to voice their opinions long before the first reviews came out.

The buying side had also long since changed. Up to 70 per cent of orders are placed a month or so before the shows take place, at private pre-collection gatherings in showrooms (Tungate, 2012).

Often, the pre-collection clothes are more commercial than those shown later on the catwalk. 'Shows are therefore becoming less commercial and more theatrical,' Tungate quotes Matthew Williamson's chief executive Joseph Velosa as saying. 'They are less and less a direct selling tool' (2012: 123).

So if buyers were ordering clothes before they hit the catwalk, and con-sumers could see the collections online without having to wait for the media to cover them, what was the point of the traditional fashion weeks?

As Jess Cartner-Morley put it in the *Guardian*:

> The bumbling way in which the fashion industry operates – with thou-sands of buyers, journalists, stylists and PR people spending a month, twice a year, traipsing around four cities, perching on endless identical rows of chairs to watch the same group of young women walk past them, wearing different clothes and different makeup each time – well, it is either sweetly quaint or plain ridiculous, depending on who you ask.
>
> (2009)

But the answer to that, as Cartner-Morley went on to acknowledge, is that a fashion show is a branding exercise – a theatrical piece of marketing – which has become even more important now that consumers around the world are watching.

It's not just about the clothes, but the celebrities in the front row, the models, the sets, whether Anna Wintour is in the audience. 'If you get everything around it right, you can change it from being merely a good product into a hot product,' Tungate writes (2012: 123).

Some editors also argue that the clothes have to be seen in real life to be fully appreciated. Grace Coddington writes in her memoirs: 'On a flat screen, things just look flat. I don't think I could recognise a great collection if I just saw it on a screen or in a look book' (2012: 325).

Those in fashion also argue that the shows are an important coming-together of the industry, where everyone mingles, networks and learns where their place is. 'It's a really important way of keeping the industry together,' says *Grazia*'s Hannah Almassi.

Luke Leitch, deputy fashion editor of the *Daily Telegraph*, went so far as to describe the shows as the equivalent of 'tribal bonding ceremonies that mean a great deal to the participants but are utterly bewildering if you aren't part of the tribe' (2011).

He might be onto something. The academic journal *Sociology* published a field study of London Fashion Week arguing that it was a 'materialization of the field of fashion', representing the social and symbolic capital of its main players and working to reproduce fashion culture (Entwistle and Rocamora, 2006).

What you can do

If you contribute to a local or university newspaper, magazine, website, TV or radio station, you could apply for accreditation and tickets to London Fashion Week.

Applying for a work placement to cover the collections for a website, to help out with PR or dress models backstage is another way of getting into the shows.

Try to attend fashion shows in your own area. Magazines, charities, stores, colleges, universities and football clubs regularly stage shows, which you could help style or review. Some cities, like Liverpool and Newcastle, also hold annual fashion weeks with catwalk shows and events.

Make sure you watch the livestreams of the four fashion weeks, to get an idea of how shows are paced and what looks are shown. It is useful to follow the Instagram and Twitter feeds of fashion journalists and editors who are actually there, to see their instant reaction to the collections and any behind-the-scenes insight they give.

Recommended reading

Coddington, G. (2012) *Grace: A Memoir*. London: Chatto & Windus.

Hallett, C. and Johnston, A. (2010) *Fabric for Fashion: The Swatch Book*. London: Laurence King.

London Fashion Week: www.londonfashionweek.co.uk.

Milan Fashion Week: www.cameramoda.it/en.

New York Fashion Week: www.mbfashionweek.com.

NOWfashion: www.nowfashion.com.

Paris Fashion Week: www.modeaparis.com/en.

Style.com: www.style.com.

Tungate, M. (2012) *Fashion Brands: Branding Style from Armani to Zara*, 3rd edition. London: Kogan Page.

8 Reporting the trends

Introduction

Trends arguably drive the fashion industry, and certainly form the basis of much fashion journalism.

By their very definition trends are new, they can be exciting, they are the perfect blend of catwalk, celebrity and high street, and they please advertisers by promoting their products. No wonder fashion publications love them.

Trends are also a useful way to organise and make sense of the hundreds of new collections shown during the four fashion weeks; they are the equivalent of the journalistic angle.

And an editor can demonstrate his or her fashion credentials by picking up on micro-trends on the street before anyone else – the equivalent of the journalistic exclusive.

E-tailers use trends as a way to edit their own collections, producing their own trend reports, grouping merchandise under trends as well as by designer and by type, and sending out emails to customers highlighting new trends.

They don't please everyone, though. Some commentators see the pushing of trends as a commercial ploy to keep the public buying in what is a very wasteful system.

Caryn Franklin, fashion editor, presenter and campaigner at All Walks Beyond the Catwalk, says:

> Fashion offers this chance for relentless selling, so the industry has created trends that we receive into our lives as the need to be regularly refreshed and updated, and be new and improved at all times.
>
> That's where the connection we have with the joy of clothes and the joy of dressing up has been corrupted.
>
> I question a system that is so wasteful we don't invest enough meaning in products we choose now.
>
> (2013)

Others wonder whether there is still a place for mainstream trends dictated by fashion editors, when more people than ever seek inspiration from

Figure 8.1 Jennifer Lawrence at the Oscars (CN/Fairchild)

blogs and street style and brands can connect much more directly with consumers.

However, fashion editors argue they are needed now more than ever to provide guidance through the maze of endless products and information now available to the public.

Their concept of the 'editorial eye' and why it's needed is an interesting one that goes to the heart of the purpose of fashion journalism, and will be explored in this chapter.

How writers and editors define trends, where they spot them and how they monitor them will also be explained, along with how they write them up into trend reports, shopping pages and recommendation pieces.

Finally, this chapter will also look at the social and cultural context of trends, and how some journalists try to bring that into their reporting to give them relevance beyond the shop shelves.

Why do trends exist?

On an industry level, a trend for a certain fabric or colour has a practical benefit. Fabrics are time-consuming and expensive to produce, and it makes commercial sense to have certain colours or textiles in demand for a particular season.

As we saw in Chapter 4, fabric trade shows are the first links in the fashion chain, and some like Première Vision in Paris produce their own trend and colour reports.

As for retailers, it's in their best interests not to go too far out on a limb. 'If retailers tacitly agree to support certain colour or fabric trends', writes Tungate, 'it means heightened customer demand, guaranteed sales and less remaindered stock' (2012: 70).

Trend bureaux like Nelly Rodi, in France, and Worth Global Style Network in London, monitor street style around the world, trade shows, graduate shows, cultural events and consumer patterns to produce trend reports 18 months in advance for fashion houses and retailers.

And although top-level designers say they set trends rather than follow them, there are advantages for them, too, to stay on message at least some of the time.

Mick Dixon, a designer who has worked with many different brands, says: 'Even at catwalk level, it's no coincidence that there are themes each season. There are colour reports, people develop fabrics, brands work with mills, and realistically, who wants to go out on a limb? There's strength in numbers' (2013).

That's on the industry side. On the journalistic side, we've already said that trends are the equivalent of an angle and a peg. They give the journalist a reason (peg) for writing about certain items, and provide a handy theme (angle) to group them into.

This works for e-tailers, too. Fiona McIntosh, who consulted for My-wardrobe. com, says:

> There is so much out there and you have to edit it for the reader or customer.
>   Why should you buy printed trousers? You buy them because they fit into this trend; this is where they've been seen before; this is what you wear them with, putting each piece into context. This is what magazines do, so why shouldn't retailers offer that as well?
>
> (2012)

On the consumer side, fashion academics have put forward a range of social, cultural and psychological theories as to why trends come and go, and why we join in.

One theory is that social class is the driver of fashion. Economist Thorstein Veblen came up with the phrase 'conspicuous consumption' in his book *The Theory of the Leisure Class* (1899, reissued 2009) to describe how the upper classes used fashion to display their wealth and continually changed styles as a sign of conspicuous waste.

This was developed into the trickle-down theory, most often associated with sociologist Georg Simmel. When the new styles adopted by the social elite are copied by the lower classes, and become mass fashion, the elite are forced to move on to another style to maintain their distinctiveness. 'As fashion spreads, it gradually goes to its doom,' Simmel wrote in a 1904 article entitled 'Fashion' (138).

The talk of social class might seem antiquated, but is easily translated into the wealthy or influential style leaders of today – musicians, film stars and models. And what is a Louis Vuitton, Gucci or Chanel logo if not a sign of conspicuous consumption and status?

Other theorists have pointed out that not all new trends come down from designers and their wealthy clients, but rather start on the street and rise up to the catwalk. This is the 'bubble-up' theory, described by writer Ted Polhemus in books like *Streetstyle* (1994), and explains the rise of garments like denim jeans and the T-shirt, and styles like Mod in the 1960s and Punk in the 1970s.

Fashion has also been depicted as a symbolic system, a way we communicate our identity, ideas and taste to others (see Holbrook and Dixon, 1985, McCracken, 1988). This is an interesting idea that underlies all those newspaper features analysing what supermodel Naomi Campbell wore to a court hearing or what politicians wear at party conferences.

It also explains why branding is so important in fashion. The clothes have to be imbued with the qualities and social values that consumers want to tap into. 'That's what you're buying in fashion, the intangible value,' says designer Mick Dixon.

He quotes sociologist Charles Horton Cooley, who came up with the idea of the 'looking-glass self' (*Human Nature and the Social Order*, 1902), to explain why people adopt a certain style: 'I'm not what I think I am, and not what you think I am. I'm what I think that you think I am.' In other words, when you're trying to construct a fashion identity, it's not how you look, but the image that you think you're putting out to other people that counts.

Trends and styles are codes that we share, via designers, the fashion media and branding. We can draw upon them to send out messages others can understand.

Interestingly, all fashion journalists comment on the fact that the general public is much more well-versed in fashion codes and trends than it used to be. The *Guardian*'s Jess Cartner-Morley says: 'Fashion has become part of the national conversation ... People in public life no longer dress to arcane codes and Savile Row tailoring; they dress in a more interesting way and people understand that' (2011b).

Academic theory is an interesting way of looking at fashion, and working out why it has such a powerful hold on us. A useful introduction is Pamela Church Gibson's chapter in *The Fashion Handbook* (Jackson and Shaw, 2006), or Jennifer Craik's *Fashion: The Key Concepts* (2009).

Defining a trend

To become a trend, a new or reworked style has to have a name – a shorthand way of describing it that catches on.

Some have gone down in history. Would Dior's New Look (1947) or A-line (1955) been so well remembered without the label? Fashion theorist Yuniya Kawamura writes: 'Certainly a name, easy to remember, is a desired feature of any new product fighting for attention in mass media reporting' (2005: 88).

Other trends are perennial – styles grouped under terms like military, florals, monochrome, masculine or neon, or particular decades like the 1960s or 1970s, are rarely far from the catwalk.

Meanwhile, others are more of-the-moment, coined by fashion editors trying to put a fresh twist on established styles or to find a cohesive movement within the new season's collections.

So instead of florals, for example, *Grazia* tagged one of the trends for autumn–winter 2013 as 'winter florals', describing them as 'the dark and moody kind that have grunge undertones' (Almassi, 2013).

It's also a chance for a publication to put its own spin on a trend by coming up with a catchy title that would appeal to its particular readers. *Vogue's* trend report for autumn–winter 2013 referred to 'a rose bouquet' (for pink) and 'the square route' (for checks and tartan).

Its Condé Nast stablemate *Glamour*, meanwhile, was more straightforward, labelling the same trends as 'pink is the new black' and 'tartan takeaway'.

Broadly, trends can be defined by the following:

- Types of fabric, like leather, tweed, denim, chiffon and fur. Most trend reports will not just focus flatly on the fabric. They will play with words for a title (the *Independent* referred to the tartan trend as 'Scotch on the frocks' and the fur trend as 'skinned' in its autumn–winter 2013 report – Fury, 2013) and will stress any new ways of wearing or new qualities of the fabric (double denim, say, or leather T-shirts).
- Colours and patterns. It's always possible to pick a colour or two out of a new season's collections and promote them as a trend. For autumn–winter 2013, *Elle* picked out navy, *Grazia* went for Yves Klein blue and *Vogue* spotted pink. Nudes, neon, pastels and monochrome are more general colour trends that resurface regularly, as are combinations like colour blocking or clashing. Prints, too, can form a trend – animal prints, camouflage, polka dots, florals, tribal prints, stars or heart prints – as can ways of wearing them, like clashing or matchy-matchy.
- Cuts, shapes and silhouettes. This can be restricted to parts of the body, like round shoulders or cinched-in waists, or to garments like the oversized coat or tulip-shaped skirt. Hemlines of skirts go up or down, silhouettes go from bodycon to slouchy, and trousers – especially jeans – can be wide, flared, boot-legged, skinny, ankle-grazing or Capri. This kind of trend tends to be more of a slow-burner, taking place over several seasons and taking longer to catch on with the majority of consumers.
- Parts of the body. One season the waist might be emphasised or on show; another the emphasis might be on the shoulders, back or legs. Sometimes, fashion writers catering for fashion-forward readers seek less traditional

areas of display to write about – the 'hidriff' (higher than the midriff), the 'side boob' and the 'side bottom' were all discussed avidly in 2012/13.

- 'Trophy items' or 'hero items'. These are key accessories or garments that are in the spotlight any particular season. Examples are underwear as outerwear, the parka, the duster coat, the high-fashion sweatshirt, the varsity jacket or the statement necklace.
- Historical eras. Designers regularly plunder the past for inspiration, often when it chimes with something current in popular culture (TV series *Downton Abbey* and Edwardian dress, *The Great Gasby* film and the 1920s, or US TV series *Mad Men* and the 1960s). Anything up to a decade earlier than the present day is fair game for a trend – 2012/13 saw a lot of 1990s-inspired clothing.
- A particular aesthetic. There is a whole roll call of styles that come in and out of fashion, like sportwear, minimalism, grunge, clubwear, boho, biker, preppy, romantic, military and safari. Like fabric, it's often offered up with a fresh twist – sports luxe, for example, or off-kilter ladylike.
- Ways of wearing clothes. Things like belts round coats, shoulder-robing, knotting a jumper round the waist, buttoning a shirt all the way up or holding a bag squashed under the arm can be defined as micro-trends if there are enough photographs of style leaders (models on the catwalk or off-duty, celebrities, street-style subjects) caught in the act.

The first trend reports come out immediately after a new season's collections, in February for autumn–winter and October for spring–summer. It's an unfortunate time lapse, but as Lucy Wood from *Look* says: 'We usually spin it as "new season changes you can start making now", then return to them nearer to the actual season and go into them in depth' (2012).

As well as referring back to catwalk collections, journalists will also be on the lookout for micro-trends that emerge during a season. These may be sparked by what a celebrity is wearing, a particular event (like a festival, or summer holidays), or a look or range that has taken off on the high street.

As always, editors and journalists bear in mind their target audience when picking out trends to focus on. Some trends, like the crop top, would be considered too young for certain readers, while publications like the *Daily Mirror* would not write about a trend that hadn't trickled down to the high street and thus become more affordable and accessible to their demographic.

Target audience also dictates the way trends are covered. In fashion magazines and websites, it's a given that readers are interested in trends, so they will be presented straightforwardly in online galleries and print spreads.

Newspapers and supplements have a more general reader, so are much more likely to deal with trends in terms of how to wear them, and why not to be scared of them. *Guardian Weekend*, for example, has a weekly section called 'How to Dress'.

They also have to bear in mind a greater age range than most magazines. Both *Guardian Weekend* and *Fabulous* regularly demonstrate trends on women from their twenties to their fifties or sixties.

Spotting a trend

A large part of a fashion writer or editor's job is monitoring and identifying trends.

Each editor will have a different speciality or emphasis, but there is a broad consensus on where trends emerge and how they can be spotted.

Catwalk

Even when it's out of the price range of most readers, the catwalk is the starting point for many trends.

The biannual shows are the consumers' first glimpse of the next season's styles and they throw up thousands of catwalk photographs which will be endlessly reproduced for the next six to seven months.

Journalists work hard to spot key themes on the catwalk, and pull together trend reports for the end of fashion week.

Fiona McIntosh, former editor-in-chief of *Grazia*, says:

> I love to sit next to the fashion director at shows, because they can always spot trends and have an eye to edit them down. They've got these real fashion antennae and a genuine excitement in trying to predict which trends will do well.

Even if a fashion editor can't get to all the shows, they watch them online and file away visuals to be used in trend reports to come. And even if they only use high-street clothes on their pages, they will still reference the catwalk for added fashion kudos.

Lucy Wood, senior fashion news editor at *Look*, says:

> Designer fashion may not seem important to us at first glance, but it's extremely important. Everything that's featured has pretty much trickled down from the catwalk or come up through street style.
>
> The catwalk completely dictates what the high streets are designing and buying in. We're not saying to our girls, 'Go out and buy the £1,000 dress,' but we are saying, 'This is the look, this is where it came from on the catwalk, and this is how to get it in everyday life.'

Tracey Lea Sayer, fashion director of the *Sun on Sunday*'s *Fabulous* magazine, also references the catwalk even when she's using high-street brands. For autumn–winter 2013, for example, she was keen to use Louis Vuitton's show featuring models stumbling out of hotel rooms as the inspiration for one of her own shoots using high-street versions of negligees and oversize coats. 'We look at the catwalk a lot,' she says (2013).

Celebrities and public figures

Fashion has always been pegged to personalities. Legendary American *Vogue* editor Diana Vreeland once said: 'A new dress doesn't get you anywhere; it's the life you're living in the dress.'

The life we apparently most wanted to emulate from the late 1990s onwards was that of the celebrity, as the fashion world became inextricably linked with showbusiness.

Louise Gannon, showbusiness reporter, says:

> I've done 15 years covering backstage at the Brits [music awards] and that used to be my realm. Now it's not – now the story is a star turning up in such-and-such a dress because the red carpet has taken over.
>
> In the past decade there's been an ever-rising fusion between celebrity, fashion and beauty. Models are out when it comes to magazine covers; now it's all celebrities. Celebrity endorsements are a huge deal with fashion and beauty companies.
>
> (2013)

That's because actors, pop stars and public figures can set trends themselves. Retailers attest that items fly off the shelves once the right celebrity has been spotted in them.

It's not just stars in the entertainment business. One of the most avidly followed public figures is Kate Middleton, the Duchess of Cambridge, who has a lookbook dedicated to her on *Grazia* online and a phenomenon named after her called the 'Kate effect'.

When she wore a Topshop dress in 2013, the brand's website crashed as people searched for it online. A dress by maternity brand Seraphine sold out within two hours of the release of an official family portrait showing her wearing it.

That's why fashion journalists trawl through agency photographs and celebrity websites each day, and keep an eye on celebrities' social media accounts. A new haircut or colour will spark a story, as will any particularly striking outfit or signs of an emerging trend.

Amber Graafland, fashion director on the *Daily Mirror*, says:

> Celebrities are inspiring trends much more than the catwalk, even though, ironically, they're getting the trends from the catwalk.
>
> But that seems irrelevant – readers are more interested when it's seen on a celebrity. I feel it cheapens fashion a bit. It gives us a lot more to write about it, so you love it, but love to hate it at the same time.
>
> (2013)

Celebrity trend stories are especially effective online, because names are what many people are searching for on the Web. 'If we do something on Rihanna or Cara Delevingne, for instance, we know it will get lots of hits,' Amber adds.

Press days

High-street stores, and brands that can't afford to show on the catwalk, hold their own previews of the coming season's collections in events called press days.

At press days, fashion editors, writers and bloggers are invited to look through samples of the clothes that will be hitting the shop floors about three months later, and talk to the PRs about any brand news.

It's an important way of forging relationships with PRs, keeping high-street advertisers happy, picking out items for future call-ins and spotting key themes and trends for the season ahead.

It's especially important to those magazines that focus mainly on high-street fashion. Tracey Lea Sayer, fashion director at *Fabulous*, says:

> I'm a real stickler about going to press days and seeing all the high-street selections.
>
> Even in recession, when the high street aren't taking many risks, brands like River Island, Asos and Topshop still go out to get real key hero pieces – you can pull your shoots in around them.

It's ideal when high-street brands use the catwalk as inspiration, giving fashion editors the opportunity to reference designers in a way that's relevant to their audience.

Emma Bigger, fashion editor at *Company* magazine, says: 'I go to all the catwalk shows, but the high-street brands are the people we use and our readers buy from. The high street makes it relevant to a younger audience – they give it a twist' (2012).

Popular and high culture

All aspects of visual culture, be they historical or contemporary, can provide inspiration for trends. It's also a useful way for editors to link fashion with everyday life for the more general reader.

The *Guardian*'s Jess Cartner-Morley says: 'We look to films, exhibitions, what's in the air. It has to have got beyond the catwalk, really, for it to be a trend for us' (2011b).

As well as sparking lots of arts coverage, big museum exhibitions are a jumping-off point for fashion features, trend reports and shoots. They can also inspire designers.

Examples are the Victoria & Albert Museum's exhibitions *Grace Kelly: Style Icon* (2010), *David Bowie is* (2013), and *Club to Catwalk* (2013–14). The New York Metropolitan Museum of Art's 2013 show *Punk: Chaos to Couture* was credited with the smattering of chains, studs and vinyl on the autumn–winter catwalks that year.

Even without an exhibition in their honour, musicians are often cited as the starting point behind trends. Debbie Harry in the late 1970s, David Bowie's Thin White Duke phase, Joan Jett, Patti Smith and Courtney Love have all inspired catwalk looks, while Jean Paul Gaultier ruffled feathers with a very literal Amy Winehouse tribute in 2012. So influential was Rihanna by 2013 that she launched an eponymous collection with British high-street store River Island.

Music festivals have become huge fashion events in themselves and are covered by most newspapers, magazines and websites in terms of what people are wearing, especially the models, actors and musicians present.

Festival season starts with Coachella, California, in April, which is particularly popular with the media, featuring as it does A-list stars in blazing sunshine. Festival dressing is not just an easy story for fashion journalists, though – it appears to have had a big impact on what people wear, with the likes of cut-off denim shorts, Hunter wellies, floral headbands and topknots all stemming from festival style.

Films and TV shows, too, can start trends. Shows like *Gossip Girl* and *The Only Way Is Essex* are credited with inspiring their own looks, while others – Baz Luhrmann's *The Great Gatsby* or the TV series *Mad Men* – create the opportunity for the revival of looks from a bygone era.

The daddy of them all was probably *Sex and the City*, which *Time* magazine said changed fashion forever; it turned shoe designers like Manolo Blahnik into household names, it promoted the Fendi Baguette and the entire 'It bag' industry, and it started micro-trends like nameplate necklaces (Pous, 2013).

Street style

Street style was largely pushed out of magazines by celebrity coverage, but became the centre of attention again with the advent of blogs like the Sartorialist and Jakandjil as well as photo-sharing websites like lookbook.nu.

By 2013, many magazines were featuring street style on their websites – *Company* found it was one of the biggest drivers of traffic to their site – and some were using street-style pictures alongside celebrity and catwalk pictures to illustrate their trend reports.

Grazia, unusually, had featured street style in its print edition from the start, but without journalistic involvement at first. 'We knew that street style was becoming really popular in the industry so we set out to make more of a big deal of it,' says Hannah Almassi, who started going out herself with a photographer to locate the perfect *Grazia* subject, someone 'individual and well put together, cool but not too done' (2010).

For her, street style is more varied than other sources of trends. 'We draw inspiration from as many different people as possible,' she says. 'We're not just going for the cool kids down at Spitalfields – we'll also get a 40-year-old woman on Bond Street who looks fantastic.'

And she believes it's more accessible and democratic, too:

> When you look at models or catwalk shows or advertising, you don't go, 'Yes, I could look like that.'
>
> Whereas if you look at a real girl, you can understand it more, and go 'Oh yes, I could do the same with my belt on my coat,' or 'I've already got that, and if I wear it like that then it makes a big difference.'

As a fashion editor by 2013, Hannah had started to use street-style pictures as the sole inspiration of some of her trend reports, eschewing the normal 'as seen on the catwalk' or 'as seen on this celebrity' photographs.

Company, meanwhile, went through a major redesign in 2012 to make it more 'streetwise', in the words of publishers Hearst, and also produces a biannual *Street Style Edit* spin-off. Emma Bigger, fashion editor, said: 'Street style is as important as celebrities for our readers. People on the street are a really strong place to see trends, and it has changed us as a magazine.'

Social media

Other than street style, bloggers and other forms of social media are monitored by fashion journalists for signs of emerging trends.

Once seen as competition, the big fashion bloggers (see Chapter 11) are now style leaders in their own right and often star in editorial features and work with brands. My-wardrobe.com, for example, asked five bloggers to style up their new London Lab collection of UK-based designers when it publicised it in August 2013 (www.my-wardrobe.com/london-lab/bloggers-picks).

So fashion editors keep an eye on style blogs from around the world, either to pick up on a new brand or trend that might be relevant to the UK or to profile the best bloggers in more in-depth features. 'I did a feature once on how fashion is the new celebrity, and people who were once behind the scenes are the new A-list stars,' says *Grazia*'s Hannah Almassi. 'You don't ignore the people doing things online, because they are helping to form where fashion is going.'

Social curation sites like Pinterest and Polyvore are also a good way for fashion editors to monitor which styles, brands and celebrities the general public are interested in at any given moment.

'I look at Instagram and Twitter, because they reflect what people are talking about or are interested in that day,' says Amber Graafland of the *Daily Mirror*. 'I look at Styloko.com to see what people are putting together, and Fancy.com too.'

Trade and graduate shows

While all the consumer publications are talking about autumn–winter, trade journal *Drapers* is already a season ahead, discussing trends for the following spring. That's because its journalists produce comprehensive reports from all the trade shows – the Copenhagen shows, Pure, Jacket Required, Stitch and Scoop.

This long-view look at trends is not aimed at consumers but people in the fashion industry like retailers, designers and buyers who need to plan further ahead. But fashion journalists do read the trade journals *Drapers* and (in the United States) *WWD* to keep abreast of what's happening.

Style forecasting agencies also use trade shows as source material, along with graduate fashion shows around Europe to spot new talent and gauge what the designers of the future are doing.

Some fashion journalists do go to the graduate shows in the UK, most notably former *Telegraph* fashion editor Hilary Alexander. Amber Graafland, of the *Daily Mirror*, says:

> If you're into fashion, it's good to go to the graduate shows, see who's up and coming.
>
> Hilary Alexander is the best example in the world of someone who's all over everything and goes to everything; that's how you get the best stories.

Monitoring the trends

Monitoring all these sources of trends requires hard work, enthusiasm and imagination.

Journalists and editors have to be familiar with all the main looks in that season's collections, know what's coming up in the high-street stores, keep on top of the glossies and the trade press, read the big blogs and find the cool new ones, look at celebrity photos online and from agencies, look at street-style blogs, be aware of what's going on in arts and culture, be all over social media, AND observe people wherever they go.

It's not a job for the faint-hearted. 'You have to have a ridiculous passion for it,' says stylist Madeleine Bowden. 'To get into the industry, you have to be obsessed with it' (2013).

Melanie Rickey, *Grazia* contributing editor, also points out that you can't stick to your comfort zone. Not only do you have to go to places you wouldn't normally go, but you have to be interested in people you wouldn't normally care about.

'You can't be snobby about who you think is interesting because everyone is influenced by different people,' she says. 'So Michelle Obama is definitely on the radar, not my personal choice but what she chooses affects people. All the Kate Middleton thing is a bit boring, but it's necessary because of the influence she has' (2012).

Trend-spotting is a science in that you take in as much information as possible and stories will emerge – as Melanie describes it, in horse-racing terms, 'following the form'.

But it can also feel like a fairly subjective and instinctive thing. The clues are there but are almost intangible, and perhaps not everyone sees what you're seeing. In her memoirs, Grace Coddington describes flying in the face of the prevailing bling style and putting together a grunge shoot just days before Marc Jacobs presented his seminal grunge collection for Perry Ellis in 1992. 'This kind of coincidence happens all the time in fashion, and it's often impossible to unravel where ideas have come from,' she wrote (2012: 224).

As with many fashion ideas (see Chapter 5), a journalist's gut feeling about a trend is often confirmed and pinned down through debate with colleagues.

Hannah Almassi describes the process on *Grazia* after the catwalk shows:

> There are the obvious trends that everyone has spotted – you find yourself writing the same words in your notebook at the shows, like peplums, metallic, 60s, and you know there's going to be a story there.
>
> But there will be other things that someone has noticed and others haven't, and that might be a cool new brand, look, person, vibe or even an idea about how to lay out a page; this all contributes to creating extra, varied content.
>
> It will get batted about for a couple of hours between us at a meeting, and something will usually prevail, and then the fashion director will really hammer out how we're going to cover it and what are the most significant messages for the introduction to the new season.

Promoting consumption?

When a trend, product or brand is tipped in a newspaper or magazine, it often has an effect on sales.

As we saw in Chapter 3, founding editor-in-chief Fiona McIntosh attributed a large part of *Grazia*'s success to women using it as a shopping guide.

That was backed up by the figures. When *Grazia* wrote about the Houlihan trouser range by American firm J Brand, Selfridges sold out its entire stock the following week (*Grazia*, 2010).

Academics and some commentators worry about this, both from the point of view of sustainability and from the way it positions women as consumers first and foremost.

In her book *Inside Women's Magazines*, for example, Janice Winship wrote about women 'being caught up in defining their own femininity, inextricably, through consumption' (1987: 39).

But fashion editors and journalists argue that it's not quite as simple as that.

For starters, they see trend reports and shopping pages as the fashion world's equivalent of news – something to keep up with, not necessarily a call to action.

Hannah Almassi says:

> We see *Grazia* almost like a dinner party, where you're aware of what the news is, what's happening in the celebrity world, what the fashion trends are, what's going on in music, art and culture. You don't necessarily go and do all of it or wear all of it, but you're in the loop and you can talk about it.

Second, they say that by using their expertise to explain a trend, and highlight its worth, they are giving readers the tools to sort the wheat from the chaff and therefore become more careful shoppers. 'I know when something is good because I've been doing it for ages,' says freelancer Melanie Rickey. 'When a trend is great, I want to share the reasons for that so people can make up their own minds.'

Third, journalists also say the really interesting part of trends is looking at how people are actually dressing and why that might be changing. That takes trend reporting beyond the products into the realm of social and cultural issues.

Throughout his magazine and newspaper career, Charlie Porter has always focused on 'looking at things as they are', he says, and is particularly intrigued by radical changes in menswear.

'I gave a talk at Central St Martins last year about the disappearance of the tie. It had never crossed their minds to design an outfit based on the central line of a tie … it's just not in their world,' he says (2013b).

> Menswear sees the suit as the uniform for the titans of power, but you just have to look at the likes of Steve Jobs and Mark Zuckerberg to see that many of the wealthiest entrepreneurs of the last decade have probably never been seen in a suit.
>
> As more men in their 20s enter employment and never have to wear a suit for work – in tech, or call centres, or the creative industries – the relationship with the suit has changed. They're now wearing it for decoration, in a dapper way.
>
> It's interesting to think about menswear in a context other than the alleged rules, which are completely false.

Instead of looking for passing trends in the new season's collections, at *Fantastic Man* he would try to identify clothes that matched the magazine's aesthetic.

'We'd always find a *Fantastic Man* look within a season, which is the way most people shop anyway,' he says. 'They find their own look within a collection.'

The editorial eye

Charlie's comment takes us to the idea of the 'editorial eye', the quality journalists believe sets them apart from brands producing their own media content.

The editorial eye is hard to define, but it's the spin that a journalist or editor will put on a trend or a story to make it relevant to their reader; it's the expertise, integrity and taste they deploy to sift out the good products or looks from the indifferent; it's the context and stories that they weave around products to turn them into fashion, and it's the imagination and point of view they bring to bear on photos and shoots.

It's why they believe fashion journalists will always be needed, even as the traditional media continue to decline.

And it's why they say they are trusted, even if the products they are writing about are from advertisers or are available through click-to-buy.

Harriet Walker, of *Never Underdressed*, says:

> There is nothing on our site that we don't like. That's honest, isn't it? It has been edited by people who know what they're talking about.
>
> Obviously it comes down to taste as well. But if you're reading that publication and you enjoy it, then it's because you can trust the people who have written it, and like their taste.
>
> People get very anxious about spending a lot of money on the latest thing, and a lot want guidance and advice.

(2013a)

Scott Schuman, who runs the hugely influential street-style blog the Sartorialist, attributes his success to having a point of view that people could relate to. It's an editorial eye of sorts.

'Without a real passionate point of view, I don't think there is anything you can do, because otherwise it just becomes a report on product, and there are a lot of blogs like that and they're incredibly boring,' he says (Big Think, 2012).

How do publications, editors, journalists and bloggers build up that authority and trust? They say it's through integrity, expertise (whether that's based on experience or on being young and cool), and having a consistent voice or point of view that audiences recognise.

Working on a fashion title bestows credibility in itself, even if sales are falling. That's why some editors will work for a magazine when the pay isn't great and take on consultancies and freelance styling jobs on the back of that.

This leverage can be transferred to the retail world – hence all the journalists employed by the likes of Net-a-Porter, Asos and My-wardrobe.com – and online, too.

'I think if the fashion editor is clever, she can still have influence in the digital age; her title means she validates things,' says Fiona McIntosh, former editor of *Elle*:

> When I did a consultancy with My-wardrobe.com, it was amazing how pieces would really fly when we did something with fashion editors like Polly Vernon or Sarah Harris from *Vogue* choosing outfits.
>
> The influence they had amongst the audience was amazing. I don't think they quite realise how much power they have.

Fashion journalists may object but e-tailers increasingly claim the editorial eye for their own. The point out that they, too, are recommending products they like – otherwise they wouldn't stock them – and have to seduce their customers with entertainment and aspiration.

'You can't just make a catalogue, because a catalogue is boring,' says Lucy Yeomans, former editor-in-chief of *Harper's Bazaar* and now at Net-a-Porter. 'Another really important constant is a point of view; a sense of curation' (in Kansara, 2013a).

Writing up trend reports

When selecting a trend to report on, you need to bear in mind how it will look on the page or screen. That's why you will barely ever see a trend piece on black trousers, however fashionable they might be.

'It has to look glamorous and exciting', says Hannah Almassi, fashion editor at *Grazia*. 'There are tricky stories like trousers, even though it's one of the biggest shifts in womenswear in recent years. You have to find a way around just having a load of cut-outs of black pants on a page.'

The first thing you'll need to stand up a trend report is pictures of style influencers wearing it. It can either be catwalk looks, pictures of celebrities on or off duty, or, in some magazines, street-style pictures.

Second, you need associated products. A trend is not usually reported on without cut-outs of garments or accessories you can buy in order to get the look.

This, too, can be tricky, especially if your trend is quite cutting edge. Hannah says:

> When I started, I'd be quite ahead in thinking of trends, but then I learned that sometimes it's too soon, because you don't have the right imagery or the right products to back it up. So you learn to pitch something at the right time.

At other times, she will ring PRs, hunt through websites and lookbooks and contact brands to ask whether they have anything related to the trend. It's essential to be familiar with which brands do what, so you can often start with them first and save time.

As we saw in Chapter 3, journalists and editors have to try to include advertisers' products to keep them happy, but insist they wouldn't compromise their editorial content if the products weren't right.

Beyond advertisers' products, they say they can choose other ones themselves. Hannah says: 'I do have quite a lot of freedom to use new brands and smaller designers if I can, which helps because my news stories about burgeoning trends are often really specific, like culottes for example.'

Some refer to this as 'confetti', and Joseph Velosa, chief executive of Matthew Williamson, attributes the British brand's success to this. He explains:

> Whether you are a buyer at Barney's or the editor of a fashion magazine, it's the same principle. You have to dedicate 80 percent of your editorial to your biggest advertisers.

So you're left with 20 percent of what's called 'confetti' – the fun, new and innovative stuff that you sprinkle around to make your store or your magazine look fresh and interesting.

(in Tungate, 2012: 55)

When e-tailers do trend reports, the products are things they stock, though they might have to take into account certain 'hero brands' that will get more marketing than others.

But that might change. In an interview in 2013, Net-a-Porter editor-in-chief Lucy Yeomans said its editorial would begin to feature brands it didn't stock. 'I don't think you can give a view of the season and I don't think you have editorial integrity otherwise,' she said (in Kansara, 2013a).

Shopping pages

Shopping pages are the pages mainly filled with products that you will often get near the front or back of the book in a magazine, and in galleries online. They have a trend as their peg, but are less time-sensitive than other types of trend report.

The subject will be very straightforward – polo-neck jumpers, for example, or two-tone accessories – and the page will include a short blurb, or even a just a sub-headline, to explain what the subject is.

Depending on the page and the publication, there may be a couple of small celebrity, catwalk or street-style pictures to establish the trend. Some pages might also show a model (or, in the case of *Company*, a reader) styled to show the full look.

But most of the page will be filled with cut-outs of products, accompanied by captions specifying the name, the brand and the price, and in some magazines the website address or stockist number.

Some magazines like *Elle* call in the actual products to shoot, once they're sure they have the right mix for the page. Others on a shorter deadline will either call in (from PRs) or download high-resolution images of the products to put straight on the page.

They will always include a couple of products from advertisers, at least. 'Advertisers are a massive thing in shopping pages; you really need to adhere to that,' says freelancer Madeleine Bowden, who styles pages for *Elle*. 'Then you can put your own stuff in there afterwards' (2013).

The fashion editor or assistant putting together the page will also have a clear brief about the price points they must stick to. It might be high street, but high street for *Elle* means £100–£150, while high street for the *Daily Mirror* means nothing above £100.

Grazia aims for a wide range of products, both in terms of price and age. 'No one else really does that mix of high and low in the same way our shopping pages do,' says Hannah. 'I try to get a mix of expensive things, cheaper things, a version that's more grown-up, something slightly younger … so it's never just a page full of cheap sequinned hot pants or completely unobtainable luxuries.'

Trend reports

Trend reports still feature product, but they're more about explaining the trend and how to wear it or do it than a simple shopping page.

They can be news-story length – 200 words, say – like *Grazia*'s in its 10 Hot Stories at the front of the magazine, or they can be feature-style and length, with room for more reflection.

But they all do the following:

- Pin down the trend – sometimes with a catchy title, always in a way that makes it seem fresh and exciting.
- Explain why it's big now – be that a cultural event, a theme on the catwalk, something started by celebrities or something spotted in the street.
- Stress why the reader should try it. Trend reports are always positive, even when their tone is slightly tongue-in-cheek. Often this encouragement comes in the form of explaining what's new about the trend, even if you think you've seen it before. So it's not just grunge – it's grown-up grunge. It's not unflattering, PE-style sportwear – it's sport luxe. You may never have suited yellow, but this year there's a choice of shades.
- Pinpoint where it's been seen on that season's catwalk, perhaps two or three references. If it's a trend report specifically based on street style, then the piece will highlight where it's been seen and on what type of person.
- Detail how it's been translated to the high street. Which brand has picked it up, and how are they doing it?
- Add in celebrity references if possible and relevant to the audience.
- Give instructions on how to wear/do the trend, with options if the reader wants to plunge wholeheartedly into it or if they merely want to dabble. If relevant, give advice related to body issues. Is the trend figure-fixing? Can you wear it if you're smaller?

The longer or more reflective reports might also trace the trend or item's history through the past few decades, and put forward a theory as to why it's making a resurgence or bursting onto the scene now. This would look at social and cultural factors, rather than just style points.

An example is a piece about the return of the waist by the 2006 winner of *Vogue*'s annual talent content, which you can read online (www.vogue.co.uk/news/2008/01/06/vogue-talent-contest-winning-entry-2006). The author, Leisa Barnett, traces the trend back to the 1950s, and explains its waxing and waning with the position of women in society.

A *Guardian* 'How to Dress' piece on grown-up grunge (Fox, 2013) talks about original grunge in the 1990s, with a nod to the fact that its thirtysomething readers were there at the time. It also explains that these days grunge is 'more of a look than a lifestyle' to make it more palatable.

Trend reports should be written in a relaxed, lively and inclusive style. Like features, they should begin with something to hook the reader and pull them in – an anecdote, perhaps, or a provocative question.

Recommendation pieces

A recommendation piece is slightly different from a trend report in that it focuses on one particular product or brand, rather than a trend, and in a timeless rather than of-the-moment way.

In what tends to be a lengthy piece of writing, the journalist explains the appeal of the product in an objective way – why they would recommend it to you, the reader – and often in a subjective way too, tying it into the history of their life with a series of personal anecdotes.

It's a way of investing the publication and the writer with a certain tone and aesthetic taste by allying with this particular product or brand. Obviously, then, the product tends to be a classic, rather than a retro horror, and there's always an interesting backstory to the brand.

A recommendation piece is structured like a feature, pulling us into the story whether we are initially interested in the brand or not. It often begins with an anecdote and writes about the product in the context of an era or a lifestyle, with lots of research and facts about its history and where it's made.

Practical details like a price and where the product is available are included but not highlighted – anything promotional would jar with the tone of the piece – and often appear in a bullet-pointed paragraph at the end.

Interestingly, recommendation pieces seem to be more a feature of men's fashion journalism rather than women's, perhaps for the reasons outlined in Chapter 6 (writing fashion news and features). Men are thought to be more interested in the story behind a product or brand, and less susceptible to being told a product is a must-have this season.

If not exactly recommendation pieces, Luke Leitch's Mencyclopaedia articles that are available to read on the *Fashion Telegraph* website are similar in focus, content and tone.

Recommended reading

Church-Gibson, P. (2006) 'Analysing fashion', in Jackson, T. and Shaw, D. (eds) *The Fashion Handbook*. London: Routledge.

Fashion Editor at Large: www.fashioneditoratlarge.com.

Lynch, A. and Strauss, M. (2007) *Changing Fashion: A Critical Introduction to Trend Analysis and Meaning*. Oxford: Berg.

Mencyclopedia: http://fashion.telegraph.co.uk/columns/luke-leitch/.

9   Styling

Introduction

Many of the best-known names in fashion journalism – *Love*'s Katie Grand, US *Vogue*'s Grace Coddington or French *Vogue* ex-editor Carine Roitfeld – are stylists rather than writers.

Styling is the traditional way into magazines, and it's the main part of the job for most of the fashion desk, from the interns through to the assistants, the editors and directors.

As well as putting together shopping pages, makeovers and get-the-look pieces, the fashion team are responsible for 'main fashion' – the big shoots that go in the well (the middle) of the magazine.

Styling for magazines, newspapers and websites is called editorial styling, which is prestigious but not always brilliantly paid. The money lies in commercial styling – celebrities, catwalk shows, advertising campaigns, lookbooks and catalogues – and many stylists aim to do both.

It's a profession that's very visible and popular now, but that hasn't always been the case. Anna Wintour was one of the first editors to credit stylists on a shoot, along with photographers and models, when she took over at US *Vogue* in 1988.

'Until that point, fashion editors were neither seen nor heard of,' she writes (in MacSweeney, 2012), though in the UK, style magazines had brought particular stylists (like Ray Petri and his trademark Buffalo look) to the fore in the 1980s.

Twenty-five years later, the stylists themselves were public figures, snapped by photographers and bloggers at the shows, giving interviews and working with brands. 'Today these fashion editors are no longer simply creating fashion images, they are themselves the living image of fashion,' writes *Purple* editor-in-chief Olivier Zahm (in Roitfeld, 2011: 5).

But what a stylist's job actually involves is not so visible. At the most basic level, they select clothes and accessories for shoots. Depending on where they work, they might also have to organise, cast, produce and direct the shoot.

And yet it's more than that still. By editing a collection of clothes they think is important that season, and putting them together in a particular way,

Figure 9.1 1950s fashion shoot (CN/Fairchild)

in a particular setting, with particular models and a particular mood, they are 'making the clothes part of a bigger story', says fashion journalist Sarah Mower.

'The best of their work has the power to transcend fashion trends, and to reflect something symbolic, joyful or, on occasion, chilling about the times we live in,' Mower adds, in a foreword to her book *Stylist: The Interpreters of Fashion* (2007: VII).

This chapter will start by looking at this bigger picture – what a fashion photograph can do beyond documenting the latest trends.

It will then go into the practicalities of what a stylist does, from coming up with ideas for fashion stories, planning them and calling in clothes to ensuring all goes well on the day of the shoot itself.

It will explore briefly what's involved with commercial styling, and ask how would-be stylists can develop their visual eye and learn practical skills.

Finally, it will look at some of the issues surrounding fashion imagery, including airbrushing, diversity and advertising.

What great styling can do

Some fashion shoots are service pieces, designed to show clothes in a simple, clear way in order to give readers advice on what's available (for example, the best winter coats) or how to put things together.

But others are real fashion stories, hung round a narrative, a lifestyle or a mood, to suggest new ways of thinking about fashion or how we present ourselves.

Robbie Spencer, fashion director of *Dazed & Confused*, told the *Business of Fashion* website that his basic job was 'to source clothes and interpret them into an image. But it's also about inspiring your readers and trying to educate or enlighten people to new ideas' (in Anaya, 2013).

As a result, because they are not trying to be timeless or classic, fashion shoots are imbued with the mood of the times – so much that they are often used in books and documentaries as visual shorthand for a particular decade.

It's fascinating to look at histories of *Vogue* magazine, for example, and see how shoots changed, from the idealistic, softly-lit aristocrats who posed for Baron Adolph de Meyer in 1914, the elegant, stately Twelve Beauties shot by Irving Penn in 1947, models rushing around city streets captured by William Klein's telephoto lens in 1955, the tall, leggy Veruschka posing in far-flung countries in the jetset 1960s, to model Lisa Taylor's predatory gaze at a topless man in a 1975 Helmut Newton shoot, the Story of Ohhh.

Anna Wintour marked the start of a new era at *Vogue* in 1988 with a cover depicting a laughing model, Michaela Bercu, on the street in a Christian Lacroix couture jacket worn with jeans. Grace Coddington recognised its importance – in her memoir, she writes: 'The cover endorsed a democratic new high/low attitude to dressing, added some youthful but sophisticated raciness and garnished it with a dash of confident energy and drive that implied getting somewhere fast' (2012: 244).

Great styling not only conveys the zeitgeist of a particular era, but can also experiment with notions of how women or men are supposed to behave and look.

Polly Devlin, in her *Vogue Book of Fashion Photography*, writes that in pictures of decades past:

> we see very clearly how women desired to look, and were expected to look, and how they were looked at. We can discern how they behaved, and how they were expected to behave. We can see what was found shocking, and how repetition of that shock lessened its impact.
>
> (1979: 59)

Sometimes this is explicit. Grace Coddington carried out a memorable shoot in 1971 that took ten rules of ladylike behaviour from a book of etiquette and depicted models decimating them. The rule 'A lady never dresses to stand out in a crowd,' for example, is illustrated with a picture of traditional nannies in Hyde Park with model Gala Mitchell in satin hot pants pushing a pram in the opposite direction.

The same experimentation underlies many of Carine Roitfeld's shoots. The former French *Vogue* editor explains in her book *Irreverent* that she's more interested in 'continually creating new images of womanhood' than portraying the latest trends (2011: 88).

Figure 9.2 Fabulous fashion shoot (Tracey Lea Sayer/News UK)

So she teams a Chanel jacket with an African gown, wraps a very conventional pussy-bow blouse round a model's breasts to give the impression of bondage, and depicts a model as a pregnant mum who smokes and tosses her baby in the air (Lily Donaldson in 'No Smoking', French *Vogue*, April 2009), or as a maniacal butcher caressing blood-smeared knives and lumps of meat (Eva Herzigova in 'The Butcher', *The Face*, 1997).

Sometimes it backfires. A shoot in the October 2009 issue of French *Vogue*, featuring Dutch model Lara Stone blacked up, sparked 'worldwide outrage', according to Voguepedia (www.vogue.com/voguepedia/Carine_Roitfeld).

While fashion photography, then, is sometimes criticised for reducing women to surface appearance and objects of the 'male gaze' – the feminist notion of the active viewer being positioned as male, the passive object as female – others see it as a more experimental and liberating force.

Fashion theorist Elizabeth Wilson writes: 'Fashion often plays with, and playfully transgresses gender boundaries, inverting stereotypes and making us aware of the masque of femininity' (2006: 187).

Not just femininity – Sean Nixon's book *Hard Looks: Masculinities, Spectatorship and Contemporary Consumption* (1996) describes how the 'new man' of the 1980s was first represented in the fashion spreads of men's magazines.

Learning how to style

Fashion editors are divided on whether you are born with a flair for styling, or whether it can be learned.

Emma Bigger, *Company* fashion editor, says:

> We have this conversation at work, and we can't agree. Because I've been doing it for so long, I tend to think it's easier than it is. I kind of think, everyone has their own style, so essentially everyone can style.
>
> But I'm not sure. Because fashion changes so much, you do have to have an eye.
>
> (2012)

Her editor, Victoria White, is more emphatic. She says none of her fashion desk have specific styling qualifications because 'you are either stylish or you're not. It's like fine art – you can make someone who is an OK artist a better artist, but you're not going to teach them how to be a true artist' (2013).

But there's a lot more to styling than being able to put together an outfit for yourself, and these other things can be learned. You have to consider your editorial stance, your readership, price points and brands you have to include because they're advertisers, and you have to learn the practical side of organising a shoot like calling in clothes and hiring a photographer.

These things you learn on the job, either by interning or assisting fashion editors. 'Being an assistant is a bit like being an apprentice,' says Elizabeth Walker, who always took time to explain to her assistants at *Marie Claire* why she'd chosen something for a shoot (2012).

Siobhan Mallen, former associate fashion director at *Grazia* and now at Asos, was an assistant for four years and says it was useful to work with people who had different styles. 'You take something from how each of them styles and approaches their job. You learn everything, then apply your own spin on it', she says (2012).

Assisting is also vital for learning how to work as a team, Siobhan says. On a shoot, you'll be working alongside a photographer, models, a hair stylist, make-up artist and perhaps a prop stylist, along with all the assistants.

'As a magazine stylist, you're an art director of sorts,' she says. 'It's all about collaboration and knowing how to get the best out of people.'

Although you need a good eye for fashion and style, you can work on developing your visual skills and understanding.

Tracey Lea Sayer of *Fabulous* looks at the shoots in all the glossies each month so she's aware of who is doing what, and can follow the big trend stories through the season.

But she's also got a good knowledge of shoots from decades gone by, which she can use for visual cues.

'Some of my mood boards aren't referencing fashion that's here now,' she says:

> A shoot that *Vogue* did on the Trans-Siberian Express had always been on my mind since I saw it years and years ago, so we took a little bit of it and did a story out in Russia on the railroads.
>
> (2013)

Beyond fashion, photography, fine art and film will also help you develop a wide visual vocabulary, a sense of proportion and ideas for shoots.

Sasha Wilkins, who blogs as LibertyLondonGirl, said her many childhood visits to art galleries and historic properties were vital in educating her eye.

'Keep looking at the world around you, and be as catholic as possible in your taste,' she advises. 'Never ever get distracted by what's cool and what's not cool, and don't be swayed by other people – have your own opinion' (2013b).

Developing your own point of view – the 'editorial eye' discussed in Chapter 8 – requires test shoots, either for your own portfolio or for publication in a local newspaper, magazine or website.

Tracey, of *Fabulous*, used to work for free with stylists on *i-D* and *The Face*. She also did test shoots at college with photography and fashion students using clothes they'd made, charity shop finds and their own wardrobes. That's why she tells interns at *Fabulous* to do their own tests at weekends.

One of the few textbooks on styling – *Mastering Fashion Styling* by Jo Dingemans (1999) – gives a whole range of suggestions for student portfolios, including making over other members of the class, offering publicity shots to small record labels, clubs and boutiques, and scouting good locations for shoots in your local area.

Dingemans advises that students don't get hung up on getting the latest clothes to shoot, and should instead learn to scour jumble sales, car boot sales, charity shops and ethnic shops, customise their own clothes and work with classics like a white shirt or denim jacket.

She especially advises against the temptation to buy a heap of new clothes on a credit card, and then try to return them after a shoot. The clothes could easily get damaged or lost and the store might become suspicious.

'It is more important to learn to put "looks" together than follow current fashions slavishly,' she writes (1999: 79).

If you're working with a photography student or local photographer on a test, make sure you agree in advance how and when they are going to send the pictures to you. Are they going to give you them all, or a selection? Will they have edited them beforehand on Photoshop, and are you happy with that?

Ideas for shoots

Fashion stories are all designed to show off the season's new collections and trends, be they designer or high street.

Editors will get an idea of which stories they'd like to do when they see the catwalk shows and the high-street press days. Already they will be mentally editing what they've seen into different trends and stories.

While some shoots will just set out to document a trend – normally against a plain studio background with no distractions – others will set the clothes in some kind of context, be it a particular setting or an unspoken narrative.

If you've watched *The September Issue* (dir: R.J. Cutler), the documentary charting *Vogue's* big fashion issue in 2007, you will have seen Grace Coddington put together a haute couture shoot against the fabulously romantic background of the Palace of Versailles.

Tracey Lea Sayer, of *Fabulous*, decided to go to Vietnam in 2013 to shoot that year's oriental trend in an imperial palace. 'It was a real career high,' she says. 'The clothes were high street, but when you get the girl there in the make-up and the clothes in that beautiful location, it looks fabulous.'

Other shoots will draw on codes from films, art, history and current affairs to weave a story or mood around the clothes.

This is where a good knowledge of the visual arts pays off. In her book *Irreverent*, Carine Roitfeld cites an eclectic mix of inspirations: the daughters of the last tsar of Russia, the Japanese artist Araki, provincial French costume, the 1962 film *What Ever Happened to Baby Jane*, erotic movie *Emmanuelle*, the Duchess of Windsor, ballet dancer Vaslav Nijinsky, artist Egon Schiele, Princess Anne, Swiss photographer Karlheinz Weinberger, 1980s TV show *Dallas*, and writer Françoise Sagan, to name but a few.

Elizabeth Walker, of *Marie Claire*, says it made a shoot more interesting when it had a story overlying it, especially if it was a basic wardrobe story like winter coats or workwear:

> You have to think of a way to make it fun. If it was a workwear story, something like the film *Working Girl* or the TV series *Mad Men* would occur to me.
>
> Looking at paintings helps. I saw a *Vogue* shoot that had a lot of black clothes, but it looked like a Bruegel or Vermeer painting. It was beautifully done.

Inspired by the Louis Vuitton spring–summer 2013 catwalk show, Tracey Lea Sayer of *Fabulous* was planning a shoot at the Regina hotel in Paris:

> I like to create an atmosphere and an ambience – it's about the type of girl she is, rather than 'Such-and-such a store has done this type of coat, and Topshop have done this.'
>
> In this story, she's an out-of-work actress living in a hotel and she probably smokes a bit too much – I obviously can't show that in my pictures, but in my mind she would.

Sometimes it's just a mood that the fashion editor wants to convey. Liz Lamb, who styles shoots for *La Di Da* magazine in the north of England, says: 'I did a little written synopsis before a shoot recently, saying I wanted it to look like the models were having the best party of their life at 4 a.m.'

Stylists will also inevitably convey some of their own personal taste, background and attitudes in the way they set up a shoot.

In fact, Anna Wintour reckons that all the great stylists draw on a 'deep pool of memory and longing'.

'The gardens, the schools, the neighbors, the light – all are signifiers that come back again and again in the work of the grown child,' she writes, in the foreword to Sarah Mower's *Stylist: The Interpreters of Fashion* (2007: V).

Mood boards

A stylist puts together a mood board before a shoot to capture the essence of the fashion, theme and look they're aiming for.

This can be shared with the photographer and hair and make-up artists to make sure everyone is on the same wavelength before the shoot itself, and is especially useful if there is no time to meet up beforehand.

Fashion editors will set to work on mood boards from the start of the season so they can coordinate stories with the rest of their team and make sure they don't overlap.

Mood boards are composed digitally so they can be easily shared. Some stylists do them on Adobe Photoshop, some on Adobe InDesign and some use social media tools like Pinterest.

They will use any picture that inspires them – an advert, a poster for a gig, a film still, a catwalk picture, a photo from the past, anything. Again, this is where having a wide visual repertoire helps. Freelance stylist Madeleine Bowden says: 'It's knowledge. An image from Calvin Klein 1995 spring–summer of a sheer, knee-length nude dress comes into your head, so you can pop that picture on your mood board' (2013).

Calling in clothes

At the same time as deciding on a theme, a stylist will also work out which clothes and accessories would work best for the shoot.

They already have a good idea of what's out there. They will probably have gone to the shows to watch the ready-to-wear collections, and will have seen both the collection and commercial lines close up in showroom appointments.

For the high street, they will have gone to the press days to see samples of new lines three to four months before they arrive in shops.

At both, they take pictures on their phones so they have a visual record of everything they've seen. They might have already asked a PR to put their name on certain samples, or they will contact the PR afterwards to 'call in' those pieces they plan to build a shoot round.

But they will also do a new trawl as they plan a shoot. For this, different publications – and different editors – have a variety of tactics.

Tracey Lea Sayer, of *Fabulous*, hand-picks every item herself:

> We do a call-in round PRs to tell them what we're working on, but to make sure I get the pieces I really want to shoot, I'll do an eight-hour day

of appointments every other week to perhaps 12 PRs and hand-pick everything for a shoot.

It's time-consuming, but in the end you can see the effort that's gone into it.

At a big glossy, fashion editors will go through catwalk photos, lookbooks and style sheets to select the looks they want, and then brief an assistant who will set about calling them in from PRs. They might select something like 40 looks, but they're likely to secure only around half of that.

If the publication is working with a freelance stylist, they will send them a brief with references from the catwalk and a mood board. 'It's then your job as a stylist to know who's done what, so if they want cut-outs or leather trimmings you know which designer has hit those this season. Then you do your call-ins from lookbooks and line sheets,' says Madeleine Bowden, who styles shoots for *Elle*.

Most clothes are samples, called in directly from the brand before they reach the stores. High-street samples are a size 10, and designer samples are often much smaller as they have to fit catwalk models (see Chapter 4).

So if a fashion editor is working on a story about fashion for all sizes, or has a much shorter deadline, he or she can also organise appointments with department stores and boutiques to call in clothes from them. That way they can get different sizes, or clothes at short notice.

There can be fierce competition for samples, and call-ins can be a cut-throat business. Fashion editors often complain that the world's top glossies sometimes call in key pieces whether or not they need them, and hold on to them for too long.

This is where friendly relationships with PRs pay dividends (see Chapter 12). Elizabeth Walker, of *Marie Claire*, says: 'If they like you, they push to get that red frock you want for your shoot.'

Freelance stylist Madeleine Bowden says that a PR might slip her an item for a couple of hours as a favour. 'I've done shoots where a look arrives at 9 a.m. and it's been picked up at 10.30 a.m., so you have to shoot it straight away!' she says.

Another constraint is the 'full look policy', where a fashion house or a store refuses to allow their pieces to be mixed with another brand's in a certain look. Fashion editors then have to shoot the full look or risk ruining relations with that brand.

This happens at the big fashion houses like Givenchy and Céline, but also at a local level. Adam Mooney, PR and marketing manager for Newcastle-based Jules B boutiques, says: 'We don't insist on a complete look, but if we advertise with a publication, we don't necessarily want to be pictured right next to a direct competitor which sells the same brands' (2013).

That raises the issue of advertising, too. As we saw in Chapter 3, publications have to use some pieces from advertisers in any shoot they do.

For a sense of this in action, read Lynn Barber's interview with British *Vogue* editor Alexandra Shulman, originally published in the *Observer* (2008).

She describes watching Shulman and her then fashion director Kate Phelan going through the Dior lookbook trying to find something that would fit into a painterly themed shoot, because the fashion house was a big advertiser.

But not all publications have this pressure. Sometimes it works the other way round, as Tracey Lea Sayer at *Fabulous* explains:

> None of the high-street brands asks us to include things.
>
> One brand did come to us when they'd noticed we hadn't used a lot of their products from April to June. I explained to them that they were releasing all their hero fashion items very early on, so we were choosing them instantly at the beginning of the season from February to April.
>
> After our discussions, they're now going to start releasing things in smaller pockets so they will get more coverage throughout the summer.
>
> We can be honest if we're questioned by a brand, and tell them their product hasn't been as strong this season.

Calling in clothes for a local publication has its own headaches. Instead of borrowing samples, stylists generally borrow direct from stores, meaning they have to take extra care with clothes that will be going back on sale. They often have to keep the sales tags on, tucking them out of sight for the photo.

'Also, we can't have them out of the stores for too long,' says Liz Lamb, who worked for the *Newcastle Chronicle and Journal* and is now editor and style director at *La Di Da* magazine, based in the north of England. 'If I was doing a shoot on Monday, I can't take them out on Friday because they'd be missing from stores at the weekend.'

Selecting clothes, calling them in and preparing them for a shoot requires a huge amount of organisation and attention to detail.

When she's borrowing from a store, Liz Lamb takes pictures of each item so she doesn't muddle them with another store's items and breach their full-look policy (see above). She checks they're not damaged before she leaves the store, so she won't be blamed.

She gets a docket from the store with a description of each item, its code and its price, which she photocopies so she's got a record. This is not only important for the captions, but also for when she's returning the clothes so she can get the PR to sign it to prove everything has come back.

Fashion editors on the national glossies have assistants and interns to help them call in clothes and prepare them for shoots. When clothes come in, the assistant will again check for damage and email the PR with a picture to protect the publication against blame.

If the clothes are for a shopping page, the assistant might have to write up each piece on a form and take a picture so they can write up the credits later on.

For a shoot, the assistant will hang them on rails so the editors can select which ones they'll use. Then the clothes are packed in tissue paper and hanging bags or cases ready to travel to a studio or on location.

Planning a shoot

Obviously, theme and clothes aren't the only things a fashion editor has to think about.

Models have to be cast, a photographer hired and a location chosen. There might be customs forms to fill out, permissions sought, and insurance organised.

On a glossy, fashion editors will have the help of bookings editors and art directors to organise a shoot, but a newspaper editor might only have an assistant to help, or have to do it all herself.

Location

Some shoots, especially the more practical ones, take place in a studio. They're booked for a certain time, and can be expensive if the shoot overruns.

Others will be shot on location abroad for more of an atmosphere, for variety and for guaranteed good weather – or, at least, more reliable weather than in the UK. That's especially important for the monthlies, shooting at least three months ahead of publication date.

One of the perks of a fashion editor's job is all the travel they do, although they don't often have the time to be a tourist when they get there.

A long-haul shoot used to mean that the team could factor in 'weather days' if they had to wait for the sun to come out.

No longer. When Tracey Lea Sayer of *Fabulous* took a team to Vietnam, they shot six different fashion stories to make it worthwhile:

> We shoot a different story every single day, sometimes eight to 10 shots a day. You might get a day at the end when you're waiting for a flight and can hop on a tourist bus, but otherwise you don't see much.

Budgets have steadily shrunk for shoots, too, and free flights in exchange for a plug for an airline have all but disappeared. Instead, a fashion team might get a media rate of about 10 per cent discount on airlines or hotels, and a certain amount of excess baggage free.

Freelance stylist Madeleine Bowden says: 'Budget is always on your mind, so if you're doing a shoot that should be set in Morocco you go to Majorca instead, because you can find a nice rocky beach there.'

Amber Graafland, fashion director of the *Daily Mirror*, often shoots in Cape Town, South Africa, because the weather is a safe bet and there's a variety of backdrops.

She says:

> We don't want to go to the most exotic beach in the world because it's not really relevant to our readers, and we have to reflect the weather that's going on here – it's not like a monthly where you're shooting a season ahead.

For that reason they also shoot a lot in Portugal, which is the type of place their readers would go on holiday.

Madeleine Bowden recommends using TripAdvisor to research locations in advance, because people post honest opinions, lots of photographs and details of tourist attractions nearby.

Closer to home, and with smaller or no budgets, fashion teams often use hotels for a location shoot in exchange for a credit on the page. In fact, hotels are useful as an emergency plan B if the weather turns nasty.

Emma Bigger, of *Company*, found herself running round hotels when it wouldn't stop raining in Miami, and ended up shooting in a hotel lobby. Liz Lamb, in the even less predictable north-east of England, always rings round nearby hotels ahead of a location shoot in case of miserable weather on the day.

Other locations Liz uses are local landmarks, stately homes, beaches and countryside, Newcastle's Theatre Royal, and an old-fashioned gentleman's club in the city.

For any venue – even a public park – you must seek permission in advance from the local council or the company or organisation that runs it. It's best to have written (or emailed) permission and the name and mobile number of the person you dealt with, in case you are challenged on the day.

You may have to work round a venue's opening hours. You will need public liability insurance in case of accidents or injury (universities and colleges have this, and you can request a copy of their certificate if required).

You will also have to consider where your models will get changed and have their hair and make-up done when you're on location, whether you need an electricity source for an iron or hairstyling implements, and where you are going to keep the clothes.

The rest of the team

Models are not well paid for editorial work, and sometimes work for free for smaller publications, but they do it to build up their portfolios and for the credibility. (Carine Roitfeld reckons she turned Eva Herzigova's image around with her 'Butcher' shoot for *The Face* in 1997. 'Before this she was the blonde Wonderbra girl. Look at her now!' she wrote (2011: 167).)

The more prestigious a publication, the more chance they have of booking top models for a story, though Grace Coddington complains it's even difficult for US *Vogue* these days with the big names tied up with lucrative advertising campaigns (2012).

A stylist or bookings editor will hire the model through an agency. It might be a top name, someone they've worked with before, someone the photographer has recommended, someone chosen at a casting or a new model spotted at a 'go see', where they are sent out to meet fashion editors and photographers.

The model is carefully chosen to appeal to the target audience. 'At the *Daily Mirror*, we don't want to use girls that are too young or too skinny, and we try to use a mixture,' says fashion director Amber Graafland.

At *Company* magazine, models are also chosen on the basis of accessibility. 'It has to be the type of girl our readers would aspire to. We don't want anyone who would alienate them,' says fashion editor Emma Bigger.

At a national level, a stylist wouldn't book a model purely from their card in case they'd had their hair cut or dyed or made other changes to their appearance. They can do castings, where models are seen, snapped and selected by the editors.

But at a local level, where models are inevitably working for free, there is no time or money for castings. Liz Lamb, who edited the fashion pages for the *Newcastle Chronicle and Journal* newspapers, says:

> Sometimes the models look amazing on the photos, and when they arrive they don't look like that.
>
> It's not like we can turn them away, but if you've got a great hairdresser and make-up artist then hopefully you'll be able to make up for that.

A newer model might need more direction with poses, too.

Depending on their brand, a publication might use people other than models for some fashion shoots. An upmarket brand might use a celebrity or a sports star – actor Kate Bosworth modelled the autumn–winter 2013 'lady-like' trend for Net-a-Porter's *The Edit* – while a younger brand like *Company* often uses real readers or their own fashion editors and interns in more straightforward service pieces.

Photographers are generally freelance, and are hired on the basis of a publication having a relationship with them or needing a certain kind of style for a particular shoot.

Like models, they tend to do editorial work for credibility and visibility even though it doesn't pay particularly well.

Phill Taylor, a fashion photographer who has worked for *Grazia*, *Elle*, *Vogue*, *i-D* and *Style.com* on the editorial side, as well as Burberry, Hussein Chalayan and Banana Republic on the commercial side, says there are three levels of job for a photographer.

'There's editorial that gives you complete creative freedom, but usually will have no budget', Phill says.

> Editorial from a more commercial fashion magazine that will commission you to shoot something the way they want it to be shot, but will usually have a budget where you can make some money.
>
> And finally a commercial job that will completely dictate the look and style of the shoot, and you are being hired because you hopefully can deliver what they need, but the rates are usually a lot higher.

(2013)

Up-and-coming photographers might offer to work for free for a local magazine or newspaper to showcase their talents and add to their portfolio.

Hair stylists and make-up artists might work for a salon or be sponsored by a hair product or cosmetic company, in which case their services are in exchange for a credit in the publication.

Locally, too, a hair salon is often willing to style models' hair for a shoot in exchange for a mention in the publication.

A photographer on a local shoot will send extra pictures to models, hair salons and make-up artists afterwards so they can use them for their own publicity.

Props

Props and accessories can make or break a shoot, so they're worth thinking about before the day.

Flowers can be a good prop, a nautical theme might require yellow sailing gear or ropes, glasses, hats or scarves can change a look, and you might even want to bring animals or bystanders into a shoot.

Jo Dingemans, in her book *Mastering Fashion Styling* (1999), advises students to become familiar with specialist dancing, hunting, army surplus, joke, craft and bike shops in their local area as a good source of props.

You can also bring things of your own to insert into a shoot. Carine Roitfeld is especially fond of using weird and wonderful things, including at one point a neck brace she was wearing after an accident. 'I often pull in something from my personal wardrobe, something that is "decalé" – totally off with the rest of the look,' she writes (2011: 286).

At the shoot

However well organised you are, a number of things can go wrong on the day or week of a shoot.

The weather can turn, clothes can go missing, get damaged or not fit, and the model can fall ill or break out in spots.

That's why stylists have to be full of invention and initiative, capable of getting things back on track and encouraging the team.

Most carry with them a bag of tricks designed to deal with minor disasters, at least. These include any of the following:

- masking tape to protect the soles of shoes, especially if they've been borrowed from a store;
- a pair of standby shoes, or boots for the model to walk in before the shot;
- bin bags, to roll up underneath a model if she has to sit or lean against something;
- a sewing kit for quick fixes, including safety pins, pins, scissors and needle and thread (though for a big publication, there may be a seamstress on hand);
- bulldog clips in case clothes are too loose;

- double-sided tape;
- spare jewellery, scarves and shawls;
- underwear, like nude thongs, nude bras and pasties (nipple covers);
- tights and socks;
- a lint roller;
- insoles;
- robe and slippers for model;
- tampons and plasters;
- shoe polish and stain remover.

If shooting on location, or a studio without facilities, they also need an iron.

Sorting out the clothes is one of the first priorities on a shoot, and this will be the job of the assistant if there is one. Ideally the clothes will be unpacked immediately, ironed and hung up on rails. They can be organised into the various looks, and also into different sections according to which brands/stores they come from to avoid contravening full-look policies.

At the same time, the models should be getting their hair and make-up done. This can be time-consuming and should never be underestimated.

Who directs a shoot – the photographer or the fashion editor – will vary according to the personalities involved. *Vogue*'s Hamish Bowles describes it as a 'subtle dance' between the two (in MacSweeney, 2012: 8).

Fashion photographer Phill Taylor says:

> Personally, it is a collaboration between the photographer, stylist, hair and make-up artists or even an art director or picture director. I will lead the way photographically and take charge of how we are approaching the story … but a good stylist is somebody who sees the creative vision and helps create a character out of the clothes.

Whatever the approach of the photographer, it's up to the stylist to focus on the clothes and whether they look right. Attention to detail is crucial.

'You've got to look for stray threads, powder on the shoulders, whether a skirt is rumpled, whether you need to pull a dress down, whether the sticker is showing on some shoes, and whether the hair is right. It's ultimately your responsibility,' says Liz Lamb.

The stylist should look after the model between shots, wrapping a robe or blanket round her to keep warm if needed. If it's an inexperienced model, the stylist might also have to give suggestions for poses and try to make her relax (some find that playing music helps). If you are doing your own test or student project, make sure you get a variety of strong poses, as well as a mix of facial expressions.

Sometimes inspiration will strike during a shoot, and the stylist will add a little detail or twist to transform a look – a belt round a coat, a rip in a T-shirt, even an odd gesture.

In *Irreverent*, Carine Roitfeld describes how she comes up with last-minute tweaks by instinct. It might be a way of hanging a Chanel bag round a model's neck ('all of a sudden, the chain strap becomes a punk S&M accessory' – 2011: 137), or it might be asking the model to fiddle with her hair or pull at her T-shirt ('all these delicate things are difficult for many male photographers to see' – ibid.: 178).

Sometimes, fashion editors might have to use their inventiveness for getting out of a hole. Elizabeth Walker recalls setting up a studio on a hotel rooftop in Monte Carlo, when it wouldn't stop raining, so they could have natural light while staying under cover.

Another time, she was on an island covered in gorse, which clashed with the colours of the new-season collections she was shooting. She had the bright idea of dying lots of backdrops like theatre canvas. 'You could see you were outside, and you could see the sky, but there was a shocking pink backdrop behind the green dress, and so on', she says.

But they can't forget the bureaucracy. During the shoot, the stylist or assistant should take notes of what's been used on each model, top to toe, for each look – the make, where it's from, the price if known. This information will be necessary for the captions.

At the end of the shoot, the stylist should check that nobody is still wearing any garments or accessories. Clothes should be hung on the correct rails and accessories wrapped, and all should be checked against the delivery note or docket to ensure nothing has gone missing.

The clothes will either go back to the publication's fashion cupboard, where interns will check for damage, organise dry cleaning if needed, mark them all up on return slips and send them to the PRs.

Or a stylist working on her own will return them directly to stores, making sure the PR or manager signs the docket to confirm that all the pieces have been returned in satisfactory condition.

It's important to take care that nothing goes missing or gets damaged, because the stylist or publication could get invoiced and it might harm their chances of getting clothes from that store or brand in future.

But if the worst happens, you have to be honest with the PR and defuse the situation. 'Common sense and damage control are two very good skills to have,' says freelancer Madeleine Bowden. A publication generally has insurance to cover the cost of any damage.

Credits, captions and layout

If you have responsibility for providing the information for captions and credits, make sure it is correct and complete.

You may have to give credits to an airline, a hotel or other venue, a hair salon and a make-up artist, along with the photographer and models.

Double-check names and addresses. Type in website addresses and call telephone numbers to ensure they're correct. Make sure you spell the photographer and models' names right and get the title of their agency.

For hair and make-up artists, make sure you include any necessary detail like the name of their salon or the brand that sponsors them.

If the clothes were samples selected from a showroom, make sure you have the retail price, not the wholesale price.

The amount of detail in a caption varies according to a publication's house style, but it will normally include a brief description of the item ('silk panel dress'), the make and the price. If it's a high-street item, some publications include the sizes available. In some, the stockists are included in the caption; in others they'll be listed elsewhere in the magazine.

When a fashion story is published, it is accompanied by a headline and a sell, a short blurb at the start setting out the theme of the shoot.

If you are laying out a spread yourself, for a student newspaper, magazine or website or for your own portfolio, bear the following in mind:

- You can vary photographs between mono and colour, full body shots and cropped shots, double-page shots, two shots to a page or even a collage.
- Edit photographs on Photoshop or similar software first (see Chapter 10) to crop, erase distracting parts of the background, change exposure and sharpen. Make sure they are a high enough resolution for the medium you are using – 300 pixels per inch is necessary for print, while online it would be more like 72.
- Catch the eye with a strong headline based on the theme of the story. Fashion headlines often play on intertextuality, referring to a film, a song or a book, or use wordplay like alliteration and puns.
- The sell, often placed on the first right-hand page, should give a quick précis of the fashion story. It can directly address the reader, telling them what to do and why, and will outline simply and clearly the key look/ trend/aesthetic involved. It should be tightly angled – too many details or side-issues will confuse the reader.
- Credits for the photographer and fashion editor or stylist (often just referred to as 'fashion') generally go at the start of the story, with the other credits at the end.
- Decide on a style for your captions on each page, and stick to it rigidly. Don't ruin the story with misspellings and mistakes; however impressive the styling, poor copy will detract from a spread's credibility.

Commercial styling

Once they have built up their reputation, an editorial stylist might get hired for commercial jobs, which mostly pay much better.

When Grace Coddington was first hired to do freelance work for Calvin Klein, she was stunned to be flown to New York and back by Concorde and was even more surprised by the one-off payment. 'It was more than I made at *Vogue* in an entire year,' she writes (2012: 148).

At their most humble, commercial jobs involve styling for advertorials, lookbooks and catalogues. After that, there are advertising campaigns – handed over to a small group of freelancers rather than the huge ad agencies that other industries use – as well as catwalk styling and generally being a muse for a particular designer or fashion house.

Stylists also work on music videos, TV shows and dressing celebrities.

Freelancer Madeleine Bowden, who does editorial work for *Elle* and others, also assisted *X Factor* style director Laury Smith and was assistant stylist to *X Factor* judge Nicole Scherzinger. That involved dressing her and going with her to auditions and shows.

'It's your job as a stylist to know what a celebrity suits, know their body and their personal style, and then try to make it current and fashion-forward,' she says. 'You stick to what they like and what they suit, but perhaps take them to up-and-coming brands they've never looked at before. You've always got to think about how it might play in the press, too.'

It requires a far greater volume of clothes than editorial styling, Madeleine says, because a personality has opinions, insecurities and a style already. 'With editorial, a model has to wear anything you put them in. With a personality, you need options because you might have 100 dresses and they don't like any of them.'

Although this kind of styling is more anonymous – Rachel Zoe and Nicola Formichetti apart – it's still very satisfying, she says.

It was Madeleine who picked out a deep maroon-purple Hervé Léger dress for Nicole Scherzinger to wear to her first *X Factor* auditions of 2013. It received a huge amount of newspaper attention, and Madeleine says: 'Nobody will ever know it's me, but I knew!'

The crossover between editorial and commercial work that is so prevalent in the fashion industry – editors also consult for brands, write for customer magazines and move between PR and journalism – is highlighted by some academic commentators as an issue for concern.

Angela McRobbie describes the fashion industry as 'an enclosed, culturally anxious and virtually self-regulating world where notions of objectivity and impartiality do not have the same impact as they do elsewhere in journalism' (1998: 168).

But fashion journalists say they are capable of keeping the two worlds – commerce and editorial – apart. *Marie Claire*'s Elizabeth Walker says: 'If you did the Prada ads and every picture you did was a Prada picture, you'd soon lose your job. You have to think separately.'

Shoots for online

At the time of writing (2013), fashion shoots were still finding a place online.

Initially, websites tended not to attempt their own shoots. Tracey Lea Sayer worked for handbag.com before joining *Fabulous* in 2008, and says: 'It was thought people wouldn't look at that kind of thing online, and that it was a bit of a luxury. Instead, it was a lot of galleries and cut-out images.'

By 2013, though, she reckoned things were changing, with tablet versions of magazines and apps acclimatising audiences to seeing digital versions of shoots.

When website *Never Underdressed* launched in 2013, it commissioned its own art-directed shoots, a mix of stills and video, as part of its attempt to reproduce the luxury experience of a glossy online.

'Visuals can come across incredibly well digitally, and not many people have figured out what to do yet,' says *Never Underdressed* news editor Harriet Walker.

'I guess SHOWstudio is a good example of that. We're trying to do something similar in terms of fleshing out what you can do with shoots, videos and gifs.'

SHOWstudio, the website set up by photographer Nick Knight in 2000, was still something of an aberration 13 years later, with no real competitors.

What the Web was still mostly associated with, shoot-wise, was street style, thanks to highly successful blogs devoted to the subject as well as popular photo-sharing sites.

According to some, street-style blogs have changed the visual codes of fashion and have influenced the way even glossy magazines shoot.

'Something about really posed, studio stuff looks very 1985,' says Fiona McIntosh, former editor of *Elle* and now a consultant. 'Street style looks so fresh and real' (2012).

When Fiona worked with My-wardrobe.com, she wanted more of a directional look to the site, to match its strapline 'everyday luxury', and she instigated a shoot with one young photographer, a stylist and a model.

> We set them up in a doorway in Camden, waited for the sun to come out and snapped them street style.
> That seemed to get that modern, sharp look to it – incidental, casual, like she's a woman who's going somewhere; she's out there looking great in clothes you can actually wear, not ones you hang in the back of your wardrobe.

Issues in fashion shoots

One of the most contentious issues surrounding fashion magazines in particular is lack of diversity in models – both in terms of body shape and ethnicity – and the amount of post-production work, i.e. airbrushing, that goes on before the photos are published.

So standardised has the perfect body shape for high fashion become that British model Jourdan Dunn said in July 2013 that she'd been dropped from Christian Dior's haute couture show because of her chest size (she's a 32, according to her agency).

Worse still, she tweeted: 'I'm normally told I'm cancelled because I'm "coloured" so being cancelled because of my boobs is minor' (1 July 2013).

The news was reported without comment, if at all, on magazine websites; see, for example, *Vogue*'s report at www.vogue.co.uk/news/2013/07/02/jour-dan-dunn-cancelled-from-dior-couture-show. Newspapers were a little more pointed, recalling that Dior's casting had previously been criticised for being predominantly white.

It's a serious issue, because campaigners believe the lack of diversity in fashion has a big impact on how audiences, particularly young people, perceive themselves.

On the question of size, the use of very thin models in fashion editorial and advertising holds up an unrealistic ideal, which leads to skewed body image for some readers and possibly bullying, depression and eating disorders, they say.

In response, the UK parliament set up an all-party inquiry into body image in May 2011. Its report, *Reflections on Body Image* (2012), concluded that dissatisfaction was on the rise, that 75 per cent of people blamed media, advertising and celebrity culture for this, and that the ideal body portrayed in media and advertising could only ever be achieved by 5 per cent of the population.

Fashion magazines and models weren't the only targets for criticism. Gossip magazines were also picked out for 'circle of shame' type stories negatively highlighting celebrities' body flaws and fashion mistakes.

Caryn Franklin, who helped set up the All Walks Beyond the Catwalk initiative (www.allwalks.org) to promote diversity in fashion, worked with the all-party inquiry.

She says that before the *The Clothes Show* started showing fashion weeks on BBC TV (1986–98), nobody much knew what catwalk models looked like.

'As a result, I grew up really unaware and unconcerned about a body ideal – this catwalk body. It wasn't until I worked in the industry that I began to see this uniform body, but now, six- or seven-year-olds see that all the time,' she says (2013).

'My daughters are bombarded with images of what it is to look good, as defined by a very powerful fashion media, and a celebrity media that takes all its pointers from the fashion industry.'

What also worries her about the fashion media, she says, are the self-appointed juries judging other women on their appearance and the handing down of 'rules' on how to look good.

> Growing up [in the 1970s and 1980s], I never questioned, 'Am I good enough? What do I have to change about myself to be good enough?' I see that all the time in young women now.
>
> Very few women get a sense that clothes are there to serve them. In fact, it often feels the other way round, that they're there to serve fashion and that fashion can tell them whether they've done it well enough.

Editors find the diversity issue difficult to address in some ways. They point to what they are doing, but say they're powerless to do more. They argue that readers claim they want diversity, but then desert the magazine in droves when they get it. And they sometimes fall back on the argument that people want to see unrealistic images, anyway.

British *Vogue* editor Alexandra Shulman has written to designers several times (as we saw in Chapter 4) complaining that sample sizes used by all the magazines in their fashion shoots are now so small that the models have to be really thin to fit them.

She has also spearheaded a Health Initiative with other *Vogue* editors whereby they don't use models under 16 or with eating disorders, and she has helped develop an educational video showing all the digital enhancement that goes on after a shoot to send out to senior schools in the UK (*BBC News*, 2013b).

But that's as far as it goes, she says. 'I don't want to pretend we are going to try to change the way we portray fashion,' she told BBC Radio 4's *PM* programme.

'Our mission in *Vogue*'s fashion pictures is to inspire and entertain while showing the clothes created by many highly talented designers. They are created with this intention in mind, not to represent reality.'

Shulman has also said that the *Vogue* cover featuring Adele, a size 16 singer, was 'one of the worst sellers we've ever had' (in Roberts, 2013).

Company editor Victoria White says her magazine uses lots of street style as well as readers modelling trends in every issue. 'Without being tokenistic, it leads to a broad mix without even doing anything,' she says.

But she does notice a lack of applications to take part from anyone over a size 14. 'People self-censor; we don't actively exclude them, but they don't put themselves forward,' she says.

Some fashion editors get impatient at the idea that magazines can brainwash people into thinking they have to look a certain way. Magazines are there to provide fantasy and escapism and we wouldn't have it any other way, they insist.

Elizabeth Walker, former executive fashion editor of *Marie Claire*, is blunt on the issue of size:

> Why would you want to see somebody not very attractive? Fashion is all about aspiration.
>
> In real terms, you know you're not going to look like Liz Hurley in that frock because you're only 5ft3 and you're a typical English pear shape, but you aspire to things.

Melanie Rickey, contributing editor at *Grazia*, says: 'It's no accident that fashion magazines are full of beautiful images, because we want them! The bottom line is you pick up a magazine because you want to look at pretty things.'

The issue of race and skin colour gets less coverage but the problem is every bit as acute.

When Prada used Malaika Firth for its autumn–winter 2013 advertising campaign, it was the first time it had cast a black model since 1994. The company, regarded as progressive in other ways, did not use any black models in its catwalk shows between 1993 (Naomi Campbell) and Jourdan Dunn in 2008.

Magazines aren't much better. Look at the archive of British *Vogue* covers on its website, and count up the number of black cover stars. In ten years, or 120 issues, from 2003 to 2013, there were three: Beyonce in May 2013, Rihanna in November 2011, and Jourdan Dunn (alongside two white models) in November 2008. Before that, you have to go back to August 2002 when Naomi Campbell last featured on the cover.

There was a brief flurry of discussion about race and fashion in August 2008 when Italian *Vogue* produced a 'black issue' that sold out so quickly it had to be reprinted. Fashion critic Sarah Mower described it as a 'a long overdue wake-up call for an industry whose precarious future will rely on reaching global markets that do not resemble the freakish army of half-starved six-foot white girls who have come to represent the Western ideal' (2008).

It perhaps explains why Jourdan Dunn appeared on both *Vogue*'s cover and Prada's catwalk that same year.

But after that, not much changed. In February 2013, black models accounted for only 6 per cent of the looks in New York Fashion Week, down from 8 per cent in 2012 (Wilson, 2013).

Somalian-born model Iman called for a boycott of fashion brands that didn't use black models, and the UK's Naomi Campbell said models faced greater discrimination than they did when she started working 27 years previously (*Channel 4 News*, 2013). 'The act of not choosing models of colour is racist,' she said.

The largely unspoken fear behind putting black models or stars on catwalks and magazine covers is that customers won't identify with them and it will have a negative effect on sales.

A fashion journalist quoted anonymously by Tungate says:

> When you put a model on the cover of a magazine, you're promoting cosmetics as well as clothes. And if most of your readers are white, they want to identify with that image. The black community has its own magazines.
>
> (2012: 102)

This not only smacks of racism, it is also damaging to young people's self-image, just like images of very thin models are. Veronica Webb, the first black model to get a contract with Revlon, said: 'This is where a lot of young women get their idea of beauty from. When you see someone that looks like you it makes women feel beautiful, and it makes women feel they belong' (in Wilson, 2013).

Recommended reading

All Walks Beyond the Catwalk: www.allwalks.org.
Coddington, G. (2012) *Grace: A Memoir*. London: Chatto & Windus.
Cutler, R.J. (dir.) (2009) *The September Issue*.
Dingemans, J. (1999) *Mastering Fashion Styling*. London: Palgrave Macmillan.
MacSweeney, E. (ed.) (2012) *Vogue: The Editor's Eye*. New York: Abrams.
Mower, S. (2007) *Stylist: The Interpreters of Fashion*. New York: Rizzoli.
Roitfeld, C. (2011) *Irreverent*. New York: Rizzoli.

10 Photography and video for online

Introduction

Even though fashion journalism has always relied on fantastic imagery, its writers and photographers were two very separate breeds.

While the journalists concentrated on the words, or the styling, the photographers took the shots using expensive kit and highly technical skills.

Digital media changed that, to some extent. The instant demands of the Web, the influence of bloggers and the popularity of street style mean that even journalists have to get in on the act.

A fashion editor at the shows might take pictures of front-row celebrities, their own outfits and anything else that catches their eye. Some will go straight on their publication's social media accounts and live blog, and others they will Photoshop and upload to the website later with their show report.

They will also take pictures of the looks as they come down the catwalk, again for a live blog and social media, and they may film short video clips using the likes of Vine or Instagram Video.

Of course, photographers are still highly-regarded creatives who bring their own brand of magic to fashion through shoots, celebrity covers and catwalk images. A fashion editor is not going to challenge them on that score.

But SLR cameras, smartphones, tablets, apps and editing software mean that they are capable of taking a decent image or video that is good enough for the Web.

More than good enough, in fact: *New York Times* photographer Damon Winter won a Picture of the Year International Award in 2012 using the Hipstamatic app on his iPhone. They were war pictures ('A Grunt's Life', of US soldiers in Afghanistan), but the film-like effects afforded by Hipstamatic's filters and the fact that he could go about his job practically unnoticed are a boon to any kind of photography.

Social media channels, too, have opened up the world of photography. Big names in fashion photography like Mert Alas and Inez van Lamsweerde are on Instagram, while up-and-coming photographers can promote their work there, build up a following and get commissions on the back of it.

Figure 10.1 Phill Taylor picture of Kellydeene Skerritt (Phill Taylor, www.philltaylor.com)

Van Lamsweerde said: 'I'm excited by the fact that social media like Instagram and Tumblr have enabled everyone to be a photographer, and made photography the number one communicator in the world' (*Nowness*, 2013).

This chapter will look at basic photography for the Web. It focuses particularly on street style, which is an easy and effective way for would-be journalists and bloggers to hone their skills and, at the same time, get used to approaching strangers and extracting information from them.

It will also discuss video, which is becoming increasingly important for bloggers, online publications and fashion brands as a way to get themselves noticed and shared online.

'Try to get all these skills going, even if you find them difficult,' advises *Grazia* fashion editor Hannah Almassi. 'Do a personal style blog, take photos of your friends, get used to it so your camera skills improve, because you never know what you're going to get thrown into' (2012b).

Kit

As a young journalist, Luke Leitch, deputy fashion editor at the *Daily Telegraph*, was told always to carry some sort of camera with him in case something happened.

It paid off when he was on his way to a masked ball thrown by Dolce & Gabbana in Venice, and happened to catch a water taxi with Japanese *Vogue*'s Anna Dello Russo.

Flamboyant as always, she was wearing a large model of a sailing ship as a hat. When the taxi went under a low bridge, she suddenly had to squat to avoid it being crushed, and Luke caught it all on his Samsung phone/camera hybrid. The pictures subsequently appeared in the *Telegraph* under the headline 'Anna Dello Russo's menace in Venice' (Leitch, 2013b).

Phil Cullen, freelance photographer and media photography lecturer at the University of Sunderland, says: 'The best camera in the world is the one you happen to have with you – and most of the time, that's your phone' (2013).

Phil says that, under ideal conditions, phones from the iPhone 5 onwards can take pictures that are good enough for publication on the web. Filters on the likes of Instagram and Hipstamatic can improve photographs.

But for pictures aimed at magazines, or those taken in low light, phone cameras are not ideal. 'If you were at a catwalk show or indoor presentation, it would be a non-starter,' he says.

'It's all about knowing the limitations of your kit; what you want to do with it is the main factor in deciding what you're going to use.' He recommends trying out any camera indoors using an ordinary light bulb and working out how you can modify the camera to cope.

The next step up from a camera phone is what he calls a 'prosumer' camera, a cross between a professional and a consumer camera, like a Canon Powershot G15 or a Canon DSLR like Sasha Wilkins uses for her LibertyLondonGirl blog. They are small enough to fit in your bag, but give you control over things like light settings to improve your pictures.

Any camera is improved by holding it properly, Phil adds.

I see a lot of people just using the screen on the back of the camera to take shots, which isn't very steady. You should put your camera to your eye and prop your elbows against your body to lessen shake.

Street style

Street style has long been a feature of fashion journalism. One of its most famous photographers, Bill Cunningham, was taking pictures for the *New York Times* from 1978 onwards. (See the documentary *Bill Cunningham, New York* from 2010 (dir: Richard Press), for a fascinating look at how he works.)

Style magazines in the UK in the 1980s celebrated the genre, but the mainstream glossies remained more interested in photographing models and celebrities than people in the street.

The Internet, however, and blogs in particular, proved a perfect medium for street style and personal style. It was a fashion genre that did not need

Figure 10.2 Phill Taylor picture of Elena Perminova (Phill Taylor, www.philltaylor.com)

insider access, there was unlimited space for photographs, and there was a potentially global audience for the results.

Scott Schuman, who began the Sartorialist blog in 2005, describes street style on the Internet as a 'digital park bench'.

'Before you were limited to the people you could see right there at your park. Now you can go on the internet and look at blogs, and the whole world's open to you' (Intel, 2011).

He says he loves street style because he can focus on the details that make up style – posture, attitude, colour combinations, the way a character shines through – rather than brands. 'It's not that I want to dress like an 80-year-old Milanese or Harlem guy, but it's the fact that they can carry themselves with such elegance which is very inspiring' (Big Think, 2012).

Not only did the glossies introduce street-style pictures to their own websites on the back of their popularity, they are also reproducing the aesthetic in their fashion spreads, too.

Phill Taylor (www.philltaylor.com), a fashion photographer whose street-style work has appeared in *Grazia*, *i-D*, *Elle*, *Vogue*, *W Magazine* and *Style.com*, says:

> Due to the popularity of this genre of photography, the art directors have sought to cash in on the aesthetic.
>
> When we look at what street style actually is, you can see how it can be manipulated to encourage the reader to buy the fashion that the editorials are promoting. When a viewer looks at an image, captured 'street

style', they believe that the person is essentially like them; therefore they, too, could look like that person if they followed the tips of their style.

It is perhaps a lot more powerful than a fashion image of an alternative world only inhabited by the visually perfect models, which lends itself more to aspiration than reality.

(2013)

Brands, too, hope this magic will rub off them. They have hired street-style photographers to shoot their advertising campaigns, including Tommy Ton of the JakandJil blog for Lane Crawford in spring 2009 and Scott Schuman's Art of the Trench campaign for Burberry (artofthetrench.burberry.com).

Choosing your subject

Street-style pages or blogs can be as general – anyone who catches your eye on the streets of your city – or as specific as you like. For example, photographer Pardeep Singh Bahra set up a blog dedicated to Sikh street style (www.singhstreetstyle.com), while What Ali Wore (http://alioutfit.tumblr.com/) chronicles the outfits of one 83-year-old Turkish man in Berlin.

As a junior on *Grazia*, Hannah Almassi used to go out with photographer Phill Taylor to get the right mix of subjects for the magazine's Style Hunter pages. She had to match the *Grazia* blend of high fashion and high street, and its cross-section of ages, so she didn't just go for East London trendsetters but also perhaps someone from Sloane Square, a young girl in central London following high-street trends, and a well-put-together 40-year-old in Bond Street.

'I'm looking for smartness – that feeling that the outfit is well thought out without being slaved over for hours,' she said at the time (2010).

Phill Taylor, who has since taken street-style photographs all over the world, says he has two main approaches to selecting a subject: either the 'style queens' who stand out because they look different, or people he's documenting as part of a familiar scene unfolding in front of him.

He has learned the names of the street-style stars – the fashion editors, off-duty models, fledgling designers and high-society women – from photographing them over the years, though he says photographers at shows often help each other out with names if they need it.

If you're doing a street-style page or blog of your own, know what kind of thing you're looking for before you go out, and focus on that. Scott Schuman, for example, says he will only see two or three images he wants to shoot each day, so he has learned to be patient and wait (Intel, 2011).

That's fine for a blogger, but would be a luxury too far for someone working for a weekly publication. When she went out on the street-style pages, Hannah Almassi said: 'I have to go and find ten really great people each week without fail. I go out whatever the weather and keep going until I find them – I'll do it on the weekend if I have to.'

Approaching a subject

Selecting a subject is only half the battle; next you have to persuade them to stop for you.

Photographers and journalists develop a sense for who is likely to be willing, and who is not. Anybody who looks in a hurry probably won't be, while people sitting, strolling or waiting at a bus stop might be more amenable.

In any case, be polite, ask them if they are willing, and always have an answer ready for when someone asks what it's for. Having some form of ID is useful.

Phill Taylor says:

> I always speak clearly and softly, and will quickly explain why I have stopped them, who I am and what I am photographing them for.
>
> In London, a lot of people think you are a charity worker when you approach them, so it's important to make sure they don't think that straight away.

Phil Cullen, photography lecturer, advises you to build a rapport quickly and put your subject at ease. 'If you converse with people while you're taking the picture and they interact with you, you'll get that unstudied moment when they're looking natural,' he says.

Framing your subject

You probably won't have much time to spend choosing the perfect background, so try to keep it simple, without unnecessary clutter. You might not want other people in the shot, and you certainly don't want trees or telegraph poles growing out of the back of your subject's head.

Sometimes, the architecture of the street can add to the image. Photographer Phill Taylor says: 'When taking candid shots, I feel that the surrounding background that you find them in can be as essential at telling the story as the clothes themselves.'

Study Scott Schuman's photos on the Sartorialist and see how he either sets his subjects against a fairly plain background or uses the perspective of the surrounding street, with his subject framed in the gap of the vanishing point of the buildings. He also has an excellent camera that allows him to blur out the background, so his subject stands out.

Media photography lecturer Phil Cullen adds: 'You can always find a great location and wait for the right person to walk into it. That gives you the advantage of deciding exactly where in the frame you want them to be.'

A general maxim of photography is to use the 'rule of thirds' to compose your picture – dividing your photo into thirds horizontally and vertically (apps and camera phones will often do this for you), and positioning points of interest along the dividing lines or where they cross.

But this is less true of fashion photography where the subject is often fairly central. More important is to ensure you don't cut off your subject's feet, top of their heads and their hands.

Try not to stand too close to your subject, as the wide angle of view makes people look short and squat. Stand further back and use a longer focal length on your lens, or zoom, so the subject fills the frame. Get on the same level as them; if you're pointing down, they will look insignificant.

Think about the light, too. Sun directly overhead might give you a desired halo or silhouette effect, but could also give you problems with contrast and shadow. Sometimes, says Phil Cullen, it's best to move into shade if there's a strong midday sun.

'You're often best with a diffused light rather than direct light, and if you've mastered the flash unit on your camera you can put a bit of light into those shadows,' he says. You can also use a reflector to bounce light into the picture; you can buy them, or use things like a newspaper, polystyrene tile or big sheet of card (white, gold or silver depending on the warmth of the tone you want.)

Whether you should pose your subject is a tricky question. 'It's bad to have people standing there like they're about to be shot,' says Phil Cullen. 'But when you pose people, you tend to end up with two stock expressions, either the cheesy grin or the sultry pout.'

If you have time, you might ask them to walk through the frame, sit down or look over their shoulder at you. Put them at their ease, in the hope of catching a natural, unstudied shot.

And don't just take one shot; if you have time, go for 10 or 12 so you have a good chance of getting a really good one. Detail shots are also interesting – a close-up of rings on fingers or a pocket scarf – as long as you've got a full-length shot as well.

Improving your work

Phil Cullen recommends looking at photographers' work and analysing it. What makes their pictures strong, and why don't yours look like that? 'If you can start answering that truthfully, then you're learning', he says.

This might mean looking at street photography of the past: Jacques Lartigue and Eugène Atget from the early twentieth century, say.

But it also means looking at blogs and magazines today, to see what's current and what's popular. A short video of the Sartorialist's Scott Schuman at work, together with his thoughts on what he does, can be seen at www. intel.com/content/www/us/en/visual-life/visual-life-sartorialist-video.html.

Other types of picture

'Selfies', or self-portraits, to show off an outfit are no longer confined to celebrities on Twitter or Instagram; they're now part and parcel of a lot of fashion journalism, which commentates on the process of covering shows and other events as well as reporting on the event itself.

So fashion editors and magazine editors post selfies on blogs, social media channels and their publication's website to show what they are wearing for, say, London Fashion Week.

Bloggers have long done this with their 'what I'm wearing today' type posts, and on the whole they do it much better.

The problem is that most journalists hold their phone out and take a picture of themselves, which means that the camera is not stable and is so close that it accentuates their nose.

If you have a timer on your camera, or a remote control, then use those to snap yourself from a distance. Try for a bigger space than a cramped bedroom, and in outdoor light rather than indoors.

Catwalk pictures are also very difficult to do well as a member of the audience, rather than the photographers' pit at the end of the runway. Again, unless you're in the front row, you'll be holding your phone, camera or tablet above your head, which won't give you a stable shot. Using a small camera with greater sensitivity, and trying to hold it closer to your body, would give better pictures.

It's normally dark, so using a flash is recommended. There's not much you can do about the movement of the models, unless you're seated near the end of the runway where they stop and pose briefly. Perhaps, though, fashion houses are taking this on board; at Holly Fulton's autumn–winter 2014 show, models posed against a giant cube in the middle of the runway before taking off down the catwalk, giving editors a few seconds to snap them.

Editing and saving your photographs

When you import your photos from your camera to your computer, make sure you tag them with keywords so you can search your files for them afterwards.

Adobe Bridge is useful software because you can rename your pictures as you import them and add data which will travel with them, like the name of the model, what they're wearing or the location. It's also a good way of archiving pictures and giving them a star rating.

But you can also import photos with the likes of Apple's iPhoto or the disk that came with your camera. If you're using the Instagram app, its blog (http://blog.instagram.com) has useful tips for hashtags.

For editing, being adept at Adobe Photoshop is an extremely useful skill to have. If you can't take a course in it at school, college or university, there are books like *Adobe Photoshop for Photographers* (Evening, 2012) as well as video tutorials on www.adobe.com and www.lynda.com.

When you open a photograph in Photoshop, you can crop it but make sure you have enough pixels (the tiny dots that make up a digital image) left for sufficient resolution.

For print publishing, a photograph should have 300 pixels per inch but for the web, 72 pixels per inch is adequate (check this under 'image size'). Most monitors are 1024 pixels wide, so if your photograph is that large it will fill the screen.

Most images need sharpening in Photoshop – though the tools can't fix a blurry picture – and you can blur the background using blur filters or erase unwanted detail with the clone stamp. You can also alter colour and light saturation, and add effects from the filters menu, though this needs care and practice. Less is generally more, when it comes to special effects.

If you don't have Photoshop, there is free open-source editing software called Gimp, which can be downloaded for PCs and Macs (www.gimp.org).

Photo-sharing site Flickr is a good way of building up a repository of photographs, as is the micro-blogging site Tumblr. Phil Cullen adds: 'Google+ is another really good resource for photographers – you can upload batches of pictures and selectively release them to whichever circle you want.'

He recommends that you are selective with which photos you share or post to a blog, keeping your mistakes to yourself. 'Even if you've only got awful pictures of the one subject, chalk it down to experience rather than publish an out-of-focus shot,' he says.

Fashion video

Fashion photographer Nick Knight is a pioneer of video, launching his web-site SHOWstudio (tagline 'the home of fashion film') in 2001 and proclaiming that print publications were on their way out.

'We're in a transition period that's almost akin to when painting went to photograph,' he said (in Jones and Enninful, 2010: 39–40). 'The best way of showing fashion is through a moving image rather than a still image.'

Certainly, video has found a natural home on the Web, where it is much easier and cheaper to disseminate than in cinemas or on television.

In 2012, video accounted for 57 per cent of all Internet consumer traffic, and this figure was expected to rise to 69 per cent by 2017, according to computer networking giant Cisco (2013).

Because of that, and because of the success of video-sharing site YouTube, bloggers began focusing their efforts on video, even to the extent of neglecting their written blogs.

It's also why Vice Media Group bought style magazine *i-D* in 2012. Andrew Creighton, president of Vice, said: 'We know digital, *i-D* knows style, and together we're going to give the world the gift of eye-catching, mind-blowing video-driven fashion content' (in Banham, 2012).

The Sartorialist's Scott Schuman signed up for a 12-part video series with AOL, and said he was excited by the new format: 'It helps me tell the story in a different way … there's a deeper story that, with video, I would go do' (in Sebra, 2013).

Grazia had already teamed up with YouTube fashion channel Fashtag (www.youtube.com/user/Fashtag), producing tutorials, trend reports, celebrity interviews and product reports in video format.

Video versions of fashion shoots were rarer, but could be found on *Never Underdressed* – one of the ways it tried to stand out from other websites – as well as Dazed Digital and Test, an experimental site set up by Jaime Perlman, UK *Vogue*'s art director.

'Almost every photographer I know feels pressure to master film and video right now, and they're keen to make a reel,' Perlman has said (in Kansara, 2010a). 'Advertising agencies don't want to hire photographers anymore, they want to hire photographers who can also direct.'

Commercial work pays far more than editorial shoots, so photographers are spurred on to master video by the enthusiasm of fashion brands for short films.

For brands, these videos are a little piece of editorial that they can send out to magazine websites, blogs and social media channels in the hope they will be shared, get the brand talked about and widen their fan base.

While some are linked to straightforward ad campaigns – see Lanvin's autumn–winter 2011 video with models dancing to Pitbull – others are more of a brand-building exercise. LVMH's award-winning website Nowness (www. nowness.com), for example, is primarily an editorial site with no e-commerce that links with other fashion brands.

Designers have also experimented with fashion film in place of catwalk shows. Gareth Pugh screened a film by Ruth Hogben for his autumn–winter 2009 presentation in Paris, for example.

One of the most popular forms of fashion video, for brands or magazines, is the behind-the-scenes action on a shoot or a show.

'You now regularly have a behind-the-scenes documentary team on a shoot, and even as the photographer find yourself being filmed as part of the story,' says photographer Phill Taylor.

While he accepts this is part of the democratisation of fashion wrought by the Web ('The readers or customers are not just satisfied with seeing the final outcome of a shoot; they are wanting to see the world behind it too.'), he also worries about the unintended effects of shining the spotlight on professionals.

'A beautiful journalist, photographer or just anybody working behind the scenes will without a doubt have a better chance of being successful and famous than somebody less attractive but equally talented,' he says.

Despite all of this, fashion video hasn't caught on as quickly as many expected when SHOWstudio launched in 2000. In his book *Fashion Branding*, Mark Tungate said brands were 'simply shooting moving fashion spreads using the same photographers they'd always used' (2012: 175).

Phill Taylor, who creates video as well as photography and used to work for SHOWstudio's Nick Knight, says: 'I really did feel that fashion film was the future. However, it certainly hasn't blown up the way I thought it would have done.'

Obstacles include the high price of creating video, compared to stills, and the lengthy editing time involved.

It's also an aesthetic issue, he believes:

> The impact of a still image is very hard to recreate in a fashion film, and this is why a lot of fashion film can sometimes be very boring and pointless.
>
> This being said, though, in the right hands, with the right budget and the right time put into the editing, some of the fashion films out there are truly amazing.

An often-cited example is *Insensate*, a film of Gareth Pugh's autumn–winter 2008 collection made by Nick Knight and Ruth Hogben to accompany a *Dazed & Confused* cover shoot. The film, however, took three months to create (Kansara, 2009).

Another obstacle slowing down fashion film is the difficulty of making it shoppable. While it's easy to attach hyperlinks to images for audiences to click through, it's more cumbersome to achieve with video.

Aaron Christian, video style editor for Mr Porter, says:

> I'm still on the fence about this. If someone wants to watch a video, do they want to be interrupted to shop? I think if you're watching a film or video, you want to be absorbed by it and watch it from start to finish.
>
> It's more of a brand exercise; it's attaching yourself to a story and selling a lifestyle.

> (2013)

At Mr Porter, Aaron says, his videos are a balance of selling product and educating the audience:

> We do interviews with experts and people behind brands. One story I pitched at the start, which has sent me to 14 countries in the last year, is to go to the factories of brands that we stock and show how products are made.

Aaron also goes to fashion weeks, but instead of filming the shows, he films a video version of street style. 'That's worked well because you get to see the movement of the clothes and get to interview people as well.'

Tips for video

On big shoots with a large budget, professionals work with kit like RED cameras, which shoot video and stills. They have a crew for lighting and sound.

But when he's out doing more of a reporting job, Mr Porter video style editor Aaron Christian prefers to use a much lighter camera like a Canon EOS 5D. 'It's more about being mobile and being able to shoot off the cuff,' he says.

For high-quality video, he recommends an SLR camera with perhaps a shoulder support rig for stability. While SLRs have an on-board mic, the sound quality will be better if you can have someone else there to record audio through a mic to a separate portable recorder.

He's also a fan of phone cameras, however. 'Instagram video works really well,' he says. 'It's so immediate – you can do a quick film, tag a brand, and it's done.'

More important than the kit, he says, is working out what you want to do and say with your video. 'Nowadays everyone is doing video, so take some time to figure out what your perspective is and what your voice is.'

He recommends finding a niche subject, or different angles and ways into stories. For social media, short videos that get to the point quickly and use comedy are especially effective.

Technically, you often learn by your mistakes. Aaron gives the following tips for those starting off with video:

- Test your kit at home before you go out. Always take two or three more batteries than you think you'll need, and take an extra SD card too.
- Audio often goes wrong, so double-check that before and during a shoot. 'I once had a mic plugged into a mini recorder for an assistant, but he pressed the wrong button!' Aaron said.
- It comes with experience, but try to edit as you shoot, rather than shoot everything. 'When you've got to cut a video for the next day, and you see 700 video clips, you despair,' he says. Think why you're choosing to shoot an image and what's different about it, and learn when not to shoot.
- Hold your shots for long enough: a couple of seconds makes it very difficult to edit. For street style, Aaron will hold a shot for 20 seconds.
- Experiment with shots. 'If you hold a shot, it's nice to get people to walk in and out of frame. So if I'm focusing on a pocket square, and they're talking and moving around, it looks good and it helps in the edit because I can cut at the point when they're turning, helping with the transition.'

Recommended reading

Concepcion, R. (2011) *Get Your Photography on the Web*. London: Peachpit Press.

Galer, M. (2008) *Digital Photography: Essential Skills*, 4th edition. London: Focal Press.

Individualism: www.individualism.co.uk.

Intel (2011) *Visual Life – The Sartorialist*. Available online at: www.intel.com/content/www/us/en/visual-life/visual-life-sartorialist-video.html.

Lynda.com (for tutorials): www.lynda.com.

Mr Porter's *The Journal*: www.mrporter.com/journal.

Press, R. (dir.) (2010) *Bill Cunningham, New York*. DVD release date 2012.

SHOWstudio: http://showstudio.com.

Schuman, S. (2012) *The Sartorialist: Closer*. London: Particular Books.

Taylor-Made (Phill Taylor's blog): www.philltaylormade.com.

Test: www.testmag.co.uk.

11 Fashion blogging and social media

Introduction

Fashion bloggers are part of the landscape now, but when they first emerged in the mid-2000s they were met with bafflement and some derision.

Designers were used to controlling visual coverage of their products by lending samples to fashion editors and suitable celebrities. They were not used to critical reviews, in magazines at least.

Then along came bloggers who could be anyone, could publish anything they wanted, and who couldn't be threatened by the withdrawal of advertising or access.

Susanna Lau, who launched her Style Bubble blog in 2006, described in 2009 how she'd been ordered by Pam Hogg's PR to take down a photo she'd taken of herself in a catsuit by the British designer because it was 'bad publicity'.

'I'm not the calibre of person Pam Hogg wants photographed in her catsuits,' a hurt Lau wrote (Lau, 2009).

Even when Dolce & Gabbana filled the front row of its spring–summer 2010 show with bloggers – considered a watershed moment in fashion and the Internet – some in the industry were unconvinced.

'It's all a bit mad, isn't it? I think it will die down though,' designer Christopher Kane told *Vogue*. 'No one who wants to read a serious review of a show is going to look at what a 14-year-old thinks' (in Milligan, 2009).

Contrary to Kane's expectations, it didn't die down. Fashion PRs saw the huge number of followers that bloggers commanded and decided they needed to care what 14-year-old Style Rookie blogger Tavi Gevinson thought, and others like her.

Bloggers were given tickets to fashion weeks, invited to launches and events, hired as 'brand ambassadors' and bombarded with products in the hope of favourable coverage.

The mainstream media, too, began to accept bloggers as style influencers, hiring them as street-style photographers, writing profiles on them and asking them to guest-edit collections.

But by 2013, there were signs that a backlash was on its way. Renowned journalist Suzy Menkes, writing in the *New York Times T Magazine* in February, lamented the fact that many bloggers took pride in accepting gifts and trips from fashion houses and thus could not call themselves serious critics.

'Judging fashion has become all about me: Look at me wearing the dress! Look at these shoes I have found! Look at me loving this outfit in 15 different images!' she wrote (Menkes, 2013).

Garage magazine followed up with a widely-discussed video called 'Take My Picture' (Zhukova and Ha, 2013). In it, *Style.com* critic Tim Blanks said the whole street-style phenomenon had gone too far. 'It makes monsters; it doesn't make gods,' he said. 'It's coarsened things.'

It reflected what some fashion and magazine editors had been saying privately: that bloggers had had their moment in the sun, there were too many of them, and they were no longer to be taken seriously.

Perhaps, though, the whole blogging versus journalism debate misses the point.

Bloggers are, like journalists, telling a story about fashion, but it's a different kind of story – not one based on technical knowledge or informed criticism, perhaps, but rather one where fashion meets real life.

In his book *Style Feed: The World's Top Fashion Blogs*, edited with Susanna Lau, William Oliver writes: 'They may offer different perspectives on fashion to the ones we are historically used to, but they highlight the excitement felt by real people who actually wear, or want to wear, the clothes featured' (2012: 14).

Whether or not journalists think this is valid, it's appealing to brands who want to harness that excitement and incorporate bloggers into their marketing strategy.

And, again regardless of what journalists think, a lot of young people are turning to blogs and social media ahead of print publications to get guidance and inspiration on fashion and beauty.

Chris Morton, chief executive of social curation site Lyst, told the *Business of Fashion* website: 'We believe the future of advertising is personal recommendation. People are much more likely to act on a recommendation than a broadcast message' (in Kansara, 2011a).

Knowing which way the wind was blowing, and keen to go where their audiences were, magazines and newspapers have worked hard on building up their presence online, on apps and on social media.

But is it enough? Take *Elle*, the prestigious fashion glossy, which describes itself as 'the most digitally innovative luxury fashion magazine in the UK market place today' (Hearst, 2013). In September 2013, it had 0.5 million Twitter followers, 200,000 Instagram followers and 3,325 YouTube subscribers, as well as over 850,000 Facebook likes.

Next, take Zoe Sugg, a 20-something fashion and beauty blogger from the UK (www.zoella.co.uk). She hadn't often been written about in the mainstream media, but she had more than 680,000 Twitter followers, almost a million Instagram followers and more than two million subscribers on YouTube.

At 235,000 Facebook likes, her page was a lot smaller than *Elle*'s, though her individual posts tended to get thousands of likes compared to *Elle*'s hundreds.

Nobody really knows what the future of fashion journalism will look like. But anybody hoping to break into the industry should be familiar with blogging and adept at social media, not least because it's vital for building up your portfolio and profile, and also because it is likely be a crucial part of any future role.

This chapter will explore the appeal of blogs to writers, brands and audiences and how they make money, if they do. It will also look at problems of ethics and transparency that swirl around blogging and were part of Menkes' attack.

Finally, it will explain how blogging and social media can be harnessed effectively – either to get a job, as tools once you're in a job, or to replace that job altogether.

The benefits of blogging

When asked what aspiring fashion journalists should do to break into the industry, many fashion and magazine editors cite blogging (after work placements).

Even if nobody looks at it much, keeping a blog is a good way to become familiar with content management systems, to hone your writing and to demonstrate passion and a point of view.

As editor of the *Sun on Sunday*'s *Fabulous* magazine, Rachel Richardson would always look at a job candidate's blog and social media sites. 'I could hire someone on the basis they had a brilliant blog that made me laugh, because I want someone who could write funny copy,' she said (2012).

Editors at *Company* and *Now* magazines say they have hired writers on the strength of their blogs (see Chapter 2). Peter Henderson believes his Hapsical blog (http://hapsical.blogspot.com), which featured in Oliver and Bubble's book, helped him get a job as fashion writer for an e-tailer at the age of 21.

'Everyone is at the point now where they realise how important online and social media is, but a lot of them are still unsure of how to go about it,' Peter says. 'If young people can offer that knowledge and awareness of what's going on online, that's to their advantage' (2013).

A blog is also a good way of building your own brand, be that as a way of getting new work or as an end in itself.

Aaron Christian is editor-in-chief of a collective men's style blog Individualism (www.individualism.co.uk) as well as video style editor for Mr Porter. He says Individualism has consciously branded itself as tongue-in-cheek, approachable and passionate.

'Now brands come to us for our voice,' he says. 'Companies are approaching bloggers that have their own personal brand, valued opinion and set audience that aligns with their own' (2013).

A well-known example of someone rebranding herself online is Anna Dello Russo, officially editor-at-large for *Vogue* Japan but much better known now for her blog (www.annadellorusso.com) and her ubiquity on street-style blogs.

She has said blogging has introduced her to a younger audience. 'It has made me feel less stiff, more approachable. It has led people to think about me differently and allowed me to get involved in many different projects' (in Oliver and Bubble, 2012: 47).

Finally, if you're really passionate about something and can convey that in a blog, it can spark opportunities you never dared dream about.

Peter Henderson was a big admirer of Belgian designer Raf Simons' menswear and wrote about it in his Hapsical blog. Simons saw the blog and invited Peter to an art festival he was curating in Berlin. 'To think that Raf Simons read my personal blog is crazy,' says Peter.

'But if you put something out there on the Internet and you're really passionate about it, I wouldn't underestimate the power of that.'

The appeal of blogs

Fashion blogs come in many shapes and sizes: personal style blogs, like the hugely successful Fashion Toast (www.fashiontoast.com); street style, like the Sartorialist (www.thesartorialist.com); photo-sharing sites like What I Wore Today (www.wiwt.com); reviews and recommendations blogs like Zoella (www.zoella.co.uk); and lifestyle blogs like LibertyLondonGirl (www.libertylondongirl.com).

Likewise, the people behind them can be anyone. Tavi Gevinson started Style Rookie in 2008 when she was 11, without her parents even knowing; for years people thought she was a spoof. Bryan Grey Yambao, the Filipino blogger Bryanboy, was a gushing fan before he was brought into the fashion industry's fold.

Others, like Sasha Wilkins of LibertyLondonGirl and Navaz Batliwalla of Disneyrollergirl, were already industry insiders who began blogging anonymously before outing themselves.

But there are certain qualities common to all blogs that give them a powerful appeal to audiences and brands. (Sometimes these qualities are more perceived than real – for example, when a blogger is paid to publish a brand's news release in the guise of a post – and that will be explored in the ethics section below.)

Freedom to comment ...

People who have worked, or do work, in the fashion industry and then start a blog say it's liberating to be able to write about what they want, how they want, without having to worry about commercial considerations.

Sasha Wilkins, who has worked as a senior magazine editor on both sides of the Atlantic, including five years at Condé Nast, says: 'On a magazine, you're always trammelled by the needs of advertisers. I love the freedom of blogging – I can write about young designers and first-time writers because I don't have to consider the advertisers' (2013b).

Peter Henderson, who doesn't accept freebies or have advertising on his site, says that the appeal of his blog Hapsical is the fact that it's 'very anti-brand'.

'There's a conflict of interest with my work where I have to like everything our brands and partners do. That's why I don't mention where I work on my blog, so I can say what I really think.'

Bloggers who do reviews of gifted products are more careful, and some say they just wouldn't write about a product that they didn't like (in the same way that magazine editors say their job is to highlight and showcase, not criticise).

But on the whole, they insist they are more transparent than traditional media. Most have disclaimers on their sites, and they flag up when a product or trip has been gifted.

Shannon Hodge, a student and one of the founders of the North East Bloggers network (http://twitter.com/NEbloggers), says: 'The thing about bloggers, especially the smaller ones, is we don't want people buying something that's not worth it, so we tend to do pros and cons in a review, to provide a balance' (2013).

... Which makes them seem authentic

Because blogs are perceived as honest, and because in most cases there's a name and a face and a voice behind them, they have an authentic quality that makes readers trust them and brands want to work with them.

'Authenticity and integrity is key,' says Sasha Wilkins of Liberty-LondonGirl. 'It took four years before my blog got any traction, meaning you have to blog because you love it.'

Shared snippets of a blogger's life beyond fashion or beauty – nights out, family gossip, favourite food – add to the sense of a personality behind the opinions or the outfit choices, and make readers warm to them more.

It's why so many bloggers end up posting pictures of themselves. Peter Henderson, of Hapsical, says: 'To really connect with readers you have to show something a bit more personal. Otherwise, you are trying to compete with big corporate sites and you can't do that as a blogger.'

And it's partly why bloggers are increasingly turning to video posts on YouTube. When vloggers sit in their bedrooms and test make-up or pull their latest fashion purchases out of a shopping bag, it recreates real-life experience and turns the blogger into something like a friend.

This is boosted by direct contact between blogs and their audiences. Individualism hosts party and club nights in London to meet its readers offline. 'Everyone from our team talks to people – being approachable is what we're about,' says editor-in-chief Aaron Christian.

The smaller bloggers pride themselves on responding to readers when they email or tweet a question, and they too have events where they meet offline.

Amy Fitzsimmons, co-founder with Shannon of the North East Bloggers network, says: 'A lot of bloggers have become really good friends rather than just online personas, and of course you're going to trust what a friend recommends you rather than a magazine that's selling to the masses' (2013).

… And audiences relate to them

A large part of the appeal of blogs is that audiences feel they can relate to them – more so than aspirational glossies.

This goes for the very biggest blogs, as well as the smallest. Scott Schuman, of the Sartorialist, says he knew his blog was taking off when:

> I got heartfelt emails from people saying they could look at my pictures and say, 'I look like this guy, I'm a little chubby like him, but he's dressed better and I want to look like that.'
>
> And they'd be able to achieve it because it's never in my blog about how expensive it is. It's just the attention to detail, and everyone can do that.
>
> (Big Think, 2012)

For school-age girls and students, posts written by similarly young, often budget-conscious bloggers can resonate with them more than a glossy magazine spread or shopping page.

'I trust a blogger's opinion more than a newspaper or magazine because they're down-to-earth people who I can relate to,' says Shannon Hodge, of the North East Bloggers network. 'Most are around my age and we all have a similar budget when it comes to products.'

Moreover, blogs can be very niche. There are successful blogs for older people, bigger people, cycling fashion, crafts, ethical fashion, weddings and even dogs, meaning audiences can zero in on someone whose looks, tastes, situation or lifestyle match their own.

A big-name example is Advanced Style (advancedstyle.blogspot.com), set up by freelance photographer and writer Ari Seth Cohen. 'I focus on men and women over 60, a demographic often ignored by the fashion media,' he says (2012: 115).

It might even be something as simple as a blogger who has the same colouring or skin type as you. 'Then I know the products they're using would more than likely work for me, and I'll go back to them again and again,' says Amy Fitzsimmons.

… So audiences are engaged

Rather like a strong magazine brand, a blogger's personality, opinions and taste can draw a reader into their world, creating a committed and engaged audience who will trust what they say.

This is a blogger's key asset, says Sasha Wilkins of LibertyLondonGirl. 'I peddle influence; I monetise influence,' she says.

She points to a 'VIP trunk show' she held at her home for fashion firm Boden, to which she invited 25 friends including models, actors, fashion editors and an Olympic athlete. She blogged about it, complete with lots of pictures of guests' children, her home, the food and flowers (2013a).

Boden made a video of the event and uploaded it online. 'The reader gets an insight into my world, without me selling out,' she says. 'It's for people who like my personal taste and viewpoint – they're a community.'

... Which gives blogs influence

Sasha says that the conversion rate for her readers who click through from her blog to retailers' websites – how many of them actually buy something, in other words – is as high as 20 per cent, compared to a normal rate of 5–10 per cent.

'My readers are very influenced by what I say, and my level of reader engagement is extraordinary,' she told *Retail Week* (Hardie, 2011).

The world's biggest blog directory, Technorati, said in its 2013 Digital Influence report that blogs were in the top three trusted sites when it comes to influencing purchases, beaten only by retail and brand sites.

And it was the same story at the luxury end of the market. A spokesman for Italian luxury foundation Altagamma told *Reuters*: 'Fashion bloggers are more and more powerful, especially in emerging markets like China' (in Ciancio, 2011).

... Which appeals to brands

For fashion brands, the opportunity to tap into the young, devoted, potentially global audience that a blog can draw is very appealing.

They do that in a number of direct ways (see below, *How bloggers make money*), but they use bloggers for branding purposes too.

High-profile bloggers design limited-edition ranges, model in campaigns, guest-blog, guest-edit and act as brand ambassadors for fashion designers and retailers.

What is especially appealing to a brand is that bloggers can create content – a key part of getting talked about online – *and* have their own communication channels to publish and share.

Aaron Christian's Individualism blog specialises in video, and has produced short films for the likes of Ted Baker, Hackett and Farah Vintage. He says:

> A lot of brands have realised the importance of their online presence and of creating their own editorial content to support e-commerce.
>
> They come to us for our voice, and because we have a team that can produce an editorial from start to finish. But we also have the audience to

push it out to people who want it. It's a kind of 360 – we can create the content and market it.

For big brands, it's a way of marketing without it looking like a hard sell. For younger brands, it's a cost-effective way of building a reputation online. Mick Dixon, a designer who works with both large and small brands, says: 'For someone not as established, it's more valuable to get peer review and word of mouth than to buy advertising. The network is the way to grow these days' (2013).

But it can go wrong if the brands aren't careful enough about which bloggers they align with, and Mick fears there is a backlash coming.

'Obviously the big brands have cottoned on to the fact that working with blogs could be a short-cut to getting some sort of credibility quite quickly. But consumers are so savvy now,' he says.

> You need a degree of social intelligence as a brand marketer or manager. A few years ago you could send your stuff out almost with the expectation that it would be featured; now, I don't think that's the case.
>
> And that shouldn't be your primary motive for doing it – it should be about engagement and discussion, getting feedback and honing your product accordingly.

In September 2013, there was a furious debate on Twitter about a Specsavers campaign, which sponsored a number of bloggers to write posts about and pose for pictures in a new range of glasses. The posts (which were flagged as paid-for) came out all at the same time and at least one of the bloggers cheerfully admitted she didn't even need glasses.

It's not only something that brands have to be careful of, but bloggers too. Aaron Christian says: 'If you don't keep a check on it, and you're always looking at the figures, you'll end up working with brands just for the money side of it and the audience will see that.'

Impact on journalism?

When blogs took off, there were some noisy debates about whether they, rather than journalists, were the future of fashion coverage.

An article in the *Independent* newspaper declared fashion blogging had lost its credibility, just one season after Dolce & Gabbana had installed bloggers in its front row (Mesure, 2010).

It quoted Robert Johnson, associate editor at *GQ*, as saying: 'Bloggers are so attractive to the big design houses because they are so wide-eyed and obsessed, but they don't have the critical faculties to know what's good and what's not.'

The following year, Italian *Vogue* editor Franca Sozzani compared bloggers to a virus. 'Do we need all these bloggers?' she asked. 'They don't offer an opinion but only talk about themselves, take their own pictures wearing absurd outfits. What's the point?' (Sozzani, 2011).

Bloggers responded angrily to the attacks, accusing the mainstream media of hypocrisy and short-sightedness (see, for example, the *Business of Fashion* piece 'What *The Independent* article didn't tell us' by Imran Amed on 3 February 2010).

And they found a high-profile champion in Lady Gaga, who used a column in *V* magazine to proclaim Tavi Gevinson's blog as the future of fashion journalism and accuse established critics of 'predictability' (in Murray, 2011).

It wasn't long, though, before bloggers and magazines, especially, began working together. Magazines hired blogging talent (like street-style photographer Phil Oh for US *Vogue*), introduced street-style and 'outfit of the day' features to their own websites, and used bloggers as the starting point of trend and style pieces.

Company magazine launched its Style Blogger Awards in 2012, with editor Victoria White declaring: 'We are harnessing and working with opinion makers and influencers online, not competing against them' (in Barber, 2012).

Emma Bigger, *Company*'s fashion editor, says bloggers are as important as celebrities for their readers. 'Also, bloggers say they use the magazine as their inspiration, so we coexist,' she adds.

But in other parts of the industry, enthusiasm for blogs was waning. In the *Garage* video, *Style.com*'s Tim Blanks said he used to find street-style bloggers charming, but 'This season, I thought "oh enough".'

In her *New York Times* article, Suzy Menkes complained about what she called the 'celebrity circus of people who are famous for being famous' who had turned fashion weeks into a 'zoo' (2013).

Some of the fashion editors interviewed for this book expressed the belief that the very top bloggers – Susanna Lau and her ilk – had demonstrated the talent to be accepted into the industry, but below that, most bloggers were not valid commentators.

Harriet Walker, former style editor of the *Independent* and news editor of *Never Underdressed*, says:

> I think a lot of the blogging stuff has descended into totally self-interested parties showing off about their lifestyle. I wouldn't call it journalism.
>
> If you want to be taken seriously, you have to make sure you're a journalist, not a blogger.
>
> You have to be able to say, 'That dress is important because they've used elements from this, this and this,' and all those things happened before I was born. You can't just say, 'That's a nice dress; I'd like to wear it.' There's a lot of that stuff and I find it pathetic.
>
> (2013a).

Stylist Madeleine Bowden says: 'Fashion editors aren't always as responsive to bloggers as there are so many out there. The only way to experience the fashion industry is to be in it, working in it, learning about it' (2013).

When journalists dismiss bloggers, unsurprisingly they do so on professional grounds. Like Harriet, above, Suzy Menkes questions their industry knowledge and critical abilities. Some bloggers, she wrote, 'go against the mantra that I was taught in my earliest days as a fashion journalist: "It isn't good because you like it; you like it because it's good"' (2013).

Some of their criticism seems also to revolve round whether bloggers have the right to take part in an industry they've worked so hard to get into. 'If fashion is for everyone, is it fashion?' Menkes asked.

But bloggers can, and do, argue that the journalists are missing the point.

First, they argue that it's not their fault they're not in the industry – yet. Scott Schuman describes bloggers as the next generation of fashion kids, and Man Repeller blogger Leandra Medine wrote, in a response to Menkes: 'Many of us couldn't land the jobs we wanted, so we just made our own' (2013).

Second, they argue that democracy – or what some journalists see as the dilution of fashion – is the whole point. They have made the scary world of fashion more approachable, and opened it up to everyone.

Third, they argue that they often have greater online influence than traditional media, which are struggling to catch up. Sasha Wilkins, of LibertyLondonGirl, believes that once brands come round to her way of thinking that advertising with her is much more effective than in a print publication – cheaper, lots of hits, more engaged readers – then magazines are in trouble.

'For example, my search engine optimisation is so good that if I write a hotel review, it goes on the front page of Google and stays there,' she says. 'If *Vanity Fair* or *Tatler* do it, it's seen by 80,000 people, then goes in the bin for recycling.'

Asked why big brands spend so much money sponsoring young bloggers, US fashion publicist Alison Brod responded that their recommendations 'can get as many hits as a feature in *InStyle* magazine' (in Storey, 2013).

And fourth, the relentless focus on themselves – anathema to a professional journalist – is their unique selling point for both brands and readers.

An article in *Adweek*, 'Bloggers mean business', describes it thus: 'It's not journalism, it's talking about oneself. Which is to say, it's branding oneself. Bloggers don't want to be editors, because they've built something more valuable: brands' (Griffith, 2011).

But it wasn't clear yet whether this new model of fashion coverage posed any kind of threat to the mainstream media.

As Charlie Porter pointed out in Chapter 3, magazines in particular will survive so long as they are supported by advertisers, and September 2013 saw the biggest advertising yield yet at British *Vogue*.

At the time, companies generally devoted 15–20 per cent of media spending to digital outlets, but there were signs of change. Burberry, which launched its fragrance Burberry Body on Facebook, told the *Financial Times* it spent 60 per cent of its marketing budget on digital media; not because it was the cheaper option, but because it led to greater engagement with consumers (Barrett and Bradshaw, 2011).

But blogs and other forms of social media were certainly challenging magazines and newspapers for the attention of young readers, as *Company* magazine acknowledged.

Editor Victoria White says:

> People ask what our main competition is. And you used to roll out a list of names, but truthfully now the main competition is anything that takes you away from reading magazines – so it's your phone, Facebook, Twitter. We've lost our stranglehold on empty time.
>
> There'll come a point soon where we have more followers on Twitter and Facebook than purchasers. But the successful brands will make the switch. As print declines, everything else will grow.
>
> (2013)

Whether those younger readers who have lost the magazine-buying habit will follow those publications online, though, is another matter.

What the mainstream media did still have was prestige. For even the biggest bloggers, a commission from a magazine, and/or a book deal, represented the pinnacle of success.

As *Daily Telegraph* fashion editor Lisa Armstrong pointed out: 'They do these projects online and then come to the journalists saying will you write about them. They still want the prestige and validation of being in print even though online gets more hits' (in Murray, 2011).

Melanie Rickey, who both blogs at Fashion Editor At Large and writes for newspapers and magazines, agrees. She questions why a 50-something journalist's opinion is considered more important than anyone else's, in these days when anyone can be a critic, but acknowledges that they get given the inside track on news from the big design houses. 'That's just how it works,' she says.

How bloggers make money

Many bloggers take adverts on their websites and YouTube channels, and are paid a certain rate depending on how many click-throughs they get.

The biggest bloggers can become part of a Web media network like Now-Manifest or Glam, which secure advertising from brands and pay bloggers a monthly share, depending on their traffic.

NowManifest provides a platform for giant blogs Style by Kling, Bryanboy, Fashion Toast and Industrie, while Glam is more like a hub of selected content from its separate partner blogs, which include Zoella.

It's not just adverts that such networks organise: they also secure advertorial campaigns, whereby partner bloggers will run their own post and pictures about a brand's product in return for payment. The Specsavers campaign, mentioned earlier, was advertorial content.

The big bloggers can work with other digital agencies, too, that match brands with blogs that can write about them. An example is Gleam Digital, which Zoella also works with (in fact her email and postal contact details are those of Gleam's London offices).

Bloggers don't have to be part of a network to earn money this way. PRs contact individual bloggers to offer them products to review (see Chapter 12) or to offer payment in return for content, like a sponsored post.

Some bloggers will simply reproduce the PR release on their site, while others make a point of producing original content that sits better with their own brand.

Any product or trip that has been gifted, or any post that has been paid for in some way, should be disclosed by the blogger. It is either flagged up at the end of the post, or by an asterix next to the headline or caption; bloggers explain how they do this on their disclosure page.

For all but the super blogs, it's difficult to make a living from advertising alone, which is why many have affiliate marketing agreements too. This is where they include a link in a post, caption or picture to an affiliate partner's website, enabling the reader to click through and buy the product in question. The blogger gets a cut (perhaps 5–15 per cent of the retail price) from any direct sale.

It's not just bloggers who do this, but magazine and newspaper websites and apps too – anywhere where you can click on a link and buy a product.

LibertyLondonGirl's Sasha Wilkins says: 'Affiliate marketing makes more money than advertising. Readers are buying into your personal style.'

The most influential bloggers can also make one-off fees from special projects with brands. That might be guest-editing and modelling in a campaign, as Sasha Wilkins did for Hunter boots and Susanna Lau did for Gap, or shooting a campaign as Scott Schuman has done for Burberry and Coach.

It could also be consulting, designing a limited-edition range, hosting events, making appearances, tweeting about a brand or any other promotional work. Some have signed up with model, talent or literary agencies to handle their deals.

Ethics and transparency

If you look at how bloggers make money, it's fairly easy to see where the fault lines lie when it comes to ethical issues.

When the whole appeal of blogs is their authenticity, what happens when they're being sponsored by a brand? Can you trust their review of a fashion show if they've been paid to go there? Can you believe their glowing review of a product when it's been gifted to them?

Not in all cases, it appears. Although bloggers should make it clear when they've been paid to feature something, or where they have received a product or trip for free, a few don't.

It infuriates Sasha Wilkins, of LibertyLondonGirl, who says it lets down those bloggers who have worked hard for years to build up trust and credibility.

'Some bloggers don't understand that creative and commercial freedom is what sets them apart from magazines,' she says.

> Instead they get flattered by the free gifts, and roll over and get their tummies tickled by brands.
>
> The worst ones create a world which is a complete lie – everything is comped [given free of charge] or sponsored or they are sent places. A lot of those blogs that present this shiny lifestyle appeal to girls in their teens, who presume that these lives are obtainable. But it's paid for by the brands.

In her *New York Times* attack on fashion bloggers, Suzy Menkes said she was continually stunned by how some bloggers boasted about free gifts and trips, which she described as 'bribes' (2013).

Bloggers have pointed out that magazines don't have to disclose freebies, or how closely they work with advertisers, and accused them of hypocrisy.

But in her response to Menkes, Man Repeller's Leandra Medine acknowledged that blogging had an image problem. 'We never should have accepted gifts in the first place. We shouldn't have bragged about the free trips, and cool events, and recognition from our industry heroes,' she wrote (2013).

In the main, bloggers say they have a right to earn a living from their work, and should be judged on the strength of their content rather than whether or not they've been paid for it.

But for this to happen, they acknowledge they have to be transparent about their links with brands, and ensure they only work with those that complement their own brand values and audience.

Scott Schuman says he is happy to work with brands he admires, and post pictures of his work that he's proud of, but won't allow advertisers to have a say in his own content. 'That idea of "I'll give you 300 words for a sweater", everyone sees through that', he told *GQ* (in Sebra, 2013).

It's fairly cut and dried for him, since it's his skills as a photographer he's selling, rather than his personality, taste or point of view.

The latter type of bloggers have to tread a fine line between working with brands and maintaining their independence, or risk losing the trust of their audience and thus their influence. 'Simply being a mouthpiece is a short-term strategy,' *Business of Fashion* editor Imran Amed wrote (2010).

Tips from bloggers

Given that would-be journalists are always advised to maintain a blog, what sort of thing should you be writing about?

Some bloggers recommend going for a niche, in order to stand out from the crowd. 'It's not like you have to invent something totally new, but you have to find a point of view,' says Peter Henderson, of Hapsical.

'I started off talking about fashion news, commenting on shows; then I realized there were so many sites doing that so much better than I was doing. So I made it a bit shoutier, with more of an attitude.'

Aaron Christian, editor-in-chief of Individualism who does street-style video for Mr Porter, agrees:

> Nowadays, everyone is doing stuff, so take time to figure out what you want to say, what your perspective is, and what your voice is.
>
> If everyone is shooting street-style stuff, you could hone it down to, say, street style on people's watches. Be the person who, if I want to look at street-style watches, I'll go to every time because you do it really well.

Or go for a different angle on an established format, he says. While many sites were videoing backstage interviews at fashion shows, Aaron was filming other street-style photographers outside, asking them what their best-ever picture was.

'It was more about personalities than the shows,' he says. 'The big sites have to report on news because they're where people go to get it. But for an individual, it's cooler to do something a bit different.'

Sasha Wilkins, from LibertyLondonGirl, believes niche blogs have been overdone, but she agrees on the need to have a strong editorial point of view. 'You have to be yourself,' she insists. 'I love blogs that tell you something you didn't already know, or show you inside the blogger's kitchen. It doesn't have to show you shiny things.'

She recommends starting with Tumblr, a picture-led micro-blogging site, as an easy way into blogging if you're unsure.

For ideas on how to blog and use social media, try books like *Social Media for Journalists: Principles and Practice*, by Megan Knight and Clare Cook (2013), and *The Online Journalism Handbook*, by Paul Bradshaw and Liisa Rohumaa (2011).

Alex Murphy, who was picked as *Elle's* intern editor in 2012 partly because of her social media campaign, also recommends engaging with other bloggers to get your work out there.

'If someone writes something, you can write something almost in response, then use social media to say "This is what I thought of your blog. What do you think of mine?" It's quite a big, interesting part of blogging' (2013).

In fact, curation of content in general – pulling in feeds and highlighting what's out there – is a big part of blogging, alongside creation of original content.

Journalists and social media

Fashion is about what's new, and fashion journalists are quick to seize on whatever the latest social media channel is. They were enthusiastic adopters of

Tumblr, Twitter, Pinterest, Instagram, Vine and Instagram video, and in 2013 were ready to pounce on whatever was next.

'Fashion people were the first to adopt Instagram, holding up their iPads at the shows to take pictures. They don't always get it right straight away, but they do have that appetite for trying new technology,' said Peter Henderson, of Hapsical.

'At the moment, everyone in fashion is desperate to be the first to get their hands on Google Glass,' a pair of glasses that allow you to take photos, film video and access online data on the move.

Platforms like Instagram, and Tumblr before it, especially lend themselves to fashion because they are picture-led and mobile-first. That makes it easy for a journalist or stylist at a fashion show, showroom, press day or fashion shoot to snap and upload instant photographs of what's going on.

These platforms don't just fit in with journalists' way of working – they're also where the audience is. Sales of smartphones and tablets overtook those of laptops and desktops in 2013 (Kansara, 2013b).

And audiences have shown a huge appetite for the added value, colour and insight that social media give them. It might be a glimpse of, say, clothes that won't be in the shops for another couple of months at a high-street press day, selfies of what fashion editors wear to catwalk shows or behind-the-scenes video of a fashion shoot.

Fashion photographer Phill Taylor says: 'The readers or customers are not just satisfied with seeing the final outcome of a shoot; they are wanting to see the world behind it too.' It's part of the 'democratising of fashion', he says (2013).

So for any aspiring journalist, it's important to keep up with social media as a professional tool. Increasingly, a strong social media presence is seen as an asset, and a necessity for some jobs at websites and e-tailers.

Loraine Davies, training director at the Professional Publishers Association, says it's the way the whole industry is going: 'Whether it's a content management system, Facebook, Twitter or apps, you have to understand how to write for your platform' (2013).

The PPA runs a New Talent awards every year, and Loraine says at least half the job categories weren't around a couple of years ago. 'Things like community managers didn't exist, and now they're an essential part of some media owners' brand delivery,' she says.

But it's not just the new type of job like online editor, social media assistant or community manager that requires a good understanding of social media.

Harriet Walker, news editor of *Never Underdressed*, says: 'I don't think you can be a fashion journalist now and not engage in some sort of conversation with the wider world, whether you're writing for a newspaper or an august glossy or a start-up.'

Jessica Bumpus, fashion features editor for *Vogue* online, says that social media is a huge part of her job. It's important for promoting content – 'Write

Figure 11.1 Madeleine Bowden Instagram pic (Madeleine Bowden)

the news; tweet it; Facebook it,' she says – but also, as Harriet says, for engaging with readers.

'Social media is more informal and you can have fun with it,' she says. 'We used to have a forum on the website that nobody interacted with – now we can have those conversations on Facebook. Twitter is a mix of news and fun' (2013b).

Journalists also use social media as a research tool when they're looking for ideas and contacting sources. Obviously they keep a close eye on celebrities' Twitter and Instagram accounts for potential stories, but they also keep track of general chatter, too.

Lucy Wood at *Look* says crowdsourcing – putting out a call for ideas, content and pictures from readers – is becoming an increasingly useful tool for the magazine.

'Say we're doing a round-up of the best charity shops around the country; we'll put a tweet out asking for suggestions. We can't be in Scotland or Manchester, so readers are very important to journalists,' she says (2012).

Amber Graafland, fashion director at the *Daily Mirror*, checks Instagram and Twitter to see what people are interested in and talking about that particular day. When she gets time, she also browses social curation sites like Styloko.com and Fancy.com to see what people are looking at.

Social media are a great promotional tool, too, whether you're a giant magazine brand or a would-be writer.

Elle, for example, live-tweeted from its cover shoot with actor Kristen Stewart for its June 2012 issue, and became the number-one trending topic on Twitter that day. It also put out teaser videos ahead of its first-ever solo male cover the same year with David Beckham.

Freelance stylist Madeleine Bowden posts pictures on Instagram of her rail of clothes when she's on a shoot, to whet people's appetite for the final spread.

And Alex Murphy used Facebook and Twitter to promote her entry to Elle's Edited by the Interns issue of October 2012. She approached people with a strong social media presence, asked them to look at her work and to share it, if they liked it.

'It's surprising how many people will get behind you,' she says. 'It's daunting at first because you really doubt yourself, but as you get a surge of people sharing your work, you gain confidence.'

Brands and social media

Social media platforms also give fashion brands a way to connect directly with consumers without having to go through traditional media or marketing channels.

The most savvy brands use it to engage people – through editorial-style, shareable content like videos, through interaction and through brand-building – rather than for the hard sell or gathering hordes of followers.

Asos is one of the most effective users of social media. It has 2.6 million Facebook likes and more than a million Instagram followers as of September 2013, and also uses Twitter, Google+, YouTube and Vine. Its own website is extremely interactive with a community of members posting their own outfit choices online, selling clothes and creating looks.

Siobhan Mallen, head of womenswear and international content, says: 'At the heart of it, it's social – Asos cottoned onto where the 20-something girl is quicker than fashion magazines did. Broadcast editorial doesn't work; girls don't respond to you just telling them something' (2012).

The Asos #BestNightEver Christmas 2012 campaign showed this strategy in action. It involved shoppable videos of music stars and models, a global feed of customers' party photos on Instagram, and a Pinterest board where fans could pin looks they liked.

Even luxury brands have latched onto the fact that engaging with fans on the likes of Facebook can get them talked about online, build loyalty and drive sales.

Cartier sent its anniversary video *L'Odyssée de Cartier* to Facebook fans in instalments in 2012, ensuring it went viral, while Tiffany developed a marketing campaign around key moments in people's lives. 'We have the best targeting tools out there, so we know when people are having babies, getting engaged, getting married, graduating,' Tracy Yaverbaun, Facebook's director of retail, luxury and fashion partnerships, said (in Amed, 2012).

Meanwhile Burberry launched its Burberry Body perfume by giving away samples to Facebook followers rather than through inserts in fashion magazines. 'You have to be totally connected to anyone who touches your brand,' Burberry chief executive Angela Ahrendts said. 'If you don't do that, I don't know what your business model is in five years' (in Barrett and Bradshaw, 2011).

As with blogs, authenticity and sharing are key. A surprise hit on Pinterest, for example, has been US designer Peter Som, who had well over 3.3 million followers there by March 2013. Instead of just pinning products, lookbooks and runway pictures, Som has collated his own boards of things that inspire him, like feathers, books, food and travel destinations.

But no platform has changed the fashion industry as much as Instagram, according to *Business of Fashion* editor Imran Amed, who said he notices a whole host of 'made-for-Instagram moments' at runway shows to encourage snapping and sharing (2013).

Tips for social media

Who you're writing on behalf of and why, as well as who you're talking to, will affect how you use social media.

But there are general guidelines and tips for using each platform, especially if you're trying to establish yourself as a blogger, stylist or writer.

Think about your reputation

People have been sacked, sued and arrested for things they've posted on social media – it's a form of publishing, after all – so be careful what you say (see Chapter 13 for the dangers of libel and contempt of court).

Even when it's not contentious, but rather you having a moan or talking about your private life, remember that on Twitter or Instagram anyone can see it (and Facebook if you haven't adjusted your privacy settings), and that it can stay online forever.

As we saw in Chapter 2, the first thing an editor will do when you apply for an internship or a job is check out your social media channels. If they see you complaining about being bored at your last work placement, joking about missing deadlines at college or confessing to getting blind drunk five nights running, your application will end up in the bin.

Treat outward-facing platforms as a professional tool, and don't post anything you wouldn't want a future employer to see.

But don't overthink it

Don't be so cautious about what you post that it turns out bland and lacking in personality. People respond to those who come across as genuine and who share experiences, opinions, passions and humour online.

Alex Murphy, of My-wardrobe.com, says: 'Even the real style insiders can be a little bit edgy, and can laugh at certain things. It makes them human, and makes them interesting.'

That's as true of the big brands as it is of individuals. Asos social media manager Sedge Beswick says her rule of thumb is: 'When you're writing for social – think to yourself, would I say this to my friend in the pub? If the answer is no, it's not right for your social channel' (Asos.com, 2013).

Be chatty, and be responsive

Discoverability is the number-one problem facing bloggers, but you stand more chance of being spotted if you're updating frequently, especially if your material is so strong, interesting or funny that people share it with others.

People also love tweeters who engage with them or bloggers who answer their questions. Have a conversation with someone and you may well have a follower for life.

Don't go for the hard sell

Whether it's a big-name publication, a freelance writer or a fashion brand, pushing out links to your work or your products without adding anything of interest will ensure you get ignored.

Instead teasers, humour, a glimpse behind the scenes or content that people can share are all much more likely to get people interested in finding out what else you've got to offer.

Sedge Beswick, at Asos, says:

> Don't broadcast, be inclusive and seek people's involvement.
> If they know what you're up to, you'll get that emotional attachment and they'll be eagerly awaiting your next Instagram snap.
>
> (Asos.com, 2013)

Make sure to post when you haven't got something to push, too. Join in a debate, make an observation, ask a question, tell a joke, have a regular feature (like Asos's #ThrowbackThursdays showing pictures of 1990s' icons on Instagram) – it will all encourage interaction and make you seem more human.

Be consistent

For a strong presence on social media, it helps to use the same handle across platforms if you can, especially if it matches the URL of your website or blog. That makes it easier for people to find you, and get a good idea of who you are and what you do.

This could also be extended to using the same bio and profile picture.

But play to the strengths of the platform

Brands, publications and bloggers use the various social media sites in different ways, depending on what they feel its strengths are.

Most will also try to put original content on each different platform, rather than push the same posts out everywhere.

So for example, Peter Henderson uses his blog Hapsical as a main page, 'almost like my online portfolio that I might show someone, where I have more polished photos and text'.

On Tumblr, the micro-blogging platform which is simpler and picture-led, Peter posts more irreverent, jokey and instant content – 'random pictures that got my attention, funny snippets, things that don't merit a whole blog post but which I want to document'.

Content on Tumblr is easily shared, and Peter has found it more effective in driving traffic to his blog than any of the write-ups he's had in the mainstream media. Showroom pictures he posted of Raf Simons' fall 2013 collection ended up all over fashion blogs and caused a wave of traffic.

Bigger or more commercial blogs, as well as brands and public figures, have Facebook pages and followers. Sasha Wilkins, of LibertyLondonGirl, says:

> Facebook gives me a lovely, engaged audience – they're worth more than Twitter followers.
>
> I put on things I haven't had room for on my blog, or things that are too commercial for my site – campaign and brand images. Brands love it because it drives traffic for them.

Again, Facebook is more chatty and personal than a blog or website. Because more people now access it via mobile than desktop, the news feed is the main thing they see, 'so create content that your followers would expect to see from their pals', says Asos's Sedge Beswick.

Twitter divides people, depending on whether they prefer working with words or pictures. It does give reach, though, it's a good way of following people and following news, and a lot of the fashion community keeps in contact with each other via its direct messaging.

Instagram, like Twitter, uses a follower model and hashtags make content searchable. People can like, share and comment on photos and videos, and it encourages a lot of interaction.

Pinterest, where users 'pin' images on themed boards, is less instant than the likes of Instagram and Tumblr but is a good way of curating visual content and sharing inspiration.

Aaron Christian has put up lots of boards for the men's style collective Individualism on Pinterest. 'There are some people who don't go to your site, so it's good if they can discover you on Pinterest,' he says.

'Really niche boards work well, and it's useful to have all our five years' worth of photo shoots on one board where people can skim through them all.'

Recommended reading

Bradshaw, P. and Rohumaa, L. (2011) *The Online Journalism Handbook: Skills to Survive and Thrive in the Digital Age.* London: Longman.

Knight, M. and Cook, C. (2013) *Social Media for Journalists: Principles and Practice.* London: Sage.

Mashable: www.mashable.com.

Oliver, W. and Bubble, S. (2012) *Style Feed: The World's Top Fashion Blogs.* London: Prestel.

Shirky, C. (2011) *Cognitive Surplus: Creativity and Generosity in a Connected World.* London: Penguin.

Zhukova, D. and Ha, A. (dirs) (2013) 'Take My Picture', *Garage* magazine, March. Available online at: http://vimeo.com/61348049.

12 Fashion journalism and PR

Carole Watson

Introduction

You won't survive for very long as a fashion journalist if you don't understand the importance of public relations (PR for short) to anyone working in the media.

There won't be a day that goes by when you aren't communicating with a PR by email, telephone, social media or, if you're lucky, over a glass of bubbly or at a breakfast meeting.

Fashion journalists need to communicate with PRs for a whole host of reasons: to provide them with sample clothes and accessories to shoot or review, for images and prices to use on product pages, for information for news stories and trends, to request interviews with designers or celebrities involved in high-street collaborations and, of course, for invitations to press events and fashion shows.

But what is public relations, what do PRs do and how can you make excellent contacts who will give you exclusive stories? And what about the much-discussed argument that fashion journalists are merely PR poodles who mindlessly write what they're told to write, namely gushing positive editorial, in exchange for expensive designer freebies and long lunches?

This chapter will give you an overview of the fashion PR industry so you can gain an understanding of all these issues, with useful hints and advice from both PR practitioners and fashion journalists.

What is PR?

The word PR is thrown about a lot but you really need to have a keen insight into what it means and what public relations executives and press officers do if you are to succeed as a fashion journalist.

Perhaps you think all fashion PRs are like *Absolutely Fabulous'* Edina Monsoon (played by Jennifer Saunders) who swans around shopping in Harvey Nichols all day, or glugging champagne and schmoozing with celebrities and important glossy magazine editors.

Well, we're not saying that never happens but there is much more to it than that.

In a nutshell, fashion PR is actually a hugely powerful industry with its professionals playing the middle man (or woman) between brands and their customers via various different types of media. Whether it's a huge designer name like Chanel, a high-street chain like Topshop, a make-up range or a small online jewellery retailer, most companies employ someone, or a whole team of people, to act as their representatives in dealings with the press. That could mean anyone from the editor of *Vogue* to a fashion intern on a newspaper style supplement or a high-profile blogger.

There is a lot of debate, in academic and professional circles, as to what public relations exactly is. One useful definition from the Chartered Institute of Public Relations (CIPR) website states:

> Public relations is about reputation – the result of what you do, what you say and what others say about you.
>
> Public relations is the discipline which looks after reputation, with the aim of earning understanding and influencing opinion and behaviour. It is the planned and sustained effort to establish and maintain goodwill and mutual understanding between an organisation and its publics.

So this means that PR executives in the fashion business are employed to positively promote their brand and its products and services to their customers, and potential new customers, using the right target media. The dream result, of course, is to sell more clothes, handbags, perfume, whatever.

As Arieta Mujay, UK PR manager for River Island for many years, defines it: 'The main part of a PR's job is to generate noise around the brand which would translate into sales' (2013).

If you think about it, what is the point of, say, Mulberry bringing out a fabulous new tote or Zara some seriously gorgeous heels if the very people who might want to buy them don't even know they exist? So PRs need to identify which particular magazine or blog or style supplement is either going to reach the largest number of potential customers, or the ones with enough disposable income to afford their wares.

Equally, you as a fashion journalist can't tell your readers about the hottest new flats or best skinny jeans on the rails if you don't have access to that information. Sadly, you can't just meander round the shops all day aimlessly hunting for the perfect products or trends to write about – you need to be ahead of the curve and find the next big thing. And it is your job to know your reader – what he or she can afford, desires and needs in their wardrobe. This will help you identify which brands you should be featuring and which PRs you should therefore be contacting.

To complicate things further, the people you will need to speak to are not always called PRs. Sometimes they are called press officers or publicists who work in press offices, or media relations, press relations, or corporate communication. But they all more or less mean the same thing and fulfil the same role.

So how does it work? Global fashion labels such as Dior and Prada usually have their own in-house press offices in key cities around the world with full-time staff employed to do their PR. So, too, do bigger high-street names such as Marks & Spencer, Selfridges or New Look, whose press offices are usually based in London with a team of press officers assigned to dealing with the media.

As River Island's Arieta says:

> As an in-house PR, you only have to push the core values of this one particular brand and ensure that brand is part of every fashion conversation there is going. So, in terms of a high-street brand like River Island, which is a lifestyle brand, we need to appeal to all sorts of customers: the aspirational customer and then your everyday customer who doesn't follow trends so much. We have a body of research so we know exactly who our customers are.

Smaller brands and fashion labels, however, usually do not have the budget to employ their own permanent staff PR teams. So they will choose to hire the services of a freelance consultant or an external public relations agency, which is an independent PR company with a portfolio of different clients whose interests they represent in dealings with the media.

There are thousands of PR agencies around the world, specialising in everything from show business to cars or charities, and of course fashion, lifestyle and beauty brands. So you may find that any given fashion PR agency simultaneously acts on behalf of a variety of different fashion-related clients, such as an upcoming swimwear designer, a handbag designer, a watchmaker and a firm specialising in yoga outfits.

Whether they work in-house for a fashion chain or for an external agency, PRs are just as keen to foster good relationships with the right fashion journalists as you are with them. It is their job to get what is basically free editorial in the right media for their clients (and ultimately reach out to potential customers), whether that is a six-page fashion shoot featuring their products in *Company* magazine or a small mention on *Grazia*'s 10 Hot pages.

Of course, a lot of fashion labels and stores buy advertising space in appropriate media platforms too. But this can cost thousands of pounds per page in a glossy monthly, so it makes sense, particularly in a tough economic climate, to ensure you receive as much free positive publicity too.

As any reader of glossy magazines knows, readers often flick past those endless pages of adverts without thinking or stopping to look at them, whereas they might take more notice of a respected fashion journalist's advice on what to buy in an editorial fashion story such as 'The 10 best strappy sandals this summer'.

The trust inspired by editorial compared to advertising is well known; in fact, it is estimated that 'the value of editorial is four times that of advertising in terms of its effect and influence' (Haid, in Jackson and Shaw, 2006: 173).

So you can see why all PRs, whether from Prada or Primark, are eager to get their positive PR message out via fashion journalists rather than just through buying pages of advertising, although, of course, unlike adverts, PRs cannot usually control exactly how much space they will be given, or what the journalist is going to write.

What do PRs do? And why do they matter to fashion journalists?

The actual role of a PR varies a lot depending on the company they work for, and their seniority.

But overall, they are tasked with making sure the right journalists receive the right information about their products, launches, collections and events. A lot of journalists complain they are bombarded with hundreds of irrelevant, badly-written emails every day from PRs who obviously do not understand who their readers are, or what their job is. Or that they receive emails with such massive image files that they crash their computers. Not surprisingly, they are usually deleted unread or unopened. Or they receive a phone call from a PR who seems bored, reading from a script and talking about something which would never make the pages of that journalist's particular publication as it isn't suitable for their readers.

Good PRs, however, are highly clued-up about the circulation, demographic and editorial requirements of all sorts of different magazines, style supplements, newspapers, websites and blogs so they can contact the right journalist with useful information.

Harriet Walker, news editor at *Never Underdressed* and the ex-style editor of the *Independent*, says:

> A good PR would know the publication really well, so they wouldn't be suggesting, if you work at a luxury publication, this thing at Dorothy Perkins. It's a big ask, but they should know the tastes and interests of the big editors or it's a waste of that editor's or PR's time to go in with things that are never going to fly.
>
> And they need to be aware of the climate in which you're launching your product – when things are difficult, it's not necessarily the right time to be going to somewhere with a general news base like a newspaper with a £3,000 handbag.
>
> Conversely, something as simple as 'the sun is out – this is the time to get people to feature your sarong', that stuff works; that stuff is useful – reactive, themed things that go along with the weather, a TV thing, what's happening in Parliament even, as long as it's tailored to the right publication.
>
> You get those blanket emails, which are 'Dear insert-name-here', and it's for a thermal vest, and you think 'Really? Why do you think I'm worth telling this to?'

(2013a)

Emma Hart, the founder and managing director of leading London fashion PR agency Push PR, used to work as a fashion writer and columnist for the *Evening Standard* newspaper before moving into public relations, so she understands both sides of the business intimately.

She says:

> When I was a journalist, I was dealing with PRs constantly on the phone, day in, day out – this was before people used email so much and I was working on a daily newspaper with three editions. What I was finding was I would phone PRs to get the information I needed, but it was unbelievable how they didn't get back to me, when I was on deadline, either because they were out or not working on that particular account that day, and I was thinking 'I am about to give you a whole column!'
>
> It was virtually impossible dealing with 90 per cent of PRs. Because I wasn't a name, they would think, 'Well who are you?'
>
> It's so, so important that fashion journalists and PRs communicate; it's the backbone of the industry. The journalist needs to trust the PR, because they are so busy and bombarded with emails. If you know someone and trust them, it cuts through the noise.
>
> It's a PR's job to know who the target reader is of each magazine and newspaper. Why would you bother contacting a teen mag with a £1,500 necklace, for instance? On what planet will a 14-year-old have the money to buy it, unless it's *Teen Vogue?*

As Emma has explained, good PRs will be contacting you because they think the information they have is relevant and interesting for your readers. She is also a firm believer in face-to-face contact and her staff are instructed to build strong relations with the right journalists over a coffee or breakfast so they can regularly discuss how they can help each other out.

But, equally, it is your job as a creative journalist brimming with ideas to track down the right PRs to help those ideas come to fruition.

Take *Grazia* fashion editor Hannah Almassi, who uses her bank of PR contacts when compiling trend and shopping pieces.

Hannah explains:

> It has to feel fresh and like we haven't already covered it, and someone else hasn't covered it in the same way. You look online, look through look books, contact PRs … it's a process of elimination, really, speaking to as many people as you can. PRs now know how much of a deadline I'm on for my news stories, so the good ones do get back to me quickly if they can.
>
> Because my stories are always really specific it can be quite difficult – a lot of PRs will phone up and say, 'What are you working on?' and the other week I started doing a thing on single earrings, which is something

we've noticed a lot of girls doing, and it's such a specific product that there are barely any PRs who are going to go, 'Oh yes, I've got that.' So it does take quite a bit of research to do some of those stories and I don't have a lot of time, so you start to get to know who's going to have the right thing, which websites are the best to check out.

I don't think I've ever had something where a PR has said, 'Oh you should do a story on this trend' because we're always ahead of any suggestions. We often have other PRs and publications follow our lead, instead.

(2010)

And she is not alone in thinking that relying on spoon-fed press releases is just lazy, uncreative journalism without the effort of thinking of any fresh or creative ideas for your editor.

Hannah adds:

I think there probably is an opportunity for people to sit back and just go for press releases, but not at *Grazia*, where things move too fast. The instances where we do get stories from PRs tend to be them contacting us saying 'We've got this new brand; you may not realise but this person and this person and this person's been out wearing it. We've got these pictures. It's really great; it's selling out on Net-a-Porter.'

That's how you may get a story from a PR. We love to see the kind of girls in the media whose style we like – it's really great to see them all wearing a certain item, because then that is a story for us. It's interesting why they're all wearing it, why is it so cool, where can we get it from.

Lucy Wood, senior fashion news editor at *Look* magazine, explains how she monitors press releases and may use them to help her identify hot trends 'almost like you put things together like a jigsaw' (2012).

She adds:

PRs are useful but they don't spoon-feed me. Nine times out of ten, they come up with an idea you've already thought of and dismissed. What you do find is one person will send an email about something and it plants a seed; then a couple of weeks later, you get another email about it, and you think, 'Maybe there's a trend here.'

I haven't ever had a release hit my inbox that I've just turned into a page – that's pretty lazy. But PRs are integral in keeping us up to speed with facts and figures. They let us know about styles that are going into stores before everyone else. It's how we keep ahead of the curve.

And we have a call-in list of all our PR contacts, so we can send them all an email saying what we're working on, and to ask if they have anything that might fit the category, so we can have a look at it and consider using it on our pages.

As we have seen, having excellent contacts with the right PRs is the life-blood of first-class fashion journalism.

Whether you are a recently-graduated intern needing to call in or return samples to fashion labels or a senior fashion director requesting a coveted front-row seat at Dior for their autumn–winter show, you will need to liaise with a PR in some shape or form.

Madeleine Bowden, a freelance stylist who worked as an assistant to *X Factor* stylist Laury Smith, says:

> I talk to PRs more than I talk to my boyfriend! I'm on the phone talking to them and emailing them all day every day.
>
> It's a give – give – they want their products in your magazine or on your client, and you want their product. I think it's the most important relationship you'll ever make in fashion. A lot of their job is to schmooze and take people out to dinner, and I think the more chatty you are, and the more personable you are – still professional but approachable – the better they will relate to you.
>
> I've just been to a few press days where it's champagne all the time. You look at the collection; then you spend 20 minutes shooting the breeze with the PR. If there's one sample and there's 50 people gunning for it, if you have a good relationship with the PR, they're more likely to let you have the sample for a few hours and work around it.
>
> (2013)

Of course, you might be contacting a PR for all sorts of reasons – to call in dresses, shoes and accessories like Madeleine, to ask if they have any appropriate products for a trend story you're researching, or to ask for an exclusive interview with the latest celebrity who's done a high-street collaboration.

How to build the right contacts in PR

But how do you initially build good contacts within the PR world in the first place when you are new to the job and it seems every other established fashion journalist has already forged strong relationships?

Emma Hart, founder and managing director of leading London fashion PR agency Push PR, has some excellent tips for both fashion journalism and PR students going for job interviews or work placements. She advises:

> Social media is so important. You should research and follow the people you're interested in, do your research via social media platforms, and look at their clients.
>
> It's amazing how many people we interview and ask which of our clients they like, and they are not sure who they are really. If you don't know that, you haven't done your research.

Also engage and interact; send a message explaining you are a student; ask if you can pop along for 20 minutes to have a look at their samples and take a few pictures.

If you have a blog, see which clients they have and offer to do a blog post on that client. Or ask to do a guest blog post on their blog and write about the brands. It's all about going that extra mile and talking about how you can engage with the brands and the agencies so it's a win-win situation.

If a PR company doesn't have a blog or Twitter account, tell them you've noticed that and would they consider it, because you could come in and help set it up for them, especially for really small brands which can't find a social media intern anywhere. It's about finding opportunities and being proactive in suggesting a solution.

Social media is an incredible information tool and if you aren't into that, we wouldn't really consider you. We've had people saying 'I don't like Twitter' but it's not about whether you like it or not: it is vitally important to the industry and to everything we do.

When you are a student you are looking for every single avenue of information. So I recommend going to fashion weeks, and events, even just hanging out, taking pictures, using the same hashtag other people are using to get yourself on the same news feed as them.

And there is nothing like good old-fashioned research to track down the sort of people you should be introducing yourself to. Any good journalist knows exactly who their reader is, perhaps by their age, their income, or where they live. Thousands of pounds are spent researching this and you can always ask to see that research and look at your employer's media packs online, which also provide this information for potential advertisers.

Once you know your reader, you will know what sort of stores, brands and websites they may use to update their wardrobes. Then it is a matter of researching who is responsible for the PR for those stores, brands and websites. This is often supplied under the 'Contact us' or 'Press' sections of their websites with a list of the PR team's names, email addresses and phone numbers. In the case of *Vogue*, for example, try looking up Chanel's press office. Or for *Woman's Own*, perhaps Monsoon's.

There is then no harm sending a press officer or PR manager a polite and friendly email introducing yourself, explaining where you work and asking to be added to their contact lists and if you can pop in sometime to say hello.

But be careful when doing this, especially if you are an inexperienced intern trying to contact a very senior PR. Arieta explains:

It's very important to get fully involved in an internship and not the glitz and glamour side of things. A lot of people are too obsessed with the celebrity side of things. For example, I was getting a lot of emails from interns during our Rihanna collection. I think they all thought Rihanna

was going to be in the office with me while I was working! When they
realised she wasn't going to be there, I was getting excuses as to why they
couldn't come and see the collection.

And don't send me emails saying 'Hey lovely' with kisses and smiley
faces when you don't know me and I'm UK PR manager of a high-street
brand. It's not professional – I wouldn't email Anna Wintour or the chief
executive of a company saying 'Hi lovely'. You need to approach people
politely and professionally. My other major bugbear is text slang in an
email.

So ensure any messages you send, whether via Twitter or email, are cor-
rectly spelt, with good grammar and, above all, courteous. The same ethos
applies to phone conversations. You may be asked on a work placement, for
instance, to call in sample products from a PR to use in a fashion shoot, or to
check prices of items being featured in the magazine.

You must always be polite, introduce yourself and take a good note of the
information to ensure accuracy, which is, of course, the cornerstone of good
journalism.

Both Emma Hart, of Push PR, and Arieta Mujay complain that there is a
growing tendency for inaccuracies, whether wrong prices, wrong websites or
missing credits, in fashion journalism, which they blame on a lack of checking
on the part of journalists.

Emma says:

> It is really frustrating because you've put a lot of work into it. In the past,
> you could ask for a correction in print but that never happens now. The
> quality control of credits and information has really gone downhill. We
> recently had some amazing coverage in a big-name Sunday supplement
> but they didn't put a credit on the product at all, so you're thinking,
> 'How is the reader going to find out how to buy it?'
>
> It makes your heart sink when they misspell a brand or they put a
> wrong phone number in. It's just sloppiness when you have given them
> the right information. Accuracy is everything.

When a PR is unhappy

It's not just sloppiness over prices and missing credits which might upset
PRs. Fashion journalists are often accused of only writing positive fluffy copy
(more of that later). However, there may be times you are required to write
something negative or critical about a brand or a collection.

You will see in Chapter 13 that journalists are perfectly entitled to be critical (and even bitchy) about any item of fashion, or a designer's latest range,
without fear of legal consequences, thanks to the honest opinion defence to
libel.

But what is more likely to be a problem is that you have upset a good contact, which may have repercussions for your future relationship with them, or upset an advertiser who spends thousands of pounds with your employer.

Fashion journalists anecdotally complain that some PRs will phone up to shout at them over negative reviews or threaten to pull their advertising spend from their company. It is never acceptable to be screamed at, but as an inexperienced fashion journalist, the best course is to politely take a note of their concerns, their contact details and speak to a more experienced colleague for advice on how to deal with it.

Good PRs, however, know how to take the rough with the smooth. They understand that some journalism involves reviewing products and that they have to take any critical press on the chin.

Emma Hart recalls:

> We had a recent situation where one of our clients was featured in a white T-shirt review in *Good Housekeeping* and they only got two out of ten. We spoke to the client beforehand and they wanted to do it, so we had to say to them when it goes out, it goes into their hands; there are no favours going on. It was a product review and that's how it should be.
>
> It was tough for the client because it wasn't an amazing review. But we had to tell them, 'We can brand-manage you to a certain extent but if you are going to put yourself up for a review, you have to embrace editorial independence.'
>
> I've had PRs screaming down the phone at me when, say, I was doing three of the best mascaras when I was working at the *Standard*. But they had put it forward as a tried and tested, and maybe they didn't get as glowing a report as the one next to it. All you can do is fully respect the opinion of the person doing that review.
>
> It is important to manage your client's expectations, which sometimes isn't done that well in PR. Sometimes you have to say, 'Yes, your product is good, but I can't guarantee I can get your product into *Vogue* or *Grazia* or whatever.'

It is much more likely you may write something negative if you decide to work on a newspaper than a traditional fashion magazine, as papers do not rely so heavily on advertising revenue from the fashion world and can therefore be much more independent when it comes to their journalism.

What is much more common, for magazine journalists, is simply not to feature a product or collection they dislike rather than write negatively about it – basically criticism by omission.

Victoria White, editor of *Company* magazine, says:

> No magazine could survive without a strong sense of identity and ethics – we would never feature something if it wasn't fabulous. At the same time, we wouldn't slag it off. Why would you give up a page to do

that, when you could highlight a great product? You have to have an environment that's right for the brand – they go hand in hand. We don't critique – we highlight and showcase.

There's so much fashion – why waste space on it if it's rubbish? Or saying this one's collection wasn't good, because the next one might be great?

(2013)

Are fashion journalists and fashion PRs too cosy?

Fairly or unfairly, the biggest criticism aimed at fashion journalists is that they are no more than the unquestioning mouthpiece of fashion PRs, who tightly control what journalists feature and write.

This accusation has many reasons behind it – lazy journalism with practitioners simply being spoon-fed press releases, the pressure to keep advertisers happy in an ever more difficult financial climate and amid falling magazine and newspaper circulations, or the thorny issue of an industry built around gifting writers with thousands of pounds worth of freebies in the hope of winning positive editorial coverage.

Fashion journalist and academic Brenda Polan suggests:

> In the often too-cosy relationship between media and advertisers, the latter long ago usurped the upper hand. PR executives, initially a conduit for information and access, have become the enforcers of the industry, doling out threats along with the champagne breakfasts.
>
> (in Jackson and Shaw, 2006: 155)

She claims that has led fashion journalists to be merely 'uncritical chroniclers of brands and labels, the corrupted or intimidated mouthpieces of a mighty PR machine that exists to part the punter from her money' (ibid.: 157).

It is a damning indictment of fashion journalism, which is fiercely denied by many writers who say their day-to-day interactions with PRs are more subtle and do involve journalistic skills such as editing out press release material not suitable for their readers.

Of claims that writers are simply spoon-fed by PRs, Harriet Walker says:

> Who isn't? At a newspaper, you see how much of the news cycle is PR driven ... and it's, what, 70 per cent? Very few publications are big enough to have roving reporters out all day looking for stories – that's just not how it works any more. No one can afford to do long-term investigative programmes very often – the *Telegraph* did MPs' expenses and that was the most expensive thing ever, and that's just not feasible, and you do rely on people sending stuff in.
>
> But obviously there's a taste level – you use your judgement. If someone sends you a thing that says 'We've taken a survey – apparently 32 per cent of women have one foot bigger than the other,' well, that's really boring,

and it's obviously been done for a horrible corporate reason. You just have to filter it. But if there are any ivory-tower academics out there thinking 'I don't want to read anything generated by PR,' then stop reading everything.

But, certainly, when a magazine's profits rely on the millions of pounds spent by advertisers, one cannot deny that they have some influence over what brands editors feature within their fashion pages. You only need to watch *The September Issue*, a documentary about the workings of American *Vogue*, to see editor Anna Wintour scanning page proofs of a multi-page fashion shoot to ensure certain designers' outfits were included.

Fashion journalist Caryn Franklin explains:

> It didn't use to be like this, but a magazine has to observe an agreed code with each of its advertisers, and advertisers are very powerful because they are the ones that fund the cost of the print and paper run. The cover price is neither here nor there these days, with many magazines heavily discounted to keep up their readership because they have huge competition online.

Emma Hart, at Push PR, says this once unspoken pressure from advertisers is less subtle post-recession, but conversely she sees no problem with positive uncritical editorial coverage of brands and labels who advertise their wares just a few pages away from that article.

She says:

> I think the industry has changed beyond recognition since I started. No one knew how good they had it. It's much tougher now we've been though two industry recessions. We used to have massive budgets where you could spend ridiculous amounts; now it's much tougher and more carefully considered.
>
> The words 'cosy' and 'gushing'? Yes, there are close relationships. But teams are limited now; you need those close relationships. Where there used to be four fashion assistants, there's now one. So to the outside world, who really is being targeted is the reader.
>
> If they are not finding it offensive, I don't really see much harm in it. There is so much negativity in the media about the economy and banks, but isn't fashion and beauty and picking up your favourite glossy about escapism and positivity?
>
> Everyone reads things with a pinch of salt. Just because someone writes you should buy this Dolce & Gabbana outfit they are wearing doesn't mean they will do that: consumers make their own choice. What they are looking for is a bit of inspiration and information.
>
> At the end of the day, fashion is a serious business and you need to support your advertisers, which is done much more blatantly now. We want print magazines and you have to play the game. Once upon a time

you couldn't have a conversation with a fashion director about this as blatantly as you can now. We've had to adapt to an industry that is very, very stretched.

Equally, Emma says the culture of gifting free clothes, handbags, jewellery and beauty items to journalists is a lot more considered and targeted in the light of financial constraints, although she accepts that senior influential fashion journalists are still the happy recipients of goodies that a fashion journalism student can only dream about.

Perhaps this is a shift away from the notorious free-for-all culture described by journalist Liz Jones, of her days as editor of *Marie Claire* in the late 1990s.

In her 2013 memoirs, *Girl Least Likely To*, Liz recounts the bounty of freebies she received in one Milan Fashion Week alone:

> A Prada bowling bag, a Tod's evening bag … in all, I counted 15 bags, all bigger than the bags received by the more junior members of the team. I received a Louis Vuitton traveller worth £1,700 with LJ on the handle, embossed in gold. I must have arrived, surely?
>
> The gifts make you feel all warm and fuzzy inside when you come to write your catwalk show review.
>
> Ever wondered why all the glossy editors applauded when animal-rights protesters were dragged by their hair from the Burberry catwalk by bouncers? They each had shiny Burberry totes at their toes, delivered to their hotels that morning.

It is easy to see why junior fashion journalists, often on low wages, trying to survive in expensive cities with huge rent bills, could be easily influenced by receiving a lovely gift. Anecdotally, the most hard-up journalists are rumoured to have sold many freebies on eBay. Others become so used to all the gifts that they simply give them away to friends and family.

Elizabeth Walker, former executive fashion and beauty editor at *Marie Claire*, recalls:

> We used to get really nice Christmas presents, and we certainly got a lot of handbags. People like Tod's, who in the beginning had no advertising money, would give out handbags to personalities so they'd be seen around with them. I used to be given an outfit by Alberta Ferretti every season. You were invited to choose and you never quite knew if you were paying or ordering wholesale and you had to bear that in mind.
>
> They're very savvy: if you never wear it and put it on eBay, you're off the list next season. Because everyone's a bit broker these days, handbags still get given to the more senior people, but you mostly dress yourself. You get quite good discounts, so most savvy editors would wear a mixture of a key blazer by someone or other mixed with Zara.
>
> (2012)

As you may expect, glossy magazines with targeted readers interested in trends and fashion are more likely to receive a fabulous gift-wrapped present than a newspaper fashion writer.

The *Guardian*'s Jess Cartner-Morley says:

> Freebie? I wish. It's a common misconception that I get to keep the clothes I wear in the 'how to wear' section. Sadly it's not the case. Of course you get lots of dinners and more champagne than you can drink, and I'm not complaining.
>
> Are we too close to PR in fashion journalism? Some are, as in all fields of journalism. PR contacts are essential – they are invaluable colleagues. If you let yourself get turned into a mouthpiece for them, though, that's sheer laziness.
>
> (2011b)

Many publishers today have ethical codes regarding receiving gifts and this is something you must check wherever you begin working, whether as an unpaid intern or salaried member of staff. In practice, many magazines simply keep all these freebies in a storeroom until they have a charity sale, selling them to staff for a much lower price and then giving the money to a good cause.

Another reason, alongside the constraints of a recession-hit fashion industry, why this freebie culture may well be changing is the recent introduction of the Bribery Act (see Chapter 13), which could potentially see journalists jailed if they accept money or gifts in exchange for positive stories. It is important not to get so starry-eyed at the prospect of a £1,500 'It bag' that you compromise your position as an independent impartial journalist. Always stop and think: would I be writing this article about this product or label in the same (positive) light if the PR hadn't sent me a nice present?

Conclusion

This chapter has discussed the pivotal role which public relations plays in helping fashion journalists access information, images and invites to media events, launches and catwalk shows.

Both journalists and PR practitioners agree it is an essential relationship which, if handled professionally, can yield the right results for both sides, namely free publicity for brands and labels, and engaging exclusive editorial copy for journalists and their readers.

It has also revealed how to ensure you build the right PR contacts for your reader, as well as the difficult ethical issues and financial constraints caused by those relationships in terms of pressure from advertisers, PR control over the industry, and the somewhat declining culture of freebies.

Jessica Bumpus, fashion features editor of *Vogue* online, says:

> I remember at university a tutor saying to us, 'Look around the room – these people will be your contacts in future.' We laughed but actually a handful are, because they became PRs and I know them.

It's a two-way relationship, a 'you scratch my back, I scratch yours' thing. After all, if you want to break the news, it's they that have it. They're also the guardians of the designers you want to interview. It's such a key relationship.

(2013b)

It is never too early, as a fashion journalism student, to start building those contacts. Start following in-house press officers and PR agencies on Twitter today, begin a contacts list of which PRs look after which stores and labels, and you will start learning how to keep abreast of the work they do and its importance to your future career.

Recommended reading

Chartered Institute of Public Relations: www.cipr.co.uk.
Finnan, S. (2010) *How to Prepare for a Career in Fashion*. London: Adelita.
Haid, C., Jackson, T. and Shaw, D. (2006) 'Fashion PR and styling', in Jackson, T. and Shaw, D. (eds) *The Fashion Handbook*. London: Routledge, pp. 172–87.
Jones, L. (2013) *Girl Least Likely To: 30 Years of Fashion, Fasting and Fleet Street*. London: Simon & Schuster.

13 Law and ethics

Carole Watson

Introduction

It may not seem as important for fashion journalists to grasp media law and ethical codes of conduct as, say, reporters covering Crown Court trials or carrying out news investigations into corruption in high places.

But covering the catwalk or commenting on the hot spring trends can take a fashion writer into dangerous legal and ethical territory which could cause your employer reputational damage or even cost them thousands of pounds in fines or damages.

You may be the best interviewer and writer in the world, with the brightest style ideas, but a good grounding in media law and ethics is essential, particularly in this post-phone hacking and post-Leveson landscape.

Further, you cannot assume, as a fashion journalist, that you may not become involved in breaking news stories with legal and ethical implications – the Kate Moss cocaine allegations, the terrible suicide of Alexander McQueen and the John Galliano anti-Jewish diatribe immediately spring to mind.

When the two planes hit New York's Twin Towers on September 11, 2001, the no-fly zone meant it was impossible for British newspapers and magazines to fly in experienced news reporters to report on the unfolding atrocity.

Instead, they turned to their fashion journalists, already in Manhattan for New York Fashion Week, to roll up their sleeves and pitch in. Some rose to the challenge and worked tirelessly round the clock on the grim news event. Others froze.

A week later, *Guardian* fashion journalist Charlie Porter wrote an article headlined 'Catwalk to carnage', reflecting:

> Should I have gone down there when it happened? It is the question that has been troubling me these past days stuck in New York. My hotel is in Gramercy Park, about 50 blocks north of the site of the World Trade Centre. With hindsight, I know that I could have started to report straight away. But at the time it never even crossed my mind. I

stayed in my hotel watching the news and not leaving my room until it was over.

(2001)

Of course, these sorts of global news events are thankfully rare. But during your day-to-day job supplying trend reports, red-carpet verdicts and runway reports, there are still legal pitfalls to consider.

Can you say a supermodel looked 'off her face on drugs' as she strutted her stuff on the catwalk? Unless you can prove it in court, those five words could cost your employer thousands of pounds in libel damages – and probably you your job.

Or you could do something as innocuous as publishing that actress Nicole Kidman's favourite perfume is Jo Malone's White Jasmine and Mint?

When the *Daily Telegraph* wrote this seemingly innocent story in 2007, Ms Kidman sued them and won substantial libel damages. Why? Because she was paid millions of pounds to be a spokeswoman for Chanel, and the inference that she was a hypocrite who took Chanel's money but snubbed their fragrances for a rival high-end brand is indeed defamatory (*Evening Standard*, 2007).

What about a scathing verdict on a high-street chain's latest womenswear collection? Or, in a round-up of moisturisers, giving one well-known brand zero out of ten, saying it gave you spots? You need to know you can be as critical, bitchy or as negative as you want in opinion and comment pieces without running the risk of a libel action hitting the editor's desk.

But how about receiving a gorgeous tissue-wrapped free £1,200 'It bag', and then writing a glowing product review as a thank you to the lovely public relations executive who sent it to you? The Bribery Act 2010, which carries a maximum ten-year jail sentence, is of growing concern in the fashion industry, where journalists are often bombarded with complimentary clothes, accessories, beauty products and other luxury items in the hope of winning favour (and perhaps free editorial mentions).

Anyone planning a career in fashion journalism should opt for a degree or similar qualification which incorporates media law and ethics, and preferably is accredited to offer the choice of sitting the professional National Council for the Training of Journalists (NCTJ) media law exam.

A large number of glossy magazine editors began their careers on local and national newspapers before moving on to the glossies, and therefore they strongly understand the importance of legal training.

Of course, most major employers have either in-house or contracted media lawyers who cast an eye over the bigger stories before publication. But there is no such safeguard for those journalists who upload their copy directly to a website, tweet on the go, blog, or work as freelancers themselves.

In this multimedia world, you can self-publish in seconds to Twitter, Facebook, Pinterest and the like without any lawyers or senior experienced colleagues as a barrier to costly and embarrassing mistakes.

So this chapter is designed to give you, at the very least, some warning signs where you may fall foul of the law or ethical codes of conduct as you go about your job.

Libel

Libelling a person, or a company, is one of the biggest worries most journalists face. If you lose a case, it can cost hundreds of thousands, if not millions, of pounds in costs and damages, so it must always be at the back of your mind. However it is not a criminal offence, so you will not get a criminal record or be jailed for this.

In the excellent media law textbook *McNae's Essential Law for Journalists*, authors Mark Hanna and Mike Dodd describe libel law as 'protecting an individual's personal and professional reputation from unjustified attack' (2012: 238). It doesn't matter if this is printed in a newspaper, magazine, or online, tweeted, or broadcast on the TV or radio.

This could be anything from calling someone a liar or a thief to, as we have seen, wrongly stating an actress uses a certain type of perfume.

Unless you can prove in court, with credible witnesses and preferably documentary proof, that what you've said is substantially true, you are likely to lose your case.

Further, most media organisations want to avoid the huge costs of going to court in the first place and are likely to reach an agreed out-of-court settlement instead.

Judges, and therefore journalists, use several definitions of libel and they are worth remembering when writing something that is potentially libellous.

Do your words tend to:

a) expose the person to hatred, ridicule or contempt;
b) cause the person to be shunned or avoided;
c) lower the person in the estimation of right-thinking members of society;
d) disparage the person in his/her business, trade, office or profession?

What you write only has to TEND to do any one of the above to be potentially libellous.

So it is unlikely that you suddenly hated actor Kate Winslet when you read in *Grazia* that she had secretly visited a diet doctor. However, Ms Winslet won substantial libel damages over this false story in 2007 because, if it had been true, she would have been a hypocrite, as she has often spoken out against Hollywood's obsession with dieting and body image (*BBC News*, 2007).

The idea that she would publicly criticise dieting and then privately visit a diet doctor would, of course, tend to make you think less of her (as in the third definition above).

You might think it would be legally safer sometimes to not name a person and avoid libelling them. But this can actually make matters much worse.

For example, think of those Wicked Whispers gossip titbits where you guess which boy band member or footballer has been dabbling in drugs or cheating on their partner.

If you print, for instance, that an unnamed up-and-coming British model is addicted to cocaine, you could be sued by several up-and-coming models, rather than just the one you were actually referring to. This is known as group libel and is a real risk for journalists.

Equally, just repeating a libel, by simply reprinting a defamatory story first published elsewhere, is not safe. This is a fresh libel in the eyes of the law, and the person defamed can sue as many publications as they wish.

Luckily, there are several defences against libel which journalists can use. The most important ones for fashion writers are those of truth and honest opinion (formerly known as justification and honest comment before the Defamation Act 2013).

Truth basically means proving your story is substantially true in court. But this is rarely used, because of the massive financial implications outlined above.

However, honest opinion is an excellent defence to use when you are writing comment and opinion pieces such as beauty product reviews, red-carpet frock verdicts and catwalk reports. It is the reason why critics can be so vitriolic and bitchy when reviewing gigs, cars, books, TV shows and so on without any legal consequences.

As long as your copy is *clearly recognisable* as an opinion piece, you can be as critical, negative and scathing as you like, provided what you write is your *honestly held opinion*.

It is important to remember this is ONLY for opinion pieces, not factual news stories and features, and must be based on *provably true facts* and not involve personal malice.

What this means is that you CAN say a designer's latest collection is her worst ever, as long as you have actually seen the clothes (a provably true fact) and you don't have any personal grievance against that designer (for example, they sacked you as an intern, or your sister is a rival designer).

If you want to slate a new fake tan for giving you a rash, ensure you have actually tried it, that it did give you a skin problem and you are prepared to prove that.

Although the prospect of a libel writ is scary, it is important that journalists are impartial and give their readers truthful opinions and verdicts on products from face creams to frocks.

As long as you are well-versed in the honest opinion defence, and seek the advice of a lawyer or experienced colleague if in doubt, you should avoid the stereotype that fashion journalists only write fluffy gushing reviews.

Privacy

Until 2000, there was no privacy law in Britain. But since then, UK courts can award substantial damages if you are successfully sued for invading someone's privacy, either by writing something about their private life, publishing a photo taken in a private place or revealing something they would rather was kept secret.

This is because, since the turn of the millennium, the European Convention on Human Rights (ECHR) became embedded in UK law. Part of the ECHR is Article 8 which says everyone has 'the right to respect for his private and family life, his home and his correspondence'.

Judges, and therefore journalists, balance this important right to privacy with the often-conflicting Article 10, which gives everyone a right to freedom of expression – i.e. the right to speak our minds and, as journalists, write what we want, within the boundaries of existing laws.

The difference between privacy and libel is that the person using Article 8 to suppress a story or sue for damages is not denying the story is true, just that they don't want that story or photograph published, or they want compensation if it already has been.

Both the law and the Press Complaints Commission's Editors' Code of Conduct stress that everyone has a right to a private life, whether famous or not.

But it has mostly been celebrities, sportsmen and public figures such as bankers and politicians who have used privacy laws to stop publication (via a court-imposed injunction) or to sue for damages after publication.

And just because someone has sold their wedding and baby pictures to glossy magazines, had their own TV reality show, written their autobiography and endlessly posed on the red carpet doesn't mean they have sacrificed any right to a private life away from the cameras.

The key test is whether a person has a reasonable right to privacy in that particular scenario. This is why no British magazine or newspaper printed the photographs of the Duchess of Cambridge sunbathing topless in a private villa. Should she have stripped off on Blackpool beach, where she should not and could not expect privacy, the pictures would have appeared on every front page!

Equally, revealing something private about someone's life is just as risky. Judges take invasion into the privacy of children and of someone's health particularly seriously and you could expect to pay substantial damages if successfully sued.

Just because a friendly fashion contact tells you that a high-profile model is battling cancer or is two months pregnant does not mean you can reveal that very private intimate information.

Just because a paparazzo has snapped a model in a hotel lobby with her children does not mean you are free to upload it.

Of course, if someone chooses to tell you something private about themselves, in an interview or by tweeting it to thousands of their followers, they have no one but themselves to blame if it is published. Just make sure you have recorded any interview and have good shorthand notes to prove the interview took place.

Equally, if they decide to parade their children on the red carpet at a film premiere, or to kiss someone other than their husband in the middle of

Trafalgar Square, they cannot reasonably expect any journalist not to publish the photos or write about it.

If you remember nothing else, just remember to ask yourself: 'Would I reasonably expect privacy in that situation?'

Famously, supermodel Naomi Campbell won damages when the *Daily Mirror* revealed she was undergoing treatment for cocaine addiction. A court ruled the paper had invaded Ms Campbell's privacy by publishing a photo of her outside a Narcotics Anonymous meeting, a place where she could have a reasonable expectation of privacy.

However, the judges believed the *Mirror* WAS right to tell its readers about the model's treatment, as she had consistently given interviews insisting she had never abused drugs (*BBC News*, 2004).

This is an important argument used by journalists for invading someone's privacy if the story is in the public interest.

The phrase 'public interest' does not simply mean the story is interesting to the public, but that it serves some public good like exposing crime or, in the Campbell case, exposing a public figure who has misled her fans.

The then *Mirror* editor, Piers Morgan, was outraged at the case, which left his paper with more than £1 million in legal costs, and famously said outside court: 'This is a very good day for lying drug-abusing prima donnas who want to have their cake with the media, and the right to then shamelessly guzzle it with their Cristal champagne.'

A journalist can always try to defend a privacy claim by saying that people who are role models (such as pop stars, models, footballers, or politicians) should be exposed if they lie to the public or, in legalese, that the media have the right to 'correct a misleading image'.

This does not mean you can write anything you like about role models. They still have a right to privacy unless they are misbehaving or lying. But it is why England footballer Rio Ferdinand lost his bid to sue the *Sunday Mirror* for up to £50,000 after they published a 'kiss and tell' story on him (*Daily Mirror*, 2011).

What all this means for fashion journalists is that they must view privacy issues just as seriously as libel problems. It can be just as expensive and embarrassing to lose such a case.

And, as with libel, it is important to consult an experienced colleague or lawyer if in doubt.

Of course, privacy does not just apply to surreptitious photographs of the likes of Prince Harry in a Vegas hotel room or publishing information about someone's health.

It is illegal to hack into anyone's phone, email or intercept their mail, and there are several different laws under which you can be prosecuted and imprisoned for doing so. The royal editor of the now defunct *News of the World*, Clive Goodman, was jailed for four months in 2007 after admitting intercepting phone messages, including some involving Prince William.

There are very rare occasions when journalists, even those from respected broadsheet newspapers such as the *Guardian* and broadcaster *Sky News*, say it is perfectly justifiable to hack into someone's phone or email, if there is a serious public interest reason. However, it would be wise to seek legal and senior editorial advice before ever taking this approach.

Copyright

An essential part of being a fashion journalist is having a eye for visuals. A picture from a catwalk or the red carpet tells a story much better than any amount of words.

So selecting images, whether for a trend report, fashion feature or Oscars frock special, will be an integral part of your day-to-day job.

If you work on an established magazine, website or for a fashion retailer, there may well be a full-time picture researcher or picture department who will work alongside you.

However, there will be occasions you might want to research pictures yourself (from designers' online lookbooks or simply via Google) to use to illustrate your article. Or you may see a brilliant picture on Twitter and decide it's perfect for you to use too.

But you cannot just pick and choose any picture you want from the Web and download it for publication. Photographers, professional and amateur, have the right for their work not to be reused without their permission and possibly a payment too.

This comes under copyright law and applies not just to photographs, but all sorts of things from other people's interviews, graphics, videos, music and sketches.

Under the Copyright, Designs and Patents Act 1988, you can be sued in court for damages if you reproduce a substantial part of anyone's work without permission, be it copying a large chunk of an interview with a top model or reusing a fashion photographer's picture available on his or her website.

Fortunately, most designers, clothing chains, cosmetic companies and public relations agencies will happily provide you with images for free. After all, it's free publicity for them! Fashion journalists spend hours poring over different websites and lookbooks trying to find just the right products needed for, say, a 'Best 10 satchels' trend report.

But it is a different matter when it comes to using a professional photographer's work without permission. *The Mail on Sunday*, for instance, paid substantial damages to Madonna in 2009 when they reproduced, without permission, pictures of her wedding to Guy Ritchie. The paper had bought the snaps after they were taken from Madonna's private album without her knowledge.

When the *Daily Mirror* secured a photo of supermodel Kate Moss allegedly snorting cocaine in 2005, they splashed it across their front page. One glossy fashion magazine thought it would be okay to reproduce that front page in a subsequent story about the scandal. However, the *Mirror* owned the copyright to that picture and the magazine had to pay them a four-figure sum as compensation.

Another complication is when photos are taken for 'private and domestic reasons' such as a wedding, christening or a birthday party. You might find these, for instance, on a social media site and think it's all right to use them.

But not only do you need the permission of the 'author', i.e. the photographer who took them, but also the 'commissioner', i.e. the person who hired the photographer to take the pictures, because they have moral rights over those images. When it comes to a wedding, for example, that is often the bride's father or the couple themselves.

When it comes to reproducing someone else's words, there is a defence called fair dealing if there is a public interest reason to report on a current news event. Say a top designer announces in a big interview in a national newspaper that she is quitting fashion to become an author – you can reuse some of her words in your follow-up story.

However, it would be ethical journalistic practice to credit the original source, the newspaper, and not use too much of the article. You couldn't just copy the whole thing, for instance. If you are working online, perhaps it would also be a good idea to insert a hyperlink to the newspaper's story.

It is important to remember there is NO fair dealing defence for still images.

Anonymity issues

It is fairly unlikely that a fashion journalist will report on crime and a court case. But there are occasions when a high-profile figure in the fashion industry becomes involved in a criminal case and you need to have an overview of some issues surrounding anonymity.

Under law, anyone who makes a complaint that they have been the victim of a sexual offence – that can range from rape to the less serious indecent assault – has automatic lifetime anonymity. You cannot reveal his or her name, address, where they work, any pictures of them, or any details which might give away who they are.

If you want to identify, interview and photograph such a victim – you may want a long human-interest feature interview, for instance – you must get their permission in writing and they must be aged 16 or over.

Similarly, any children under 18 usually have anonymity when they appear in courts as defendants, witnesses or victims under the Children and Young Persons Act 1933.

Victims of blackmail also have lifelong anonymity, along with a few notorious criminals who could face reprisals if their new identities were revealed once they had been released from jail.

If any of your stories involve these sorts of cases, it should ring alarm bells immediately.

Contempt of court

At first glance, you may not think issues involving court cases and prejudice will matter in your line of business.

But, as before, you could find yourself reporting on fashion figures caught up in crimes, either as the accused or the victim. Or, as explained in this chapter's introduction, you may just find yourself in the wrong place at the wrong time when a big story breaks, such as the September 11 attacks.

Under the Contempt of Court Act 1981, a journalist can be jailed for up to two years and/or fined an unlimited amount if they publish anything which could cause a 'substantial risk of serious prejudice' to a case which is active. This usually means when someone is arrested.

This is to stop 'trial by media', that is, prejudicing potential jurors and witnesses by publishing something that makes the accused person look guilty when they have the right to a fair trial and are innocent until proven guilty in the eyes of the law.

There have been several well-publicised cases of the media being heavily fined for prejudicing cases, such as the terrible Joanna Yeates murder in 2010.

Even if you never find yourself covering a murder hunt or a court case, you may well be asked to get a human-interest interview with a witness or a victim in a case. It is best not to approach them before the case ends, and certainly not before they give evidence in court. It is also ethically wrong to offer payment to a witness before a case, as this might affect their evidence.

Also under contempt law, it is illegal to approach jurors to ask them about their experiences and how they voted in their deliberations.

Freebies

When you are a student, the prospect of lots of lovely free clothes, make-up and expensive lunches is probably an exciting one. And influential fashion journalists are bombarded daily with tissue-wrapped gifts from designers and public relations executives who want them to look favourably on certain brands (and hopefully get some free publicity too).

Of course, it's human nature to want all these luxury goodies, especially if you are just getting by on a lowly wage. But there are legal and ethical considerations.

Columnist Liz Jones is almost alone in exposing the freebie culture enjoyed by fashion journalists. She told the *Independent* in 2010 that one of the reasons she was sacked as editor of *Marie Claire* was because she had revealed a long list of freebies she'd received in just one month, including a week on a yacht in Capri courtesy of luxury handbag designers Tod's (Ross, 2010).

Ms Jones added: 'If a Westminster reporter took money from the Government or a football reporter took money from a club, it would be a scandal.' She also claimed she is now barred from attending shows by Armani, Louis Vuitton, Chloé, Chanel, Marc Jacobs and Victoria Beckham.

Another anonymous fashion writer told how she had thousands of pounds' worth of freebies under her desk, ranging from a £850 leather handbag to sparkly diamond earrings (in Pugh, 2011).

The Bribery Act, which came into force in July 2011, has raised concerns that accepting such presents when you are supposed to be an impartial journalist could put you, and the company which sent them, at risk of committing a criminal offence.

The law defines bribery as giving a financial, or other, advantage (which would include clothes and accessories) with the intent to persuade someone to 'improperly' do their job, which they would normally perform impartially. Giving or receiving such a bribe carries a maximum ten-year prison sentence.

Ethically, many magazines and publishing companies already had stringent policies about freebies long before this became law. Many insist all gifts sent to their editors and writers are given to charity. Others hold staff sales and give the money raised to charity.

Of course, some do keep these gifts, and less scrupulous journalists have been known to sell them on eBay to supplement their wages.

Fashion journalism is often criticised for being too fluffy and positive to keep advertisers happy. This is not a legal issue. Writing a gushing review of some £200 designer heels because you have been given a free pair and would not ordinarily write that is much more problematic.

Ethics

As well as abiding by a whole slew of laws, journalists need to bear in mind how they conduct themselves as professionals while going about their job on a daily basis. This is ethics.

Most newspapers, magazines and accompanying websites are signed up to a clear code of conduct which outlines acceptable and unacceptable behaviour ranging from accuracy to harassment.

In the light of the *News of the World* phone-hacking controversy and subsequent Leveson report into the media, the whole issue of how the press is regulated was still under debate at the time of writing.

However, it was widely considered that the Press Complaints Commission's long-established Editors' Code of Practice and its 16 clauses were a solid responsible model for journalists to follow. It is reproduced in full in the twenty-first edition of *McNae's Essential Law for Journalists*.

Journalists, whether reporting on Chelsea FC or Chanel, are under more scrutiny and regarded more warily than ever before.

As a journalist, you are expected to be accurate, impartial and professional at all times.

On duty or off, you represent your employer and your behaviour must reflect that.

When going about your job, you should be polite, and always announce your name and who you work for. There are circumstances when reporters use subterfuge and disguise their identities, but that is really the domain of the investigative journalist.

Further, you should ensure your spelling is immaculate and you always check how to spell someone's name. Imagine misspelling the name of a major beauty advertiser in your article. This would be hugely embarrassing for your editor, who won't be offering you a promotion any time soon.

To ensure accuracy, it is important to have learned shorthand to keep a good note of any interviews and conversations (100 words a minute is recommended) and to also record your interviews.

Legally, you do NOT have to tell the person on the other end of the phone that you are recording the conversation. You must, of course, tell them who you are and where you work.

Of course, most celebrities and fashion figures used to dealing with the press would expect you to use a recording device if they are sitting down for a face-to-face interview with you.

A good shorthand note and a recording of any interview should be stored for at least 12 months as evidence in case you are later sued for libel.

A hugely important ethical issue for journalists is protecting your sources. People secretly give you stories for all sorts of reasons – they want revenge, they want money, they genuinely want to expose some wrongdoing. Whatever their motive, they are risking their jobs, reputation and sometimes a jail sentence by giving you confidential information.

Morally, journalists must protect the identities of these sources at all costs. Say, for example, a friendly contact gives you documentary proof that a well-known high-street fashion chain is putting staff at risk by not adhering to health and safety guidelines.

It is important to investigate this story. But if the company, or even a court, demands to know who gave you this information, you must refuse to name them.

You would be extremely lucky to go through your career as a journalist without receiving a single complaint from either a reader or a person involved in one of your stories. Someone may complain that they have been misquoted by you, libelled by you, or that you have got the price wrong on a product review.

Certainly as a junior journalist, you should not try to deal with these complaints by yourself. Everyone's first thought is to say sorry, hope it goes away and that your boss never finds out! That is the worst thing to do.

For a start, by apologising, you could be admitting legal liability if it is a serious complaint and you have only made matters worse. The best practice is to simply take a note of the complainant's name and all their contact details (email, mobile phone, other phone numbers) along with the nature of the complaint and say you will pass this on to someone more senior to handle.

If you are in a full-time job, your boss will know what to do, sometimes after seeking advice from a media lawyer. If you are freelance, it may be worth seeking legal advice if it appears to be a serious costly issue.

Hopefully, if you are a responsible and accurate journalist, these scenarios will be extremely rare. As a student, regular attendance at your media law and ethics lectures will ensure you have a good grounding in all the issues which may crop up throughout your career.

And keeping up to date with changes in the law and press regulation will mean any employer will have confidence that you are a legally safe and ethically responsible person to hire.

Recommended reading

Hanna, M. and Dodd, M. (2012) *McNae's Essential Law for Journalists*, 21st edition. Oxford: Oxford University Press.

Hold the Front Page: www.holdthefrontpage.co.uk/category/news/law/.

Keeble, R. and Mair, J. (2012) *The Phone Hacking Scandal: Journalism on Trial.* Bury St Edmunds: Abramis Academic Publishing.

McNae's Essential Law for Journalists website: http://fds.oup.com/www.oup.co.uk/general/mcnaes/index.html.

Quinn, F. (2013) *Law for Journalists*, 4th edition. London: Pearson.

Rozenberg, J. (2010) *Privacy and the Press*. Oxford: Oxford University Press.

Glossary

Audit Bureau of Circulations: ABC for short, an industry body that audits and publishes the *circulation* figures of newspapers and magazines, and the user figures for newspaper websites.

ABC figures: the audited *circulation* figure for a magazine or newspaper. The *Audit Bureau of Circulations* publishes newspaper circulation figures every month, and magazine circulation figures every six months.

ABCe figures: the daily and monthly user figures for newspaper websites, published monthly by the *Audit Bureau of Circulations*.

advertisements (or **ads**): written, illustrated, photographic or video material which appears in a newspaper or magazine, or on a website or app, paid for by the advertiser. In print, these can take the form of display ads (often photographic, normally a page, half page or double page) or classified ads (smaller, text-based ads appearing in their own section). Online, they can take the form of banner ads (box on website), pop-ups (displayed in new window), floating or expanding ads (appear on top of editorial content), or interstitial ads (display before user gets to the content).

advertorial: words and pictures paid for by an advertiser but designed to look like *editorial*. Also known as advertisement features or special features or 'native advertising' on the web.

angle: the slant or main aspect of a story that the journalist thinks is most important or attention-grabbing. The story will start with or build up to the angle, and it shapes the way the whole article is written.

appointment: where a fashion journalist, editor or stylist arranges to meet a designer or brand *PR* to look at a new range, carry out an interview or select clothes for a shoot.

autumn–winter: one of the two main seasons a year, together with spring–summer. Designer *ready-to-wear* ranges for autumn–winter are shown on the catwalk in February/March, and land in stores in August to September. Known as 'fall' in the United States.

book: a production term for a magazine. 'Back of the book' is near the end of the magazine; 'front of the book' is near the start.

brand extension: when a newspaper or magazine branches out into another line of business – like awards ceremonies, exhibitions, retail, radio and television. Also, when a designer or retailer puts their name to another type of product, such as sunglasses, T-shirts or perfume.

Broadcast Journalism Training Council: BJTC for short, accredits some university courses.

business-to-business: also known as B2B, or the *trade press*. Publications targeted at members of a particular trade, focusing on news and analysis relevant to that profession. Examples are *Drapers* (for the fashion trade) or the *Press Gazette* (for journalists).

byline: the name of the writer that appears with their story. A picture by-line has a headshot (photograph of subject's head and shoulders) next to the name.

calling in: the process of selecting and borrowing samples of clothes and accessories from brands and stores to use in product or fashion shoots.

caption: sentence or short paragraph accompanying a picture or illustration, explaining what it shows. On a fashion story, a caption lists the garments, gives prices and specifies brands.

circulation: the number of copies of a newspaper or magazine that are sold or otherwise distributed (for example, given away for free, or sent to customers).

comp: short for complimentary, i.e. provided free of charge.

consumer press: publications targeted at the general public, rather than a trade, providing them with entertainment and news about a hobby, interest or general lifestyle.

content management system: CMS for short, a web application and tools that make it easy for non-technical users like (most) journalists to upload content to a website, edit it and publish it.

content marketing: when a brand creates *editorial* content, such as a blog post, a video, an article or a whole magazine, to attract and engage a targeted audience.

contract publisher: a company that produces customer magazines for brands which don't have in-house publishing staff.

copy: words written by journalists for publication.

coverlines: the headlines on the front cover of a magazine, highlighting the stories, interviews and fashion inside.

cover mounts: free gifts given away with a magazine (often bagged with the magazine, or stuck to the cover).

credits: the names of photographers, stylists, hair and make-up artists, models, and assistants who worked on a shoot, which will appear at the start or the end of the story. Credits are also given to travel companies, hotels and other locations that helped with the shoot.

cruise: a collection that normally arrives in stores in November to fill the gap between autumn–winter (in stores from August) and spring–summer (in stores from February). Traditionally aimed at those going abroad for winter sun, now more of a commercial, mid-season collection. Also known as *resort*.

customer magazine: a print or digital magazine produced by brands (like Asos, John Lewis or Tesco) as a form of *content marketing*, sent to customers or available to pick up or buy in store.

diffusion line: a secondary range produced by a design house, typically at more moderate prices. Examples are McQ by Alexander McQueen, and Versus by Versace.

double-page spread: DPS for short, a story, shoot or advert taking up two facing pages.

editorial: content (text, video, photographs, audio) produced by journalists for a newspaper, magazine, website or brand. Anything that's not an *advert*.

editorial mention: the inclusion of a picture or name of a product on an editorial page, as opposed to an advert.

e-tailer: a retailer which sells clothes via a website. Some are e-tail only (like Asos or Net-a-Porter); some are bricks-and-mortar stores which also retail online.

fashion cupboard: a room, area or cupboard where clothes and accessories are stored before and after a shoot. Normally the interns' job to keep it tidy and well-organised.

flatplan: a plan showing each page of a magazine – or screen of an app – as a small rectangle with planned content marked on it (or a cross through it to represent an advert).

freelance: anyone who is self-employed, contributing to a range of publications or mixing editorial and commercial work. On a *masthead*, freelance journalists or stylists appear as 'contributing editors' or 'editors-at-large'.

go-sees: appointments where models go to meet fashion, art or bookings editors in the hope of being cast for a particular shoot or earmarked for a future one.

haute couture: the creation of made-to-measure garments for individual clients. Design houses have to meet certain standards to be legally entitled to use the term.

house style: guidelines about spelling, grammar, voice, tone and editorial policy that every publication and website has, to ensure consistency.

intro: the introduction, or first paragraph, of a feature or news story.

inverted pyramid: the traditional way of structuring a news story, with the most important facts at the start, narrowing down to less important details at the end.

lead time: the time that elapses between a newspaper or magazine being 'put to bed' or completed, and its actual publication.

line sheets: photos or sketches of a designer's or brand's range, accompanied by style names or numbers, colour and fabric information, and prices. Used by editors and stylists for *calling in* clothes for shoots, and by buyers for making orders.

lookbook: a book or digital collection of catwalk or model photographs showing off a designer's or brand's upcoming range. Sent to editors and used for *calling in* clothes for shoots.

main fashion: the big fashion shoots for any particular issue of a magazine.

masthead: either the title/logo of a magazine or newspaper, or a panel near the front of a publication listing the staff members and contributors, and contact details.

media pack or **kit**: information compiled by a publisher giving details about circulation and readership of a magazine, newspaper or website, together with the cost of advertising in it.

model card: a card printed with pictures from a model's portfolio, their vital statistics, eye and hair colour, and contact information. Used as a type of business card.

National Council for the Training of Journalists: NCTJ for short, a charity for the media that sets qualifications and awards, and accredits some university and college courses.

National Readership Survey: an industry body that measures and carries out research into the *readership* of newspapers and magazines in the UK.

news release: an announcement of new collaborations, new ranges, company news, financial figures, etc., written by a PR and sent (normally by email) to journalists and bloggers. Also known as a press release.

nub paragraph: the part of a feature, normally a couple of paragraphs in, that explains what the story is all about and why the reader should be interested in it, now.

paywall: a system whereby a newspaper or magazine charges for access to all or some content on its website.

peg: the timely aspect of a story which justifies why it's being published now.

PR: short for public relations. People employed to promote a brand and its products, and handle its dealings with the media.

pre-fall: a mid-season collection that normally drops in stores around May, filling the gap between spring–summer (February) and autumn–winter (August/September) collections. Like *cruise/resort*, often more commercial than the main collections and increasingly popular with customers.

press days: previews of upcoming collections by high-street retailers or other brands that can't show at London Fashion Week. Useful for fashion journalists and stylists to see future trends, earmark items for upcoming shoots, meet brand *PRs* and keep advertisers happy.

prêt-à-porter: garments produced in standard sizes and bought off the peg, as opposed to made to measure. Known in English as ready-to-wear (RTW).

primary source: somebody that a journalist has talked to or swapped messages with, for the purpose of a story.

Professional Publishers Association: PPA for short, the trade body for magazine brands. Accredits some university courses.

pull quote: a quote taken from a story and printed in larger type or in a panel or box to break up the text and pull the reader into the article.

rate card: a list of the rates a publication charges for advertising space, depending on the size and position of the advert.

readership: how many people read a print publication. Different from *circulation*, as it's generally estimated that at least two to three people read every copy distributed. Measured and analysed by the *National Readership Survey* (NRS) in the UK.

ready-to-wear: or RTW for short, garments produced in standard sizes and bought off the peg, as opposed to made to measure. Known in French as prêt-à-porter.

resort: a collection that normally arrives in stores in October or November to fill the gap between autumn–winter (in stores from August) and spring–summer (in stores from February). Traditionally aimed at those going abroad for winter sun, now more of a mid-season collection. Also known as *cruise*.

returns: the process of checking clothes or accessories and sending them back to *PRs* once they've been used for a fashion shoot. Normally the job of an intern or fashion assistant.

samples: items of clothing, or accessories, produced to show on a catwalk, exhibit in a showroom, show to buyers and lend to fashion editors/stylists for shoots.

search engine optimisation: often shortened to SEO – techniques used to make web pages more visible in search engines, in order to rank higher in lists of results for popular search terms and so get more hits.

secondary source: information that a journalist draws upon for facts for a story, for example a *news release*, a report, a book or an article that has already been published.

seeding: when a brand sends free products to celebrities, journalists and bloggers in the hope they'll be spotted wearing or carrying them, and might write about them.

sell: a sentence or two of text, normally in large or bold type, or in a box, that introduces a feature. Also known as a *standfirst*.

shopping page: a page showing various products available in stores at that time, normally grouped around a product type or trend (e.g. winter coats, or cobalt blue).

showrooms: rooms owned or leased by designers or brands to house *samples* of their latest collections.

sidebar: additional material (text or photos) that complements the main story and sits alongside it on a panel or in a box.

source: a person, organisation or published material that a journalist draws upon for quotes and information for a story. See *primary source* and *secondary source*.

splash: the main story on the front of a newspaper or news magazine.

spring–summer: one of the two main seasons a year, together with autumn–winter. Designer *ready-to-wear* ranges for spring–summer are shown on the catwalk in September/October, and land in stores around February.

standfirst: a sentence or two of text, normally in large or bold type, or in a box, that introduces a feature. Also known as a *sell*.

strapline: a subsidiary headline that runs along the top of a page, expanding on the main headline. Normally has slightly more detail than a *subhead*.

subhead: a subsidiary headline that runs just below the main headline, giving a little more detail.

tear sheets (or tears): articles or photographs ripped out of newspapers or magazines by a journalist to keep because they might prompt a follow-up story or feature.

trade press: publications targeted at members of a particular trade, focusing on news and analysis relevant to that profession. Examples are *Drapers* (for the fashion trade) or the *Press Gazette* (for journalists). Also known as *business-to-business* publications, or B2B.

trade shows: exhibitions of yarns, fabrics or garments aimed at those in the fashion trade (design houses, high-street brands that manufacture their own ranges, buyers and trade press) rather than the general public.

treatment: how a writer handles a feature story, e.g. whether it is written in the first person or third person, as a diary, as a series of pictures with captions, or as a series of mini-interviews.

trend forecasters: people or companies who research future trends for clients, on the basis of trade and graduate shows, industry analysis, consumer and retail trends, and scouting in cities around the world.

trunk shows: a special sale where a small business or designer presents their range to select customers at a store or other venue.

vox pop: short for vox populi ('voice of the people'), where a journalist puts the same question to various members of the public and publishes a quote from each one, together with a headshot, or edits them together on a piece of audio or video.

well: the middle section of a magazine, where main fashion spreads or longer features appear, as opposed to smaller pieces and shopping pages near the front or back.

Bibliography

Advertising Association (2013) 'UK advertising's bounce-back continues', 9 July. Available online at: www.adassoc.org.uk/write/UK_advertising's_bounce_back_continues.pdf.

Agins, T. (2001) *The End of Fashion: How Marketing Changed the Clothing Business Forever*. London: HarperCollins.

Alexander, E. (2013) 'Marion Cotillard BAFTA interview exclusive', *Vogue* online, 11 February. Available online at: www.vogue.co.uk/news/2013/02/11/marion-cotillard-baftas-style-and-rust-and-bone-interview.

All Party Parliamentary Group on Body Image (2012) *Reflections on Body Image*. Available online at: www.ncb.org.uk/media/861233/appg_body_image_final.pdf.

Almassi, H. (2010) Interview with the author, 18 December.

——(2012a) 'Queen of bling hits H&M', *Grazia*, 17 September.

——(2012b) Fashion masterclass at Sunderland University's Canary Wharf Campus, 2 November.

——(2013) 'From Jennifer Aniston to Florence Welch, winter florals are the print trend for all!', *Grazia*, 15 August. Available online at: www.graziadaily.co.uk/fashion/tips/from-jennifer-aniston-to-florence-welch-winter-florals-are-the-print-trend-for-all-pick-your-bouquet.

Amed, I. (2010) 'What the Independent article didn't tell us', *The Business of Fashion*, 3 February. Available online at: www.businessoffashion.com/2010/02/fashion-2-0-what-the-independent-article-didnt-tell-us.html.

——(2011) 'Is Burberry's digital prowess really waning?' *The Business of Fashion*, 6 June. Available online at: www.businessoffashion.com/2011/06/is-burberrys-digital-prowess-really-waning.html.

——(2012) 'BoF interviews Facebook's Tracy Yaverbaun at Decoded London', *The Business of Fashion*, 5 November. Available online at: www.businessoffashion.com/2012/11/bof-interviews-facebooks-tracy-yaverbaun-at-decoded-london.html.

——(2013) 'Fashion's made-for-Instagram moments', *The Business of Fashion*, 3 July. Available online at: www.businessoffashion.com/2013/07/fashions-made-for-instagram-moments.html.

Anaya, S. (2013) 'Creative class: Robbie Spencer, fashion director', *The Business of Fashion*, 17 June. Available online at: www.businessoffashion.com/2013/06/the-creative-class-robbie-spencer-fashion-director.html.

Armstrong, L. (2009) 'Why Vogue still wields such power', *The Times*, 2 July. Available online at: www.thetimes.co.uk/tto/life/fashion/article1753909.ece.

Asos.com (2013) '5 questions: Sedge Beswick, social media manager for Asos.com', *Seller Blog*, 18 July. Available online at: https://marketplace.asos.com/community/sellerblog/2013/07/5-questions-sedge-beswick-social-media.

Ballaster, R., Beetham, M., Frazer, E. and Hebron, S. (1991) *Women's Worlds: Ideology, Femininity and Women's Magazines*. London: Palgrave Macmillan.

Banham, M. (2012) 'Vice acquires style bible i-D magazine', *MediaWeek*, 19 December. Available online at: www.mediaweek.co.uk/article/1164922/vice-acquires-style-bible-i-d-magazine.

Barber, L. (2008) 'The world according to garb', *The Observer*, 10 February. Available online at: www.theguardian.com/lifeandstyle/2008/feb/10/fashion.features1.

Barber, L. (2012) 'Company magazine unveil redesign', *MediaWeek*, 13 January. Available online at: www.mediaweek.co.uk/article/1112068/company-magazine-unveils-redesign.

Barrett, C. and Bradshaw, T. (2011) 'Burberry in step with digital age', *Financial Times*, 31 August. Available online at: www.ft.com/cms/s/0/70689408-d3f2-11e0-b7eb-00144feab49a.html?siteedition=uk#axzz2fYOYYfJh.

Barthes, R. (1967) *The Fashion System*, translated by M. Ward and R. Howard, New York: Hill and Wang.

BBC News (2004) 'Naomi Campbell wins privacy case', 6 May. Available online at: http://news.bbc.co.uk/1/hi/uk/3689049.stm.

——(2007) 'Winslet accepts libel settlement', 9 March. Available online at: http://news.bbc.co.uk/1/hi/entertainment/6434081.stm.

——(2013a) 'Burberry profits rise as Asian sales grow', 21 May. Available online at: www.bbc.co.uk/news/business-22605706.

——(2013b) 'Vogue sends fashion tricks film to schools', 5 September. Available online at: www.bbc.co.uk/news/uk-23979809.

Beaty, Z. (2012) 'We hit the shops with the Far Eastern-istas', *Grazia*, 6 February, pp. 43–5.

——(2013) 'A day at the races, Scouse style', *Grazia*, 22 April, pp. 51–4.

Big Think (2012) 'A Big Think interview with Scott Schuman'. Available online at: http://bigthink.com/users/scottschuman.

Bigger, E. (2012) Interview with the author, 25 October.

Blanks, T. (2011) 'Spring 2012 ready-to-wear: Alexander McQueen', *Style.com*, 4 October. Available online at: www.style.com/fashionshows/review/S2012RTW-AMCQUEEN.

Bletchly, R. (2012) 'Tramp to vamp … we give mum banned from nightclubs for skimpy clothes a chic makeover', *Daily Mirror*, 25 January. Available online at: www.mirror.co.uk/news/uk-news/lisa-woodman-given-a-chic-makeover-190035.

Bowden, M. (2013) Interview with the author, 5 July.

Bowe, H. (2013) 'Are seasons out of fashion?', *The Industry London*, 8 August. Available online at: www.theindustrylondon.com/are-seasons-out-of-fashion.

British Fashion Council (2010) 'Value of the British fashion industry', *British Fashion Council*. Available online at: www.britishfashioncouncil.com/content.aspx?CategoryID=1745.

——(2012) *Future of Fashion: Strategic Considerations for Growth*. Available online at: www.britishfashioncouncil.co.uk/uploads/media/62/26140.pdf.

Bruton, J. (2013) Speech to Professional Publishers Association annual conference, 8 May.

Bumpus, J. (2013a) 'Autumn/winter 2013-14 ready-to-wear: Anna Sui', *Vogue* online, 13 February. Available online at: www.vogue.co.uk/fashion/autumn-winter-2013/ready-to-wear/anna-sui.

——(2013b) Interview with the author, 27 June.

——(undated) 'Jessica Bumpus, Vogue Online,' University of the Arts London. Available online at: www.arts.ac.uk/fashion/people/alumni/jessica-bumpus.

Cartner-Morley, J. (2009) 'Eyes front', *Guardian*, 13 March. Available online at: www.theguardian.com/lifeandstyle/2009/mar/13/fashion-shows-front-row.

——(2011a) 'Autumn fashion forecast: after the catwalk storms come the calm', *Guardian*, 11 March. Available online at: www.theguardian.com/lifeandstyle/2011/mar/11/autumn-fashion-catwalk-sexy.

——(2011b) Interview with the author, 14 September.

——(2011c) 'Mary Portas and Melanie Rickey: fashion's power couple', *Guardian*, 7 October. Available online at: www.theguardian.com/fashion/2011/oct/07/mary-portas-melanie-rickey-fashion-power-couple-intervierw.

——(2011d) 'Tom "God" Ford has off day: fashion world in denial', *Guardian*, 19 September. Available online at: www.theguardian.com/fashion/fashion-blog/2011/sep/19/london-fashion-week-tom-ford.

——(2012) 'Haute couture shows: nice frocks – but no shocks', *Guardian*, 25 January. Available online at: www.theguardian.com/fashion/2012/jan/25/haute-couture-nice-frocks-no-shocks.

——(2013a) 'New York Fashion Week: the return of Diane von Furstenberg', *Guardian*, 11 February. Available online at: www.theguardian.com/fashion/fashion-blog/2013/feb/11/new-york-fashion-week-von-furstenberg.

——(2013b) 'New York fashion week: John Galliano makes his presence felt at Oscar de la Renta', *Guardian*, 13 February. Available online at: www.theguardian.com/fashion/fashion-blog/2013/feb/13/new-york-fashion-week-john-galliano-oscar-renta.

——(2013c) 'Christopher Kane marks ascent to fashion's top flight by hitting sweet spot', *Guardian*, 18 February. Available online at: www.theguardian.com/fashion/2013/feb/18/christopher-kane-fashion-top-flight.

——(2013d) 'Paris Fashion Week: Alexander Wang makes confident debut at Balenciaga', *Guardian*, 28 February. Available online at: www.theguardian.com/fashion/2013/feb/28/paris-fashion-alexander-wang-balenciaga.

——(2013e) 'London fashion week kicks off with call to support fashion education', *Guardian*, 13 September. Available online at: www.theguardian.com/fashion/2013/sep/13/london-fashion-week-education.

Channel 4 News (2013) 'Naomi Campbell: fashion industry "guilty of racist acts"', 16 September. Available online at: www.channel4.com/news/naomi-campbell-fashion-london-show-bethann-hardison-video.

Chartered Institute of Public Relations: www.cipr.co.uk/content/about-us/about-pr.

Christian, A. (2013) Interview with the author, 13 July.

Church-Gibson, P. (2006) 'Analysing fashion', in Jackson, T. and Shaw, D. (eds) *The Fashion Handbook*. London: Routledge, pp. 20–28.

Ciancio, A. (2011) 'Fashion bloggers to spur online luxury sales – report', *Reuters*, 15 September. Available online at: http://uk.reuters.com/article/2011/09/15/uk-italy-luxury-idUKTRE78E4LA20110915.

Cisco (2013) 'Cisco visual networking index: forecast and methodology', 2012–2017, 29 May. Available online at: www.cisco.com/en/US/solutions/collateral/ns341/ns525/ns537/ns705/ns827/white_paper_c11-481360_ns827_Networking_Solutions_White_Paper.html.

Cocozza, P. (2012) 'Smile! It's the hot new fashion accessory', *Guardian*, 10 January. Available online at: www.theguardian.com/fashion/shortcuts/2012/jan/10/smiling-back-in-fashion.

——(2013) 'Skinny jeans: the fashion trend that refuses to die', *Guardian*, 9 January. Available online at: www.theguardian.com/fashion/2013/jan/09/skinny-jeans-fashion-trend-refuses-to-die

Coddington, G. (2012) *Grace: A Memoir*. London: Chatto & Windus.

Conboy, M. (2004) *Journalism: A Critical History*. London: Sage.

Core, C. (2013) 'Haute couture fact file', *Daily Telegraph*. Available online at: http://fashion.telegraph.co.uk/news-features/TMG10147014/Haute-Couture-fact-file.html.

Cowles, C. (2013) 'Hedi Slimane's controversial Saint Laurent clothes sell like hot cakes', *New York Magazine's The Cut* blog, 18 April. Available online at: http://nymag.com/thecut/2013/04/hedi-slimanes-saint-laurent-sells-like-hotcakes.html.

Craik, J. (2009) *Fashion: The Key Concepts*. Oxford: Berg.

Crisell, H. (2012) Fashion masterclass at Sunderland University's Canary Wharf Campus, 2 November.

——(2013) 'In London, Tom Ford launches "luxury" T-shirts', *New York Magazine*, 18 June. Available online at: http://nymag.com/thecut/2013/06/london-tom-ford-launches-luxury-t-shirts.html.

Cullen, P. (2013) Interview with the author, 15 July.

Currie, S. (2013) Interview with the author, 23 May.

Cutler, R. J. (2009) *The September Issue*.

Dacre, K. (2013) 'Meet team ASOS', *Evening Standard*, 8 July. Available online at: www.standard.co.uk/news/uk/meet-team-asos-theyre-in-their-20s-or-30s-hit-the-pub-together-on-fridays-have-epic-staff-parties–and-work-their-butts-off-8695194.html.

Daily Mirror (2011) 'Rio Ferdinand loses privacy case over Sunday Mirror kiss and tell', 29 September. Available online at: www.mirror.co.uk/news/uk-news/rio-ferdinand-loses-privacy-case-273703.

Davies, L. (2013) Interview with the author, 3 July.

Devlin, P. (1979) *The Vogue Book of Fashion Photography: 1919–1979*. London: Simon & Schuster.

Diderich, J. and Wynne, A. (2011) 'Too much pressure, Galliano tells court', *WWD*, 23 June. Available online at: www.wwd.com/fashion-news/fashion-features/too-much-pressure-galliano-tells-court-3678311.

Dingemans, J. (1999) *Mastering Fashion Styling*. London: Palgrave Macmillan.

Dixon, M. (2013) Interview with the author, 15 July.

Drapers (2012) 'Media information'. Available online at: www.drapersonline.com/Journals/2012/04/23/z/s/x/Drapers-Display-Media-Pack-2012.pdf.

Drew, W. (2009) 'London's front row comes of age', *The Times*, 19 September. Available online at: www.thetimes.co.uk/tto/life/fashion/article1754051.ece.

Edwards-Jones, I. (2007) *Fashion Babylon*. London: Corgi.

——(2009) 'Fashion's big secret is out of the bag as Beyonce reveals how stars are deluged with freebies', *Daily Mail*, 28 May. Available online at: www.dailymail.co.uk/femail/article-1189043/Fashions-big-secret-bag-Beyonce-reveals-stars-deluged-freebies.html.

Enoch, N. (2012) 'Mother-of-four, 28, banned from every nightclub in town for being "too old to wear skimpy outfits"', *Daily Mail*, 23 January. Available online at: www.dailymail.co.uk/news/article-2090547/Mother-28-banned-towns-nightclubs-old-wear-skimpy-outfits.html.

Entwistle, J. and Rocamora, A. (2006) 'The field of fashion materialized: A study of London Fashion Week', *Sociology*, 40(4): 735–51.

Evening, M. (2012) *Adobe Photoshop for Photographers*. London: Focal Press.

Evening Standard (2007) 'Nicole Kidman accepts "substantial" damages over perfume claim', 14 December. Available online at: www.standard.co.uk/showbiz/nicole-kidman-wins-substantial-damages-over-perfume-claim-6619614.html.

Fashion Monitor (2013) Jobs: Style Editor – *Metro International*, June. No longer available online.

Fitzsimmons, A. (2013) Interview with the author, 9 September.

Fox, I. (2010) 'Country jacket gets streetwise as urban Britain goes for rural look', *Guardian*, 5 November. Available online at: www.theguardian.com/lifeandstyle/2010/nov/05/country-jackets-urban-fashion

——(2011) 'Your guide to the autumn/winter 2011 fashion shows', *Guardian*, 10 February. Available online at: www.theguardian.com/lifeandstyle/2011/feb/10/shows-fashion-week-new-york.

——(2012) 'Victoria Beckham goes from strength to strength with New York show', *Guardian*, 12 February. Available online at: www.theguardian.com/lifeandstyle/2012/feb/12/victoria-beckham-new-york-show.

——(2013) 'How to dress: grown-up grunge', *Guardian*, 23 August. Available online at: www.theguardian.com/fashion/2013/aug/23/how-to-dress-grown-up-grunge.

Franklin, C. (2013) Interview with the author, 11 May.

Freeman, H. (2008) 'Torn off a strip', *Guardian*, 19 June. Available online at: www.theguardian.com/lifeandstyle/2008/jun/19/fashion.catwalk.

——(2009) *The Meaning of Sunglasses: A Guide to (Almost) All Things Fashionable*. London: Penguin.

Fury, A. (2013) 'Winter forecast: French frocks to Highland flings – the key trends for autumn/winter 2013', *Independent*, 18 August. Available online at: www.independent.co.uk/life-style/fashion/features/winter-forecast-french-frocks-to-highland-flings–the-key-trends-for-autumnwinter-2013-8773091.html.

Gabrillo, J. (2012) 'It's a man's world at MrPorter.com', *The National*, 27 June. Available online at: www.thenational.ae/lifestyle/fashion/its-a-mans-world-at-mrporter-com.

Gannon, L. (2010) '"I didn't think I'd make it to 40. I'm not proud of what I've done," Naomi Campbell on her regrets', *Mail on Sunday*, 22 March. Available online at: www.dailymail.co.uk/home/moslive/article-1258631/Naomi-Campbell-I-didnt-think-I-make-40-Im-proud-Ive-done.html.

——(2012a) Interview with Carole Watson, 1 October.

——(2012b) Fashion masterclass at Sunderland University's Canary Wharf Campus, 2 November.

——(2013) Interview with Carole Watson, 15 July.

Graafland, A. (2013) Interview with the author, 2 July.

Grazia Daily (2010) 'Grazia Ignites Houlihan Fever!', *Grazia*, 10 June. Available online at: www.graziadaily.co.uk/fashion/archive/2010/06/10/grazia-ignites-houlihan-fever.htm.

Greene, L. (2010) 'The boom in branded magazines', *Financial Times*, 8 January. Available online at: www.ft.com/cms/s/0/82754772-fbe0-11de-9c29-00144feab49a.html?siteedition=uk#axzz2fHTshwGi.

——(2011) 'Online retailers discover the joy of journalism', *Financial Times*, 4 February. Available online at: www.ft.com/cms/s/2/4dc5e92c-2fe3-11e0-a7c6-00144feabdc0.html#axzz2f5b1LjlZ.

Griffith, E. (2011) 'Bloggers mean business', *Adweek*, 13 September. Available online at: www.adweek.com/news/advertising-branding/bloggers-mean-business-134757.

Guardian online (2013) 'Punk fashion: get the look – in pictures', 23 April. Available online at: www.theguardian.com/fashion/gallery/2013/apr/23/punk.

Halliday, J. (2013) 'Condé Nast's style bible is still in Vogue as upmarket publisher sits pretty', *Guardian*, 18 August. Available online at: www.theguardian.com/media/media-blog/2013/aug/18/conde-nast-vogue-upmarket-magazine.

Hanna, M. and Dodd, M. (2012) *McNae's Essential Law for Journalists*, 21st edition. Oxford: Oxford University Press.

Hanna, M and Sanders, K (2007) 'Journalism education in Britain: who are the students and what do they want?', *Journalism Practice*, 1(3): 404–20.

Harcup, T. (2009) *Journalism: Principles and Practice*, 2nd edn. London: Sage.

Hardie, C. (2011) 'The power of the network', *Retail Week*, 24 January. Available online at: www.retail-week.com/multichannel/the-power-of-the-network/5021426.article.

Hart, E. (2013) Interview with Carole Watson, 5 July.

Hearst (2013) 'Elle launches its first ever beauty online shop', 5 August. Available online at: www.hearst.co.uk/magazines/011-1213-ELLE-UK-Launches-Its-First-Ever-Beauty-Online-Shop-SHOPELLEUK-COM.html.

Henderson, P. (2013) Interview with the author, 1 July.

Hines, T. (2006) 'The nature of the clothing and textiles industries: structure, context and processes', in Jackson, T. and Shaw, D. (eds) *The Fashion Handbook (Media Practice)*. London: Routledge, pp. 3–19.

Hodge, S. (2013) Interview with the author, 9 September.

Holbrook, B. and Dixon, G. (1985) 'Mapping the market for fashion: complementarity in consumer preferences', in Solomon, M. (ed) *The Psychology of Fashion*. Lexington, MA: Lexington Books, pp. 109–26.

Horyn, C. (2010) 'Beyond Twitter: what's next for designers in 2011', *New York Times*, 23 December. Available online at: http://runway.blogs.nytimes.com/2010/12/23/beyond-twitter-whats-next-for-designers-in-2011.

Intel (2011) *Visual Life – The Sartorialist*. Available online at: www.intel.com/content/www/us/en/visual-life/visual-life-sartorialist-video.html.

Jackson, T. and Shaw, D. (2006) *The Fashion Handbook (Media Practice)*. London: Routledge.

Jones, D. (2012) 'The Donatella interview', *Vogue* online, 31 May. Available online at: www.vogue.co.uk/news/2012/05/31/donatella-versace-oxford-union-talk-and-interview.

Jones, L. (2012) 'Cathy Horyn is as rare as a size 16 model on a Victoria Beckham catwalk: Liz Jones on why most fashion critics are terrified of writing an honest review', *Daily Mail*, 4 October. Available online at: www.dailymail.co.uk/femail/article-2212974/Cathy-Horyn-rare-size-16-model-Victoria-Beckham-catwalk-LIZ-JONES-fashion-critics-terrified-writing-honest-review.html.

——(2013) 'Confessions of a front row fashionista: in the final part of her unmissable memoirs, Liz Jones looks back in horror at her days as a glossy editor', *Daily Mail*, 22 June. Available online at: www.dailymail.co.uk/femail/article-2346566/Confessions-row-fashionista-In-final-unmissable-memoirs-LIZ-JONES-looks-horror-days-glossy-editor.html.

Jones, M. (2012) Interview with Carole Watson, 15 September.

Jones, T. and Enninful, E. (2010) *i-D Covers: 1980–2010*. London: Taschen.

Kansara, V. (2009) 'In conversation with Ruth Hogben, fashion filmmaker', *The Business of Fashion*, 11 August. Available online at: www.businessoffashion.com/2009/08/fashion-20-in-conversation-with-ruth-hogben-fashion-filmmaker.html.

——(2010a) 'Jaime Perlman tests the future of fashion editorial', *The Business of Fashion*, 18 January. Available online at: www.businessoffashion.com/2010/01/fashion-2-0-jaime-perlman-tests-the-future-of-fashion-editorial.html.

——(2010b) 'Digital scorecard: Telegraph fashion', *The Business of Fashion*, 13 October. Available online at: www.businessoffashion.com/2010/10/digital-scorecard-telegraph-fashion.html.

——(2011a) 'Social curation start-ups target fashion industry', *The Business of Fashion*, 20 April. Available online at: www.businessoffashion.com/2011/04/fashion-2-0-social-curation-start-ups-target-fashion-industry.html.

——(2011b) 'The trouble with iPad magazines', *The Business of Fashion*, 23 May. Available online at: www.businessoffashion.com/2011/05/fashion-2-0-the-trouble-with-ipad-magazines.html.

——(2013a) 'The long view: Lucy Yeomans says it's time to change the rules of fashion media', *The Business of Fashion*, 17 February. Available online at: www.businessoffashion.com/2013/02/the-long-view-lucy-yeomans.html.

——(2013b) 'The store is everywhere', *The Business of Fashion*, 17 July. Available online at: www.businessoffashion.com/2013/07/the-store-is-everywhere-frog-forrester-google-nike-apple-steve-jobs-the-fancy-joe-einhorn.html.

Kawamura, Y. (2005) *Fashion-ology: An Introduction to Fashion Studies*. Oxford: Berg.

Kennedy, V. (2012) Interview with Carole Watson, 15 September.

Lafferty, C. (2010) 'Dolly Jones on internships', *Arts London News*, 20 May. Available online at: www.artslondonnews.co.uk/20100518-interview-with-dolly-jones.

Lamb, L. (2011) Interview with the author, 18 April.

Langmead, J. (2013) 'Op-ed: is church and state obsolete?', *The Business of Fashion*, 7 April. Available online at: www.businessoffashion.com/2013/04/is-church-and-state-obsolete.html.

Lau, S. (2009) 'Hogg roasted', *Style Bubble*, 2 June. Available online at: www.stylebubble.co.uk/style_bubble/2009/06/hogg-roasted.html.

Lea Sayer, T. (2013) Interview with the author, 15 July.

Leitch, L. (2011) 'A man's guide to a woman's wardrobe', *The Economist*, Sept/Oct. Available online at: http://moreintelligentlife.co.uk/content/lifestyle/a-mans-guide-a-womans-wardrobe?page=full.

——(2012) 'Becoming Mr fashion', *Vogue*, October issue, pp. 125–6.

——(2013a) 'Paris Fashion Week: Chanel autumn/winter 2013', *Daily Telegraph*, 5 March. Available online at: http://fashion.telegraph.co.uk/news-features/TMG9909597/Paris-Fashion-Week-Chanel-autumnwinter-2013.html.

——(2013b) 'Anna Dello Russo's menace in Venice', *Daily Telegraph*, 10 July. Available online at: http://fashion.telegraph.co.uk/news-features/TMG10169610/Anna-Dello-Russos-menace-in-Venice.html.

——(2013c) Interview with the author, 11 July.

Look Media Kit (2012) Available online at: www.ipcadvertising.com/resource/ws1q539gzzjskgql0yvnkpih.pdf.

LOVE Media Kit (2012) Available online at: www.condenastinternational.com/country/united-kingdom/love/.

McCaffrey, J. (2012) Interview with Carole Watson, 1 October.

McCracken, G. (1998) *Culture and Consumption: New Approaches to the Symbolic Character of Consumer Goods and Activities*. Bloomington, IN: Indiana University Press.

McDowell, C. (2013) 'Why fashion needs its fourth estate', *The Business of Fashion*, 31 July. Available online at: www.businessoffashion.com/2013/07/colins-column-why-fashion-needs-its-fourth-estate.html.

McIntosh, F. (2012) Interview with the author, 1 May.

McKay, J. (2013) *The Magazines Handbook*, 3rd edition. London: Routledge.

McLoughlin, L. (2000) *The Language of Magazines*. London: Routledge.

McMahon, B. and Churcher, S. (2012) 'The British fashionista on a mission ... to make America have more sex', *Mail on Sunday*, 23 September, pp. 34–5.

McRobbie, A. (1991) *Feminism and Youth Culture: From Jackie to Just 17*. London: Macmillan.

——(1998) *British Fashion Design: Rag Trade or Image Industry?* London: Routledge.

MacSweeney, E. (ed.) (2012) *Vogue: The Editor's Eye*. New York: Abrams.

Malik, S. (2011) 'Unpaid website intern celebrates court victory,' *Guardian*, 23 May. Available online at: www.theguardian.com/media/2011/may/23/unpaid-website-intern-court-victory.

Mallen, S. (2012) Interview with the author, 25 October.

Marr, A. (2004) *My Trade: A Short History of British Journalism*. London: Macmillan.

Medine, L. (2013) 'Blog is a dirty word', *The Man Repeller*, 18 February. Available online at: www.manrepeller.com/2013/02/blog-is-a-dirty-word.html.

Menkes, S. (2013) 'The circus of fashion', *T Magazine*, 10 February. Available online at: http://tmagazine.blogs.nytimes.com/2013/02/10/the-circus-of-fashion/.

Mesure, S. (2010) 'Fluff flies as fashion writers pick a cat fight with bloggers', *The Independent*, 31 January. Available online at: www.independent.co.uk/life-style/fashion/news/fluff-flies-as-fashion-writers-pick-a-cat-fight-with-bloggers-1884539.html.

Milligan, L. (2009) 'Kane and Able', *Vogue* online, 1 December. Available online at: www. vogue.co.uk/news/2009/12/01/christopher-kane-interview.

Mintel (2011) 'Online fashion clicks with Brits as market increases 152% over past five years', *Mintel*, 15 April. Available online at: www.mintel.com/press-centre/fashion/online-fashion-clicks-with-brits-as-market-increases-152-over-past-five-years.

Mooney, A. (2013) Interview with the author, 15 July.

Mower, S. (2007) *Stylist: The Interpreters of Fashion*. New York: Rizzoli.

——(2008) 'Fashion world stunned by Vogue for black', *Observer*, 27 July. Available online at: www.theguardian.com/lifeandstyle/2008/jul/27/fashion.pressandpublishing.

Mujay, A. (2013) Interview with Carole Watson, 9 July.

Murphy, A. (2013) Interview with the author, 28 June.

Murray, A. (2011) 'Fashion week: the ordinary people who stole the show', *BBC News*, 9 September. Available online at: www.bbc.co.uk/news/magazine-14813053

Mustafa, S. (2013) 'Dhaka factory collapse: can clothes industry change?' *BBC News*, 25 April. Available online at: www.bbc.co.uk/news/world-asia-22302595.

Neil, B. (2012) Interview with Carole Watson, 1 October.

Nikkhah, R. (2009) 'Vogue's Alexandra Shulman: LFW designers ignore size-zero problem', *Daily Telegraph*, 13 September. Available online at: http://fashion.telegraph.co.uk/news-features/TMG6175998/Vogues-Alexandra-Shulman-LFW-designers-ignore-size-zero-problem.html.

Nixon, S. (1996) *Hard Looks: Masculinities, Spectatorship and Contemporary Consumption*. London: Routledge.

Nowness (2013) 'Abstracting beauty: Inez & Vinoodh', 13 July. Available online at: www.nowness.com/day/2013/7/13/3170/abstracting-beauty-inez-and-vinoodh.

Oliva, A. and Angeletti, N. (2006) *'In Vogue': The Illustrated History of the World's Most Famous Fashion Magazine*. New York: Rizzoli.

Oliver, W. and Bubble, S. (2012) *Style Feed: The World's Top Fashion Blogs*. London: Prestel.

Oxfam (2004) *Play Fair at the Olympics Report*. Available online at: www.oxfam.org/en/policy/olymp-report.

Phillips, A. (2007) *Good Writing for Journalists*. London: Sage.

PPA (2012a) *Internships Made Easy*. Available online at: www.ppa.co.uk/careers/ptc-work-experience-guidelines/.

——(2012b) *Tap Report: A Study of Tablets and Publishing*. Available online at: www.ppa.co.uk/marketing/research/the-tap-report.

——(2013) 'Publishing futures 2013: at a glance'. Available online at: www.ppa.co.uk/marketing/features/publishing-futures-2013-at-a-glance.

Polan, B. (2006) 'Fashion journalism', in Jackson, T. and Shaw, D. (eds) *The Fashion Handbook (Media Practice)*. London: Routledge, pp. 154–71.

Polhemus, T. (1994) *Streetstyle: From Sidewalk to Catwalk*. London: Thames & Hudson.

Porter, C. (2001) 'Catwalk to carnage', *Guardian*, 17 September. Available online at: www.guardian.co.uk/media/2001/sep/17/mondaymediasection.charlieporteronmensfashion.

——(2002) 'The truth about mags and ads', *Guardian*, 15 November. Available online at: www.theguardian.com/lifeandstyle/2002/nov/15/shopping.pressandpublishing.

——(2013a) 'Milan menswear show: runway report 2', *Financial Times*, 24 June. Available online at: www.ft.com/cms/s/2/ce850ca0-dc6b-11e2-a861-00144feab7de.html#axzz2fSUCy9YX.

——(2013b) Interview with the author, 19 July.

Pous, T. (2013) 'Carrie's return: four ways Sex and the City changed fashion', *Time*, 14 January. Available online at: http://style.time.com/2013/01/14/carries-return-four-ways-sex-and-the-city-changed-fashion.

Press, R. (dir.) (2010) *Bill Cunningham, New York*.

Press Gazette (2003) 'Tips of the trade: fashion journalism', 25 June. Available online at: www. pressgazette.co.uk/node/28220.

——(2013) 'Mag ABCs: big circulation drops for most paid-for women's lifestyle magazines', 15 August. Available online at: www.pressgazette.co.uk/mag-abcs-big-circulation-drops-most-paid-womens-lifestyle-magazines.

Pugh, A. (2011) 'Could accepting freebies land journalists in jail?', *Press Gazette*, 26 August. Available online at: www.pressgazette.co.uk/node/47771.

Richardson, R. (2012) Fashion masterclass at Sunderland University's Canary Wharf Campus, 2 November.

Rickey, M. (2012) Interview with the author, 30 April.

——(2013a) 'British-made fashion is back in business', *Guardian*, 30 January. Available online at: www.theguardian.com/fashion/2013/jan/30/british-made-fashion-clothing-manufacture.

——(2013b) 'The autumn/winter 2013 fashion weeks showed us clothes we can really love', *Guardian*, 11 March. Available online at: www.theguardian.com/fashion/fashion-blog/2013/mar/11/autumn-winter-2013-fashion-weeks.

Roberts, P. (2013) 'Popular girls', *Vogue* online, 17 May. Available online at: www.vogue.co. uk/news/2012/05/10/alexandra-shulman-talk—fashion-and-fantasy.

Roitfeld, C. (2011) *Irreverent*. New York: Rizzoli.

Ross, D. (2010) 'Liz Jones: "All writers betray people. It's tricky"', *Independent*, 9 July. Available online at: www.independent.co.uk/news/media/press/liz-jones-all-writers-betray-people-its-tricky-2022107.html.

Rousselle, S. (2012) 'An interview with Jeremy Langmead', *New York Times*, 13 January. Available online at: www.nytimes.com/video/2012/01/13/fashion/100000001281587/an-interview-with-jeremy-langmead.html.

Roy, R. (2010) 'An interview with fashion editor of the Guardian Jess Cartner-Morley', *Stylist Stuff*, 26 March. Available online at: www.fashion-stylist.net/blog/2010/03/26/an-interview-with-fashion-editor-of-the-guardian-jess-cartner-morley.

Sayer, J. (2013) 'Half-naked American Apparel advert banned by watchdog', *Sun*, 10 April. Available online at: www.thesun.co.uk/sol/homepage/news/4881225/half-naked-american-apparel-advert-banned-by-watchdog.html.

Schuman, S. (2013) 'Repost: on the street, Centro, Mexico City', *The Sartorialist*, 28 May. Available online at: www.thesartorialist.com/photos/repost-on-the-street-centro-mexico-city.

Sebra, M. (2013) 'The GQ+A: The Sartorialist's Scott Schuman', *GQ*, 13 May. Available online at: www.gq.com/style/blogs/the-gq-eye/2013/05/the-gq-a-whats-next-for-the-sartorialist.html.

Shah, O. (2013) 'Asos: not always the perfect fit', *Sunday Times*, 21 July, p. 7.

Sheridan Burns, L. (2002) *Understanding Journalism*. London: Sage.

Simmel, G. (1904) 'Fashion', *International Quarterley*, 10: 130–55. Available online at: www. modetheorie.de/fileadmin/Texte/s/Simmel-Fashion_1904.pdf.

Simone, C. (2013) Interview with the author, 29 September.

Small, M. (2013) Interview with the author, 23 May.

Smith, K. (2012a) 'A point to pre-Fall? A reason for Resort?', *Editd*, 16 January. Available online at: http://editd.com/blog/2012/01/a-point-to-pre-fall-a-reason-for-resort/.

——(2012b) 'Q&A: Duncan Edwards of Asos magazine', *Editd* blog, 5 November. Available online at: http://editd.com/blog/2012/11/qa-duncan-edwards-of-asos-magazine/.

Sozzani, F. (2011) 'Bloggers: a culture phenomenon or an epidemic issue?', Italian *Vogue* online, 28 January. Available online at: www.vogue.it/en/magazine/editor-s-blog/2011/01/january-28th.

Sparks, I. and Todd, B. (2012) '"She is a little too fat": Karl Lagerfeld slates Adele's size before backtracking on his comments about her image', *Daily Mail*, 8 February. Available online at: www.dailymail.co.uk/tvshowbiz/article-2097488/Karl-Lagerfeld-slates-Adeles-image-backtracking-comments.html.

Stevenson, S. (2012) 'Polka dots are in? Polka dots it is!', *Slate*, 21 June. Available online at: www.slate.com/articles/arts/operations/2012/06/zara_s_fast_fashion_how_the_company_gets_new_styles_to_stores_so_quickly_.html.

Storey, K. (2013) 'The rise of the power blogger', *New York Post*, 5 September. Available online at: http://nypost.com/2013/09/05/the-rise-of-the-power-blogger/.

Sweney, M. (2012) 'Vice Media buys style publication i-D', *Guardian*, 18 December. Available online at: http://www.theguardian.com/media/2012/dec/18/vice-media-buys-i-d.

——(2013) 'Mirror's online traffic soars in wake of Sun paywall', *Guardian*, 19 September. Available online at: www.theguardian.com/media/2013/sep/19/mirror-traffic-sun-paywall.

Taylor, P. (2013) Interview with the author, 9 September.

Technorati Media (2013) *Digital Influence Report*. Available online at: http://technorati.com/business/article/technorati-medias-2013-digital-influence-report.

Thomson, R. (2012) 'Analysis: how the weather is changing retail', *Retail Week*, 25 October. Available online at: www.retail-week.com/analysis-how-the-weather-is-changing-retail/5042047.article.

Travers-Spencer, S. and Zaman, Z. (2008) *The Fashion Designer's Directory of Shape and Form*. London: Quarto.

Tungate, M. (2010) *Fashion Brands: Branding Style from Armani to Zara*, 2nd edition. London: Kogan Page.

——(2012) *Fashion Brands: Branding Style from Armani to Zara*, 3rd edition. London: Kogan Page.

Tunstall, J. (1971) *Journalists at Work: Specialist Correspondents*. London: Constable.

Veblen, T. (2009) *The Theory of the Leisure Class*, reissue edition. Oxford: Oxford University Press.

Vernon, P. (2003) 'King of bling', *Observer*, 17 August. Available online at: www.theguardian.com/theobserver/2003/aug/17/features.magazine27.

——(2012) Interview with the author, 25 October.

——(2013) 'I'll have what she's wearing', *The Times Magazine*, 9 February, pp. 18–23.

Walker, E. (2012) Interview with the author, 5 October.

Walker, H. (2013a) Interview with the author, 22 May.

——(2013b) 'Kate Moss has dinner with Fergie', *Never Underdressed*, 3 August. Available online at: www.neverunderdressed.com/fashion/news/kate-moss-has-dinner-with-fergie.

Wallop, H. (2011) 'UK stores boosted by Chinese shoppers,' *Daily Telegraph*, 1 August. Available online at: www.telegraph.co.uk/finance/newsbysector/retailandconsumer/8675915/UK-stores-boosted-by-Chinese-shoppers.html.

White, V. (2010) 'Webchat', *Company.co.uk*, 17 September. Available online at: www.company.co.uk/community/forums/thread/990916.

——(2011) Magazine masterclass at Sunderland University, 16 May.

——(2013) Interview with the author, 23 May.

Watkins, N. (2012) 'Why shouldn't we dress like this?', *Sun*, 31 January.

Wilkins, S. (2013a) 'Boden and LibertyLondonGirl VIP Trunk Show in London', *Liberty-LondonGirl*, 17 June. Available online at: www.libertylondongirl.com/2013/06/17/boden-libertylondongirl-vip-trunk-show-in-london.

——(2013b) Interview with the author, 1 July.

Wilson, E. (2006) 'Fashion and postmodernism', in Storey, J. (ed.) *Cultural Theory and Popular Culture*, 4th edition. London: Prentice Hall, pp. 430–9.

Wilson, E. (2013) 'Fashion's blind spot', *New York Times*, 7 August. Available online at: www.nytimes.com/2013/08/08/fashion/fashions-blind-spot.html.

Winship, J. (1987) *Inside Women's Magazines*. London: Pandora.

Wood, L. (2012) Interview with the author, 30 April.

Young, R. (2013) 'Stripped bare: brands move toward transparency and traceability', *The Business of Fashion*, 23 July. Available online at: www.businessoffashion.com/2013/07/nikenudie-honest-by-bruno-pieters-stripped-bare-brands-move-toward-transparency-and-trace-ability.html.

Zhukova, D. and Ha, A. (dirs) (2013) 'Take My Picture', March. Available online at: http://vimeo.com/61348049.

Index

advertising 39, 51–7; advertorials 53, 209–10; digital 56–7
affiliate marketing 45, 57, 60, 210
airbrushing *see* diversity
Almassi, H. 3, 14, 15, 18, 32–3, 55, 56, 84, 96, 98, 107, 154–5, 157, 160, 188, 191, 223–4
apps 47–8
Asos 50, 57, 58, 215
audience 49–51
Audit Bureau of Circulations 6, 38, 41, 42

Barthes, R. 36
Beaty, Z. 114–15
Bigger, E. 16, 17, 22, 153, 168, 175, 176, 207
Blanks, T. 132, 200
blogs 27–8, 125, 155, 199–202; appeal 202–7; ethics 210–11; impact on journalism 206–09; monetising 210–11; tips 211–12
body image *see* diversity
Bowden, M. 14, 16, 20–1, 171, 172, 174, 181, 214, 225
brands: fashion 75–6, 148; media 45, 48–9
British fashion 66–7, 74–5
Bruton, J. 47, 92, 135, 138
Bumpus, J. 7–8, 18, 60, 118, 119–20, 134, 141, 213–14, 232–3
Burberry 79
business-to-business magazines *see* magazines

call-ins 171–3
Cartner-Morley, J. 14, 25, 43, 58, 77, 92, 107–8, 143, 232
catwalks: reports 85, 135–42; shows 128–32, 142–4
celebrities 54, 75, 91–2, 101–2, 136, 138, 151–2

Christian, A. 27, 123–4, 197–8, 201, 203, 205, 206, 212, 218
circulations 6, 38, 41, 42
Coddington, G. 127, 156, 166, 180
collaborations 76–7
Company 2, 41–2, 48, 155, 207
Conboy, M. 38
conference 84–5, 92, 93
consumer magazines *see* magazines
consumption 157–8
contacts 89, 95–6
copy approval 100–1
covering letter *see* internships, applying for
Crisell, H. 6–7, 11, 132, 134
criticism 56, 141–2
Cullen, P. 189, 192, 193
customer magazines *see* magazines
CVs *see* internships, applying for

Daily Mirror 4, 49–50, 91
Daily Telegraph 1, 4, 45
Davies, L. 15–16, 50, 213
degrees *see* qualifications
Dello Russo, A. 189, 202
designers 69–71, 133–4; process 72–5
Devlin, P. 166
diversity 73, 182–5
Dixon, M. 69, 70, 72, 74, 75, 76, 147, 148, 206
Drapers 7
dress codes 32–4

e-commerce 9–10, 28, 57–8, 77–8, 122–3
editorial 2; editorial eye 158–60; editorial mentions 51–2
Edwards-Jones, I. 5, 52, 75
Elle 46, 83
ethics 43, 231–3, 235, 242–5
exclusives 84, 87

Fabulous 3
Facebook *see* social media
fashion cupboard 2, 20–1
fashion weeks *see* catwalks
fast fashion 37, 68
features 113–18; angles 114; intros 115–16; nub paragraph 116; peg 114; treatments 114; writing 115–17
finance 71–2
Franklin, C. 35, 61, 73, 145, 183, 230
freebies 231–3, 235, 242–3
freelancing 10–11
Freeman, H. 34, 63, 77, 142

Gannon, L. 15, 44, 85, 87, 98, 100, 101–2, 152
Graafland, A. 4, 11, 23, 49, 76, 91, 132, 152, 156, 174, 176, 214
Grazia 83, 87, 92, 107, 154, 161–2, 191

Hart, E. 223, 225–6, 227, 228, 230–1
haute couture 62–4; shows 128–9
Henderson, P. 27–8, 77, 78, 201, 202, 203, 211–12, 213, 217–18
high street 66, 68, 70

ideas 32, 88–93
imagery 88, 94, 160
Instagram *see* social media
internships 16–17; applying for 17–19; dress codes 32–3; pay 22–4; tasks 19–21; tips for success 21–2
interviewing 96–102
inverted pyramid *see* news

jobs 1–3, 25–9; art desk 27; consumer magazines 5–6, 26; customer magazines 6–7; CVs 19; e-commerce 9–10; editorial 2; Freelancing 10–11; news agencies 26; newspaper supplements 5; newspapers 4–5, 25–6; office politics 32–4; personal qualities 29–32; pros and cons 11–12; styling 2; trade magazines 7; websites 7–9
Jones, L. 131, 142, 231, 242
Jones, M. 18, 82

Kawamura, Y. 36, 149
Kennedy, V. 18, 27

Lamb, L. 4, 24, 70–1, 170, 173, 175, 176
Langmead, J. 55, 57, 58, 123
law 234–6; anonymity 241; Bribery Act 243; contempt of court 242; copyright 240–1; libel 236–7; privacy 237–40; public interest 239
Lea Sayer, T. 22, 23, 151, 153, 168, 169, 170, 171–2, 173, 174, 181
lead times 82–4
Leitch, L. 1, 4, 25–6, 69, 87, 124, 136, 188–9
licences 77
Look 5, 45–6, 50, 83

magazines 26–7; biannuals 36–7, 40–1; consumer 5–6; customer 6–7, 57; future 59–60; history 37–40; men's 39; monthlies 41–2; trade 7; weeklies 37, 41
Mallen, S. 50, 57–8, 168, 215
manufacturing 73–5
McCaffrey, J. 97–8
McDowell, C. 142
McIntosh, F. 9, 37, 46, 54, 147, 151, 159, 182
McRobbie, A. 181
media kits 18, 49
Menkes, S. 199–200, 208, 211
menswear 71; reports 123–5; shows 131
mood boards 171
Mooney, A. 10, 122, 172
Mower, S. 165
Mujay, A. 220, 221, 226–7
Murphy, A. 9, 83, 122, 212, 214–15, 216

National Council for the Training of Journalists 14, 15, 235
Neil, B. 99
Never Underdressed 8, 46–7, 182
news 85–6; angles 110–11; intros 111–12; inverted pyramid structure 112–13; values 86–8, 112; writing 109–13
newspapers 4, 42–4; advertising 52–3; history 40; jobs 25–6; supplements 5

Oliver, W. 200

photography: editing 194–5; kit 188–9, selfies 193–4
pitching 102
Porter, C. 14, 25, 36–7, 52–3, 60, 62, 71, 99, 105, 113, 121, 124–5, 134, 136–7, 139, 140–1, 142, 158
press days 90, 152–3
prêt-à-porter *see* ready-to-wear
Professional Publishers Association 14, 15–16, 213

PRs 20–1, 54, 90, 101–2, 219–25; making contacts with 225–7; relationship with journalists 227–32

qualifications: accreditation 14–15; degrees 13–16, 235; shorthand 15, 100, 244; styling 167–9

racism *see* diversity
ready-to-wear 64–5; shows 129–30
research 93–6, 115
Richardson, R. 31, 33, 86, 126, 201
Rickey, M. 28, 29, 43, 69, 81, 84–5, 89, 156, 158
Roitfeld, C. 55, 65, 166–7, 170, 177, 178–9

samples 72–3, 172
Schuman, S. 68, 70, 159, 190, 193, 195, 204, 211
search engine optimisation 119, 122
seasons 67–9
seeding 75–6
sells 117–18
Sheridan Burns, L. 110
shoots 166–7, 177–9; captions 179–80; layouts 180; online 181–2; tests 31, 169
shopping pages 21, 85, 161–2
shorthand *see* qualifications
SHOWstudio 182, 195
Shulman, A. 55, 73, 172–3, 184
sidebars 118
Simmel, G. 147–8
Simone, C. 19
social media 31–2, 155, 187–8, 195, 212–18, 235; tips 216–18
sources 95–6; protecting sources 244
standfirsts *see* sells
street style 154, 182, 189–93
styling 2, 164–7; commercial 180–1; inspiration 169–71; kit 177–8; locations 174–5; props 177; on a shoot 177–9; team 175–7; tests 31, 80, 169; training 167–9

tablets 47–8
Taylor, P. 176, 178, 190–1, 192, 196–7, 213
tests *see* styling
tone 106–7
trade fairs 67, 155
trade magazines *see* magazines
training *see* education
trends 67, 145–8; reports 85, 148–157, 160–1, 162–3; spotting 151–7
Tungate, M. 65, 70, 75, 77, 78, 79, 147, 185
Tunstall, J. 2
Twitter *see* social media

universities *see* qualifications

Veblen, T. 147
Vernon, P. 5, 10–11, 53, 55, 84, 92, 93, 94, 96, 102, 105–6, 125
video 195–8
Vogue 184; history 38–40; online 7–8, 118–19; tablet edition 47

Walker, E. 27, 33, 51–2, 141, 170, 179, 181, 184, 231
Walker, H. 2, 8, 24, 33–4, 42–3, 46–7, 56, 58, 84, 108–9, 120–1, 159, 207, 213, 222, 229–30
websites 7–9, 44–7; 118–21
White, V. 2, 17, 18, 26, 41–2, 48, 51, 184, 209, 228–9
Wilkins, S. 29, 59, 169, 202, 203, 205, 208, 210, 212, 218
Wood, L. 5–6, 11–12, 23, 33, 45–6, 50, 53, 58, 109, 150, 151, 214, 224
work placements *see* internships
writing 105–9, 125–6; for e-tail 122–23; for features 113–18; for men 123–5; for news 109–13; for online 118–21; vocabulary 132–3